Motivating
Human
Behavior

Motivating Human Behavior

Ernest Dichter
President, Institute for Motivational Research
Croton-on-Hudson, New York

McGRAW-HILL BOOK COMPANY

new york   st. louis   san francisco   düsseldorf
johannesburg   kuala lumpur   london   mexico
montreal   new delhi   panama   rio de janeiro
singapore   sydney   toronto

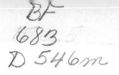

MOTIVATING HUMAN BEHAVIOR

07-016781-8

1 2 3 4 5 6 7 8 9 0 MAMM 7 5 4 3 2 1

This book was set in Baskerville by the Monotype Composition Co., Inc., and printed and bound by The Maple Press Company. The editors were Dale L. Dutton and Carolyn Nagy. The designer was Naomi Auerbach. Teresa F. Leaden supervised production.

To my wife, Hedy, who often practices better than I what I preach, and Fannie Friedman who helped me with many of the unpleasant chores of writing this book.

Contents

Preface

Lately it has become very fashionable to deplore the fact that machines and computers are taking over our lives, that mechanization and scientific procedures are attempting to dehumanize our environment, distorting our views, and making the future something horrible to contemplate. We are being threatened with the effects of "the future shock," the contamination of our planet, the rape and biological destruction of Mother Earth.

The viewpoint which I defend in this book is an optimistic one. We don't need less science—we need more. It is true that we have failed in many areas because we neglected to anticipate many of the negative side effects of progress. However, it is absolutely untrue that the good old days were really good.

Today, we are suffering from many fears and frailties. Our awareness of these fears and frailties has been heightened by the increase in information the mass media provides of what goes on around us and what is happening in many remote parts of the world. We are also caught by a number of conflicts. We are still proclaiming old-fashioned puritanism from pulpits and political platforms, although we present it in a more modern form. We are frightened because in looking around us we notice that we must choose between two alternatives: either we can try to turn the clock backwards, live in communes, and reject the machine and the computer as intruders in our supposedly peaceful life, or we can accept our machines as necessary, unavoidable elements of progress and make them our servants rather than our masters.

What we are really afraid of is the inevitability of having to adapt ourselves to the new world, since in reality we really cannot flee from all the new possibilities which surround us. We are going to have more leisure time, we are going to have more and more of our daily unpleasant chores taken over by machines, and we will learn to control time and space. We are like frightened children who don't feel at home yet in this new world. We would like to run back to the bosom of a supposedly more quiet, peaceful, and less hectic time. We tend to forget too easily that man's life span used to be much shorter, that he had to suffer from many more diseases. We forget that man had to spend from twelve to fourteen hours a day on menial tasks and that the vast majority of people did not enjoy anything even faintly comparable to what can be called civilization or culture.

While we tremble at the thought of being able to control our destiny as far as the physical and scientific world is concerned, we become enraged and feel even more threatened in the inner core of our personality if it is suggested that we are beginning to get the means—if we only have the courage—to influence man's behavior. In this book are discussed some of the techniques of motivating human behavior for definite purposes. My viewpoint is that many of the problems we are faced with on a personal, national, and international level lack solutions because we have not dared to enter the forbidden land of how to get people to do what we want them to do.

First, we are immediately confronted with the question of who is going to decide what people ought to do. The first chapter of this book explains that a goal for man that can be universally accepted is the one of continuous growth, self-discovery, and expansion of one's own horizons. In every one of the tasks that daily challenge us, whether they concern pollution, combating drug addiction, more intelligent behavior in voting or consumerism, we are setting goals. We are admonishing, demanding, and cajoling people to do certain things. Thus, there is an overall agreement about what is right and what is wrong.

While values may change as far as economic, social, or work goals are concerned, I am really less concerned with the outward manifestation of these values than I am with the basic psychological meaning of a happy life. I doubt very much that copping out, standing still, or running away from the realities of living can bring about true satisfaction. I am ready to defend the idea that constructive discontent, rather than paradisiacal fulfillment of all of man's desires should represent the real goal underlying our aspirations. I am also convinced that the vast majority of educational techniques or attempts at motivating people which utilize purely factual triggers, threats, exortations, and similar approaches are ineffectual and do not represent a sophisticated enough approach as far as the complex goals which we have set up for ourselves and others are concerned.

In this book I have collected all those techniques of motivating human behavior which I have found to be effective in my more than thirty years' experience at an institute which specializes in motivational research. It is obvious that none of the techniques are perfect solutions. They have to be adapted to each individual case in a new way. Nor do I pretend that they have been tested through large-scale, statistical experiments. However, most of these techniques have been utilized in many organizations and large corporations and have been used when we have been called upon to help find solutions to many daily problems brought to our attention. The various techniques are discussed in each chapter, and organized in such a way that the most primitive methods of motivating human behavior are discussed in the beginning, leading gradually to more and more sophisticated approaches.

My main purpose in writing this book is to make people who are involved in motivation in one form or another—and most of us are involved in having to motivate, even if it is just ourselves—try a psychological double-take, think twice before simply trying to tackle a problem in a direct, head-on fashion. I hope to demonstrate that motivating human behavior is a more complex task than just waving a threatening finger and can be more readily and more effectively accomplished by finding the proper channels of motivation and thinking through the reactions of the person who is to be persuaded. We are too often guided by our own convictions about what another person ought to do rather than by trying to understand first why the other person is not behaving the way we think he or she should. Throughout the text, I cited as many concrete case histories as possible to impress the reader with the feasibility of my approaches. And in the second part of the book I demonstrate how these techniques have been translated into practice in specific areas.

Properly translated, motivating human behavior means finding out the best methods of convincing people rather than persuading them. Just as I have stated about the field of physical sciences—that we need more science rather than less—I am sure that the same thing applies as far as our psychological and social problems are concerned. We are still suffering from many social diseases because we have not yet learned to develop our techniques a few steps further instead of being frightened by new possibilities. I hope that this book will represent a small step further in mastering not only our physical environment, but also our psychological contacts and personal relationships.

Ernest Dichter

*Motivating
Human
Behavior*

Part One

Motivating Human Behavior

PRAGMATIC THINKING—PRAGMATIC ACTING

We are mastering the physical world more and more. We have landed on the moon, but the progress we have made in dealing with human behavior and in changing attitudes has not kept pace with our progress in the physical sciences. One reason may be the attitude of many scientists themselves, who still teach that the "why" and "how to" questions are not worthy of the true academician's interest —that all he should concentrate on is the objective facts.

I think there is a fallacy in this philosophy. Intelligent and meaningful observation is not possible without interpretation. Rather than having such interpretations sneak in in an inadvertent and often subconscious fashion,

1

however, it is much more honest to state the concepts which have been utilized in introducing meaningful interpretation. For example, Claude Levy-Strauss, in his book entitled The Savage Mind, *states that savages are not as savage as all that, but have a fairly high degree of intelligence. He introduces psychological interpretation.*

Motivational research, the techniques of which are often referred to in this book, is basically applied cultural anthropology. Instead of neglecting the "why" and the "how to" problems, it has made those two areas its main concern. In a sense, therefore, it is our business to develop viable methods of changing human nature. Instead of going thousands of miles to New Guinea or Africa to find topics of investigation, motivational research considers that the day-to-day behavior of the twentieth-century man—even when he lives in Brooklyn, on the outskirts of Paris, or in the south of Italy—is as worthy of study as the Samoans or the Trobrianders. Motivational researchers feel that interpretation of observed behavior needs to go into depth. *It is not sufficient to ask the member of a tribe why the tribe has instituted a particular type of initiation rite. More likely than not, he won't know himself. The only honest answer he can give is that they have practiced these ceremonials since time immemorial.*

I admit right from the start to a biopsychological bias— if, indeed, it is one. I am convinced that most aspects of human behavior have as their final goal adaptation to, and conquest of, the difficulties of life. First among those difficulties are physical protection, security, shelter, and satisfaction of hunger; secondarily they include regulations and guides to make living together easier and to avoid hardship.

Whether these symbols of security in our contemporary world are a Rolls-Royce, a swimming pool, or a vacation home in the tropics does not matter psychologically. They are not very far removed from the more colorful feathers of a tribal chieftain or the large size of his hut. They guarantee him respect from other competing members of his family and clan. They are usually indications of his greater physical or mental powers and ability as a hunter or fighter.

More important even than this need to recognize the basic relationship between the dwellers of an apartment house and the inhabitants of a tribal village is the fact that

*motivational researchers feel that social scientists have to
begin to accept their responsibility as major promoters of
progress, whether this consists in introducing more effective
measures of birth control in India, in getting the average
citizen to accept urban renewal programs, in controlling
drug addiction, or in changing the food habits of Africans
or, for that matter, even those of so-called more advanced
civilized Americans and Europeans. What we urgently need
is a list of techniques of social engineering.*

*I am called upon almost weekly to give practical solutions
to imminent problems, ranging from how to bring about
better understanding between Europeans and
representatives of new African countries and improving
racial relations to how to change the attitude of the police
force in an American city. Some of the problems have to
do with food, population, and birth control. Others, again,
are more mundane, such as how to change attitudes toward
men's suits in Italy, France, Germany, or the United States.
Another question concerns how to modernize a religion
and bring it in line with the increasing likelihood of a
three- to four-day leisure-time period every week and with
the fact that 2 percent of the population may be able,
through their productive work, to provide for all the needs
of the rest of the population.*

*Many of these pragmatic problems involve a change in
our moral and religious concepts. Increased leisure time
will mean that people can read more books or take up new
hobbies. They will need outlets for creativity. If they are
not properly motivated, however, they may simply loaf or
drink more. In many of our dealings we are within the
domain of easily accepted, legitimate, and so-called ethical
goals—when, for example, a company hires us to get
Frenchmen to eat cellophane-wrapped cheese or when the
vice-president of a government wants to find out how to
improve his image so that he will have a better chance to
become president. However, some people begin to question
the manipulative nature of motivational research. I tried
to answer these fears in a previous book,* The Strategy of
Desire, *(pp. 12–14):*

Ever since we built the first fire or devised the first clothing, we
have attempted to improve upon the world. Each faster plane or
better fertilizer or electronic computer represents another step
forward in this evolution. We have made some progress in understanding human nature, but we have been painfully slow in

learning how to bring about behavioral change. We have no qualms about tampering with nature in many of its manifestations. We use artificial insemination in cattle breeding and discuss seriously the fact that plowing, although practiced for thousands of years, may be a poor agricultural technique.

For a long time we simply did not have the tools to bring about behavioral change. As the social sciences have progressed, we are evolving these tools very slowly. The mass media developed over the last few decades have given us the means of reaching millions of people with the verbal and non-verbal cues which could bring about changes and the utilization of the human factor. Applying these techniques, however, to the commercial and social problems on the list of assignments has aroused fears of hidden persuasions, manipulation.

In these discussions various issues are raised. Some people consider any kind of interference with human nature wrong and immoral; others object to the goals for which these persuasive techniques are used. It is interesting that there is so much emotional anxiety connected with this subject of persuasion. Why are we so afraid of being influenced, of being persuaded? Maybe what we are really afraid of is the growth and evolution of the individual and of the human race. The story of Adam and Eve repeats itself in our individual lives and in the evolution of human groups. It symbolizes the eternal conflict between the desire to stay in the paradise of ignorance and static tranquility, and the desire to live in the world of knowledge, striving, challenge, and growth. Who did the first persuading? Was it Eve, was it the apple, or was it the serpent? And why did Adam take the apple?

Ideally, we may wish that people should never be influenced. The truth is that they are continuously being influenced, and not only by people (parents, teachers, clergymen, friends) but also by the poverty or wealth of their society, and even by their physical environment, the landscape and the climate.

In Handbook of Consumer Motivations: The Psychology of the World of Objects, *I tried to draw attention to the fact that in a world of objects, each one of them has a deeper meaning going far beyond its purely utilitarian description. We live in a world of symbols. By better understanding them, we can adjust ourselves to this more instrumental, "real," although hidden world. In this book, I try to concentrate on what I feel represents an important need in the techniques of changing human nature. Many of these techniques were developed by our organization as we tried to solve concrete problems posed by other companies;*

others I have collected from many scientific sources. I have tried to develop a sort of manual of social and human engineering, based on my own experience gained in the course of doing thousands of studies for many different governments, organizations, and commercial companies— all of them interested in bringing about a major or minor change in human attitudes, depending on their particular interests and goals. I also scanned the world literature in the field of social and behavioral sciences—approaches that have worked in political campaigns, community approaches, those used by religious organizations, and techniques used by the Communists—to combine here a comprehensive summary of applicable and usable pragmatic ideas that have proved to be instrumental in bringing about change.

No progress is truly possible unless we introduce some "upside-down" thinking—unless we break through barriers and destroy rigid and often false concepts which surround us, whether they are thousands of years old or not. We have to reappraise aspects of social structure and standards of behavior; otherwise we cannot truly make progress. Interfaith marriages can still cause us great concern, and we can become really fanatic on the subject of interracial marriage. Yet many such problems could be solved if we had the right techniques.

This book is organized in such a way that we start with the most direct and almost brutal ways of changing human nature and gradually, chapter by chapter, work our way through until we arrive at more illustrious and more exciting ways of bringing about reorientation such as through inspiration, the setting of examples, and the sacrificing of our own goals for the good of others. Only if we learn to think pragmatically can we begin to act pragmatically and in a goal-directed fashion. In Part Two of the book I apply the principles developed in the first part to a collection of twenty major human problems, ranging from motivating for social progress and the satisfaction of newly developed human needs to making people do things that are good for them, bridging the generation gap, combating racial and national prejudices, obeying recommendations, motivating communities, helping people to decide, and many other areas; the book ends with some pragmatic ideas on how to create a more unified world and to work toward peace.

1

Motivational Principles

CHANGE IS GROWTH

You cannot be a brother without having one. You cannot change human nature without knowing or thinking about what you're changing to—and from what. Our life tendency is to learn certain adaptations and to stick with them. These learned rules help us to live our life with as few complications and hurts as possible. An attempt to change human nature, even if the goal is clearly to achieve better adjustment, is usually resisted.

For at least a decade, modern Spain has tried officially to change working hours, cut out the two- to three-hour siesta, and have people eat their lunch and dinner at what other countries consider normal hours. In France, "la journée continuée" (or uninterrupted day) is being discussed. Apparently, in both countries attempts to change even simple eating habits have not met with too much success as yet. Everybody is in agreement that such changes would be desirable; people would get home earlier and would have more time to themselves.

Are other tasks easier? A gasoline company wanted its attendants to make more money. To do so they had to work harder. Very quickly the philosophical question presented itself: Why should they change—even assuming that the techniques for bringing about such a change were available? We shall discuss such techniques throughout this book. However, before entering into these more technical questions, it is best to remove any resistance which might exist in the mind of the reader, making him less receptive to the recommendations that will be put forth. He may be convinced that change per se is not really desirable. He may feel that the lazy person is quite happy and that making him more diligent will result simply in making him *work harder*.

Indeed, first we have to answer the question of why we even bother discussing such a possible change. Without wanting to, we find ourselves very rapidly involved in a discussion of human happiness. What is life all about? A whole series of presumptions and rather arrogant definitions is necessary. Yet without these we cannot answer our basic query as to why we want to change people and what we want to change them to.

A native of Zululand sits in front of his hut and does a few hours of work, and the rest of the time he dreams, sleeps, makes love, and apparently enjoys himself. The same thing is true of some Brazilian fishermen and the inhabitants of a Samoan village. Why do we want to change them? My point of view is—that we want to because change will make them happier. And here's the defense. Life itself is changing continuously. Conscious living consists of mastering difficulties. Being happier, and not knowing that you are, means not being happy. We have not really been chased out of paradise, where we lived in blissful ignorance. Having eaten from the tree of knowledge, we became conscious and awakened, and it was after that that the paradise of *struggle* and *conquest* really started.

We need a major revision of our educational goals. We teach and practice a lot of "platform thinking." We talk about the time when we will have passed our exam, when the children will be grown up, when we will have paid off the mortgage on our house. We continually set ourselves goals without having gotten wise to the fact that once we reach those goals, a good part of the pleasure that we had in trying to get there will be eliminated. Getting there is not only half the fun but, possibly, all the fun.

All progress depends on our willingness to develop, to live consciously, to get up from our squatting position in front of the hut, for only conscious living is really "fun" and can be called "living." Therefore, when we set out to change human behavior, one of our first tasks is to defend the proposition that salvation and pleasure consist to a large degree of continuous, purposeful change and growth. I have been preaching up to now that it is our job to reach a goal. I shall make it clear that behind each goal is another one—that in a sense we never "get" there.

During his administration President Eisenhower set up a Commission for the Determination of American Goals. As far as I know, no clear-cut definition was ever reached. The real purpose of this commission, however, should have been to state that our goal is one of continuously running with a goal flag. Just when we get nearer to the finish line, we should plant it a few hundred "human miles" ahead again.

It is frightening to tell ourselves that happiness lies in the fact of never attaining it. Yet, this is a basic truth that we simply have to learn to accept. If we call it "continuous growth," it becomes a little more palatable. We have to grow, change, develop, and adapt ourselves until the last second of our life. The more experiences we have accumulated, the richer our life has been; the more things we have done, the more we have learned; the more skills we master, the more lives we have lived.

I believe that appealing to patriotic, moral, and religious considerations is only half as effective as promising people more fun. This sounds sacrilegious. Knowledge, for example, is not just worthy in itself. Knowing history not only makes you more educated but also makes you more proud of yourself and permits you to interpret the world that existed before your time and to predict, to a certain extent, what developments might take place in the future. Your life becomes richer. The newspapers you read, the discussions you carry on, and the chain of associations produced in your mind are more vivid and extend in many different directions. You're having more fun in living. The same thing is true about acquiring a knowledge of mathematics, physics, or geometry. It certainly is true about traveling.

Maybe one of the basic factors we have been suffering from is that we have been portraying learning as a *duty* rather than a *pleasure*—which it really is. Recently, a Protestant minister proposed a "fun religion" to fit in with our modern world and to get religion back into the mainstream of life. There are still far too many educators who feel that only discipline will bring rewards and that laughter is sinful. We enjoy physical growth. We're proud of the fact that we're getting stronger, that we can jump higher. Why should we not be equally proud of the fact that we have become more intelligent and know more things?

It may sound unconventional to suggest that in order to have children understand the life of Napoleon better, it may be all right to have them watch the film *Desirée* in which he is played by Marlon Brando. Maybe some scenes would have to be cut out, but I don't see anything wrong in creating, through such a film, real identification and three-dimensionality and thus bringing a part of history to life. We have marvelous modern means and media of communication, and yet few of them are being used in our customary channels of communication. How many courses are given in "how to have fun in a museum"? Why haven't we yet made a visit to a museum as much fun as going to a baseball game? We want to change people not because some global educator has ordained it so but because we can promise people a more enjoyable and a better life.

In motivating the African to get up, to chop some trees down, to build a sturdier home, and to earn money—and possibly with the money to buy appliances, clothes, and a radio for himself and his family—we are not making him unhappy; we are making him, for the first time, truly happy. Most underdeveloped countries are underdeveloped primarily as far as their desires are concerned, not in terms of their resources. Once we get people to want things, to become constructively dissatisfied, we've begun human progress and growth.

While we are all dreaming of the South Pacific islands and a return to paradise, reality is quite different. People would not have gone to the moon and into the depths of the earth, developed lasers, split the atom, or created artificial hearts if they had not had fun doing it. They can accomplish such things because technological help has been developed. Their wives don't have to wash dishes; they can let the dishwasher do it. They have central heating. They have cars and planes. We still court and admire a caveman type of philosophy and morality which makes us look upon these things as bad. We do not realize that by developing them, we have freed ourselves. We have developed not only disposable income but also, what is even more important, *disposable time.*

It has become the task of the behavioral scientist—the professional changer of human nature, the social engineer—to point out first that his profession is practiced not because it is better for the economy or because it will result in the achievement of some moral or religious goal but because it helps us reach the basic, eternal summit of human achievement —the Olympian goal of happiness.

All change of human nature, therefore, is change for growth, and without growth life is not worth living. The techniques that can be used successfully to bring about this change are discussed in many chapters in this book. None of them will work, however, unless the willingness to change has been established and accepted, not because "big, moral brother" says so, but because it provides a better life.

2

Changing You—the Tough Way

CARROT OR CANE?

In a recent experiment, a psychiatrist succeeded in stopping men from having extramarital experiences or dreaming of other women by administering electric shocks to them each time a picture of a woman other than their wives was shown to them. At the same time, sweet music was played when a picture of their wives was shown. The psychiatrist reported that within a few weeks, these "unhappy" men lost all interest in other women—at least as goals of amorous pursuits. This is, indeed, a successful method of changing human attitudes. It is one of the oldest techniques in training and education. Our whole process of civilization is brought about with more or less success as a result of scolding the child and lauding it.

Fear is probably one of the most powerful techniques for changing human behavior. The majority of neuroses are caused by anxiety, and neurosis can be considered an enforced change of attitude and outlook on life. We normally consider it to be a disease and negative. In reality, it is an attempt by the individual to adjust to the difficulties he faces. Neurotic behavior is a form of adaptation.

Behavioral engineers are often called upon to choose between reward and punishment as techniques. Is it better, for example, when trying to get people to drive more safely to threaten them with the possibility of their death or to use a positive approach? On the basis of my experience, I defend the reward technique. For many years, the National Safety Council has been warning people—threatening them, begging them—to drive more carefully, with very little success. If anything, the accident figures, particularly during long weekends, have gone up rather than gone down.

The first attempts have been made to praise people, to tell them that this weekend there were six fewer accidents than expected. This has meant the saving of several hundred thousand dollars of the earning capacities of these motorists. It made it unnecessary for the police department, the hospital, and the ambulance to spend $15,000 or more to take care of the victims.

In combating pilferage in department stores, we in our organization also found that a positive approach was much more effective than a threatening one. For a long time, warning signs had been posted all over, threatening would-be thieves with six months in jail. We suggested that the threats be changed—first of all, by making them much more dramatic and talking about *180 long days and long nights.*

We also used the fear of embarrassment as a powerful deterrent to pilfering. Our study showed that being thrown in jail or getting caught in the act is considered a really shameful thing. Many people, however, think that stealing is almost like a sport. We showed photographs of pilferers being apprehended with crowds assembling around them, and we used as a slogan: "Was it worth it?"

Another approach was to show photographs of eight different ways to steal in a department store—the idea being that "We are just as smart as you, Mr. (or Miss) Thief; we know all your little tricks and some additional ones, too." Thus, we changed the pure threat to a more "experience-able" and more human one. In a way, our contest was a more positive form of communication with the potential lawbreaker.

Another case concerned the local corps of ambulance drivers. They desperately needed voluntary drivers. They had appealed to the public spirit of the local citizens and had threatened that if they did not volunteer one of these days, they themselves might be in the precarious situation of needing an ambulance for which there was no driver and thus losing their lives.

Instead of using a threat, we showed a situation in which all ambulances were fully staffed and manned by volunteers. The value of such a positive approach was further demonstrated by showing that participating in this community activity was a form of insurance policy that did not cost very much—and, indeed, was free—and which paid a very high dividend.

Getting people to give money to charity provides another important example of ways of changing human nature. Basically, nobody likes to part with his money—no more than anyone wants to be reminded of the misery of other people. Charity is a very laudable, a very Christian activity, but as everyone knows who has been involved in such drives, it is a difficult idea to sell. There is a great difference between accepting the principle of giving and actually parting with hard cash. Here, too, we found that showing starving children in India or Africa, while appealing for contributions, was the customary approach. It often resulted in rejection, however, of the appeal. People did not want to be too closely identified with these dreadful situations.

Many times when we ourselves are doing all right and are asked to help poor relations, for example, there is a deeper fear involved. We are afraid that we might be drawn back by them to the original state of poverty that we escaped from not too long ago. We therefore refuse to give, not because we are uncharitable, but because by avoiding contacts of that type we feel we can surround ourselves with a protective wall. We try to combat our fear of contamination. To the international organization "S.O.S. Kinderdoerfer," which builds villages for orphans and underprivileged children in various parts of Europe, we suggested that a smiling child be shown instead of an abandoned or starving one—that this smile was the beautiful thing the giver was buying. Our headline then was: "How much is this human smile worth to you?"

In his book entitled *Battle for the Mind,* William Sargeant describes religious conversion and primitive techniques of converting behavior. He starts out by saying that all religious conversion and all primitive attempts have one thing in common: Some physiological technique is always necessary, whether it is beating, chastening of the flesh, some kind of physical discomfort, drugs, incense, or dancing. He points out drumming in particular and the fact that customs in primitive cultures lead to great excitement and emotional release.

The primary method used in conversion or in establishing a new pattern of behavior in these cases is to create anxiety. One particular religious sect in the South utilizes snake handling. These are poisonous snakes—which creates a great amount of anxiety. This, says Sargeant, guarantees your undivided attention and exposes you to more suggestibility. As examples, he cites the primitive methods of initiating young boys into adulthood. In the Poro tribe boys are taken away from their homes. First there is a kind of brainwashing process. The young boys are made to feel that the camp they are taken to is so important that if they should not make the grade, life wouldn't be worth living. The only way to live a worthwhile life is to be a Poro. They are then placed in a very threatening situation in which monster heads lunge at them. They are not allowed to show any fear and they are put into the jaws of a monster head and almost eaten; then they are subjected to very painful tattooing. They are told that the demon has attemped to put an end to them. This monster that comes at them attempts to swallow them, but the Poro society saves them and raises them to a new life. Then they are retrained, now that they are interested in this new life, in all the attitudes and feats associated with being an adult in the Poro society. They receive training in sex, and they learn the handicrafts. Dances are used to get them into a semiconscious state in which they feel that they have become one with the new spirit they have adopted.

Electroshock therapy brings about the same response in that people subjected to it become completely exhausted; old patterns are broken away, making room for newer patterns.

Robert J. Lifton, a psychiatrist, writes on thought reform in the psychology of totalism and a study of brainwashing in China. This gentleman went to Hong Kong shortly after the Korean War to learn the technique of brainwashing. He reports on several cases, but the one of most interest is that of an American doctor. According to Lifton, the process goes something like this. First, you are placed in an 8- by 12-foot cell with about eight other people. This is called the "struggle." The other people denounce you as a spy, tell you to confess, and threaten you by saying the government has the goods on you. These persons are motivated and engaged in this struggle because they will gain merit points and perhaps be released.

Next you go for your first interrogation, at which point you learn that the crime you committed was "against the people." You are told to confess, and you talk about your own activities, the people you know, what you do, and the organizations you belong to—for approximately ten hours. A judge then gets angry at you for not confessing and orders you to be put in handcuffs. You are brought back ten minutes later, and he orders you to confess. When you cannot do so, he orders chains to be put around your feet. These are never removed. You live in your cell this way. The interrogations continue interminably, so you get very little sleep. You have no privacy; only your basic needs are taken care of. You have to eat by pushing your food along with your nose. A basic motivation then sets in, which is the seeking of comfort, and you try to make up wild confessions. However, these never seem to do. They always have loopholes in them, and they are not acceptable.

During the period of time when you are called on, you are constantly interrogated. During your off time you are called upon to dictate your confessions, when you are not actually confessing. At this time, you are asked to add more than you told and to sign your confession with a thumb since your hands are in chains.

Next you are forced to betray your friends. You are asked to tell whom you know, what they do, and what conversations you had with them. Then the next stage sets in. You learn what people's "standpoint" is. Basically, it is any kind of news. Any information or intelligence is considered proof that you are an espionage agent. In other words, if you report that you told a friend the price of shoes, it wasn't just news you were confessing; you gave away intelligence. Every conversation you have with other people is interpreted as intelligence.

The next stage is leniency. All of a sudden one day you find that you are suddenly being made more comfortable. The judges and the people around you are friendly. The effect is that you suddenly have hope for the future. You are then instructed to rewrite your confession with guidance. Every time you disagree with the guide, you find yourself back in chains.

You then find that you are becoming part of the cell routine. You belong. You do things with your compatriots. You are one unit. Your cell life consists of study periods. You take Communist readings and discuss them. Everyone is motivated to look well; there is great zeal to succeed in these discussions. You are "encouraged" to interpret what you understand of what is read or discussed in terms of the "people's standpoint." You are also told that you are to examine yourself constantly and demonstrate your own reform. As a result, you learn to think out loud.

You become very spontaneous. You talk about your wrongs and your faults, asking others for facts. If you don't like those facts, you present others. You learn to communicate your most basic thoughts with a group of people. Any time you make a mistake, your old culture is thrown up to you. If you happen to be a Westerner and you drop a plate on the floor, you are told that you are inconsiderate, that you are wasting the people's money. If you want more food, you are told that you are being greedy. If you take up too much space to sleep, you do so because of your imperialistic background. After one year, you have a new interrogation and confession. This confession becomes more solidified.

Later on, you become a helper to others in your cell. You try to educate them. You are motivated to try to make them come through the "struggle." After three years, in most cases, you sign a confession in front of cameras and newsmen; you read it aloud, and it is recorded. You are thrown out of the country almost immediately following this discussion. What sets in then is a kind of feeling of being lost—a longing for discussion, a meaningful use of time, and a measure of progress that you had in the very organized cell life. In many cases you are too weak to try to reconvert yourself, and it is easier to remain a Communist.

Dr. Lifton describes twelve basic steps that each person goes through in the process of being brainwashed:

1. The assault upon your identity. You thought you were a doctor, but you really were a subversive agent. Everything you were and did comes under attack.

2. The establishment of guilt, showing you that in your most casual conversations you weren't really casual—you had ulterior motives.

3. Betrayal. You are forced to talk about your friends.

4. The breaking point—a total conflict in a basic fear. You wonder what is truth and what will happen.

5. Leniency and opportunity. Your life becomes more comfortable. You have an opportunity to confess and to learn how to get yourself out of this situation.

6. A compulsion to confess—to get rid of that bad element that all people feel is within them—and to take on the new values that will be more rewarding.

7. The channeling of guilt. You really learn to see and express to others your personal evil.

8. Reeducation. You undergo a logical dishonoring of yourself. Through group study, you throw out your old self.

9. Progress and harmony. You adapt to your new surroundings. You become comfortable in the routine.

10. Final confession, a summing up—making it a fact in front of cameras and tape recorder.

11. Rebirth. There emerges a new self—plus selected elements of the old self which the brainwashing group usually gives back to you. You can continue to be a doctor or a clerk, but your new self is impinged on top of the old one.

12. Release—a transitional state in a feeling of limbo. You become suspicious of both sides—the Communist and your old side. You even distrust yourself. What you do there is very significant. Do you try to go back? Do you stay in limbo? Do you remain a Communist?

We cannot use these techniques in our everyday life. They have to be accepted, however, as powerful approaches in the task of changing human behavior, which is the topic of this book.

In a minor way, many of us use a sort of autobrainwashing approach when we want to accept unpleasant tasks. We tend to routinize unpleasant tasks in an effort to minimize their importance. By making a habit out of shaving or using Kotex or tampons, for instance, a person can practically forget about what he or she is doing.

In a study on shaving, for instance, we found that men usually shave at the same time in the morning and that they also shave the same side of their face first and go in the same direction. They go through the same preparations before shaving and the same ritual after shaving, and they usually request the same blade when they are at the drugstore. In this regard, women usually ask for the same sanitary protection product. In order to break such habits and get the user to buy a different product, one must appeal to his sense of *self-preservation*. Specifically, one must point out that what the buyer is currently doing is, in fact, self-destructive and therefore warrants attention. This is almost like the situation in brainwashing—like accusing the victim of being a capitalist.

For instance, men have been induced to switch blades when they were made to realize that they were using a metal that was completely out-dated and damaging to the skin. When the Wilkinson stainless blade came into existence, the company claimed that older blades nicked a man's face unnecessarily and that men were spending their money wastefully—that is, that they were being self-destructive. Similarly, women can be convinced to buy tampons instead of napkins when it is pointed out to them that napkins are old-fashioned, cause unnecessary aggravation and irritation, and, in fact, are somewhat socially unaccept-able.

In summary, by appealing to people's desire *not* to destroy themselves, one can motivate them to change habitual behaviors which are protective devices in the first place.

People in teaching, advertising, political, and puplic relations fields very frequently have to decide whether to use the carrot or the cane. Recent scientific research shows that using intermittent rewards and punishment for behavior is a better teaching device than systematic com-mendation and punishment. Many experiments have been conducted in the field of so-called conditioning. Scientists distinguish between classical conditioning and instrumental conditioning. Classical conditioning is best exemplified in the experiments conducted by the Russian physiol-ogist Ivan Pavlov, who trained dogs to salivate by ringing a bell each time he presented them with a meal. After awhile, it was enough to ring a bell to get them to salivate. Instrumental conditioning involves a sys-tematic relationship between reward and punishment and learning of new behavior. If you punish somebody each time he does something wrong and reward him each time he does something right, sooner or later he is going to learn to do the right thing.

The interesting and new discovery that intermittent reward and punishment is better than consistent reward and punishment has many applications. Gambling provides probably one of the most outstanding examples of the value of intermittent conditioning. If people were to win —even if this were legally possible—each time they played a certain number or a certain horse, a lot of the pleasure of gambling would dis-appear. Indeed, it would not be gambling any longer. This can be carried over to other examples. In a psychological analysis of people's attitude toward lighters, for instance, we found that the fact that a lighter does not function every time actually represents a positive element. Each time a flame is produced, this is taken as a reward for one's effort, while failure to produce a flame constitutes intermittent punishment. One can even think about the possibility that it would be wrong to produce a perfect lighter.

The problem of potency in the human male is governed by similar psychological factors. If the act of love were possible to all males at all times and under all circumstances, a good part of its attractiveness and desirability would disappear.

The carrot-and-cane, reward-and-punishment aspect of changing human behavior is therefore very closely related to an element of doubt. You want to induce people to drive safely. If you promise them that by doing so they will never have an accident again, you may be overdoing it and remove this element of excitement and of never being quite sure— which seems to be, according to the latest studies, closely tied up with the carrot-and-cane method of changing human behavior.

Conditioning can be used in several different forms. In France, we in our organization recently approached the problem of how to get Frenchmen to have their clothes cleaned more often. We found that they were afraid that the cleaning process would somehow take something away from the individuality of their clothes. They would return diminished in some form. We used the method that can be referred to as *progressive desensitization* to stimuli. We asked people first to think about the cleaned clothes in order to get them accustomed to the idea of this process. We then asked them to designate a day when the cleaner could pick up the clothes. He would be given only one garment at a time. Bit by bit, the French family and housewife were accustomed not to be afraid any longer of the dreaded punishment, which they imagined would happen if their clothes were cleaned.

Another form of conditioning is to *exaggerate* the reward and the punishment to a ridiculous degree. Our task was to get young people to clean their shoes. Appeals to logic did not help. Instead, we went along with them and acknowledged their desire not to clean their shoes, but showed, in an exaggerated cartoon form, that by letting dirt accumulate on one's shoes, one could eventually grow radishes on them.

In psychotherapeutic practice if someone states that he detests people, one can take him at his word and call his bluff. The therapist would then forbid him to see anybody for a period of two or three weeks— usually with the result that the patient recognizes in this exaggerated form of reward and punishment that he really is not ready to accept the logical consequences of his behavior. Similar methods are involved in forcing alcoholics to get drunk or stutterers to stutter more.

Another method is to *combine rigid instrumental conditioning;* every time you do something right you are rewarded, until the pattern has been well established. Then, only *intermittent reinforcement* may be necessary. We used such an approach in training workers in coal mines to become more careful in their operation of machines. They received various training lessons resulting in an admonition to think twice before making a dangerous move. This admonition was accompanied by a bell signal until this behavior had been properly learned; then at regular intervals throughout the day only the bell signal itself was played. No intellectual reaction was necessary any longer. In a way, we achieved a success similar to that of Pavlov with his dogs.

3

Changing Environments
and Values

The use of threat or reward constitutes the most positive and widely employed method of changing human behavior, but it is not always possible.

How do you bring about the unification of Europe or the world or a successful operation of the Organization of African Unity? This will be discussed in detail in the second part of the book. Many people feel that such unification will be brought about only as a result of a common threat from the outside or by a sort of benevolent dictator. Promising the citizen economic or other advantages or waving a threatening stick at him won't work. A better method is to effect a major change in values, a change in environmental pressures. Not much can be achieved by intellectual admonition. Reality will have to be brought to bear on the individuals whom we want to change. This three-dimensional approach is often necessary when major changes in philosophy and outlook are desired.

A book entitled *The New Man and Soviet Psychology* by R. A. Bauer presents interestingly the effects of a changed philosophy on the part of those who govern the lives of people. It points out, for instance, that before the revolution in Russia, there was a great deal of concern about man's subjective reactions to his experiences: great depth of meaning in literature, intensity of feelings, introspection, and great emphasis on the freedom of will. Then in the twenties, right after the revolution, Marx's philosophy placed Soviet individuals in the role of creatures of their environment, controlled by it. The study of man was restricted to this study of reactions. Subjective reactions and introspection were thrown out as irrelevant. Freedom of the will was not considered to be a useful concept. Today the more modern Soviet thinkers picture Soviet man as a lonely master of his own environment. He is personally responsible for himself and his actions. His actions, of course, must serve the interest of the Soviet country. However, he is in a state of conflict. Although he is responsible for serving the country's interests, he must strive for the goals as set by the party. He must strive to be a conscious individual, since the unconscious is not considered as important (although it is not as completely thrown out as before). He must be a person of action with ideals, and yet he is now responsible for himself; he is not so much a creature of his environment.

This is an example of the psychological tensions that occur when a new philosophy of government or control impinges itself on the individual. In about a hundred years, the Soviet person has gone through three states: the deep introspective soul, the soul controlled by his environment, and a soul who is now master of his environment. He must make it yield so that he can be a success.

This brings up the question of the psychological barriers that could arise in individual countries as a result of the unification of Europe, assuming there would be a government made up of individuals from different countries like Germany, Italy, France, Holland, Belgium, and Luxembourg. This in itself would become a threat to the other countries —just as in our country people often fear that a President from the South will bring in Southern attitudes or that a President from the East will bring in Eastern attitudes. They feared that under Kennedy we would be ruled by the Pope, for instance.

Another very fascinating book on this subject is *Nations Have Souls,* by Andre Siegfried. Siegfried points out first of all that today's European has received quite a shock psychologically because he has had to become aware that today's world is more extra-European than it is European. He says that in many ways, the European of today is possibly harkening back to the nineteenth century, when things really were ideal, whereas in the nineteenth century Europe continued to philosophize about progress and advancement with an optimistic feeling that things would get even better. However, during the twentieth century Europe suffered the consequences of two world wars, and now there is a harkening back to the good old days of the nineteenth century. Europeans, Siegfried says, are aware that the civilized world is growing less and less European and more and more Asiatic and American.

Siegfried then goes on to discuss three major groups in Europe and how they differ, talking in terms of national characteristics and the psychology of the Latins, the Germanics, and the French and pointing out problems they have in the way they deal with life. He starts with the Latins and what he calls "Latin realism." He characterizes them as mature, older people with the psychology of adults, a clear idea of the past, a deep and keen sense of individuality, and a great wealth of resourcefulness. They make good businessmen and diplomats. This is in contrast to Anglo-Saxon countries and to some extent Germany, where the state is perceived as an expression of the community. Thus Siegfried feels that the Latins would have difficulty assimilating into a culture where there would be any chance that they would lose their sense of individuality and would have to give in to the state in an idealistic sense.

In direct contrast, Siegfried talks about the Germanic efficiency. He points out that the Germanic concept is not one of a country with boundaries; rather, the German concept of self is based on a people, on a race. The main contrast he makes here is that the German spirit is always looking for form; in this regard he brings up the example of Pirandello's play *Six Characters in Search of an Author.* He feels that Germans are always looking for a savior, always looking for someone to give them identity.

A further problem in this three-dimensional approach to changing human behavior would be the fact that the cultural heritage and the discussion of generalized principles are, according to Siegfried, of great value to the Latin and to the Frenchman, while the Germanic type looks upon life as movement, dynamism, and a constant searching for form. To him, what has been realized is dead. In a sense, many of us represent these two types of attitudes—the French looking for closure and the Germanic fearing enclosure.

"He is a changed man," exclaims a person's friend. What does he mean by that? "Are we still the country of the poets and thinkers?" asks the title of a recent German book. "He has mellowed a lot," we say. Discussing Tommy, aged thirteen, his parents say, "He's almost a man. See how mature, how quiet, how self-assured he is." All of them are talking about change in human behavior that is due to environmental forces. It is part of the definition of change and the techniques applicable for his goal that willful and controlled change is usually a change for the better. It requires often a change of basic values and of a frame of reference.

A German leasing corporation was interested in getting industrialists to lease trucks and equipment rather than buying them. The desire for possession was a major obstacle, we found. By describing the results of leasing as a much greater ownership, although of a different nature, we could overcome the fear that leasing involved deprivation and lack of ownership. The industrialist now could own three times as many trucks and have them at his command. The change brought about was the freeing of the individuals involved from the obsession with possession. We changed their way of thinking to a freer and more modern outlook.

A new British women's magazine has been created for the declared purpose of addressing itself to more intelligent English women and actually functioning as an educational instrument, enlightening and broadening the minds of these women. We helped by proclaiming that it is fun to be smart and by giving encouragement to the pursuit of educational goals. It is clear that from a certain viewpoint, education is a very desirable and laudable goal. On the other hand, there are many men and, astonishingly enough, quite a number of women who do not feel that it can lead to anything good if their own sex becomes too well educated. Recently Swiss women voted against receiving voting rights. Changing human behavior thus inevitably involves one in a discussion of values.

Were men and women not truly happier when both knew their place? The male ruled, and the woman obeyed—until somebody came along and educated her or, as some might say, put the wrong ideas into her head. Things moved along peacefully and satisfactory in many areas—and might have done so for many hundreds of years had not "villainous" changes come along. Revolutions purport to and undoubtedly often do change human behavior, but they are often, if not always, followed in history by counterrevolutions—a change directed backward when looked upon from the position of revolutionary dictatorships. There are some people who would say that humanity would have been better off if fewer changes had been introduced over the last few centuries. Men and women might have been happier if everybody had been left alone. The spontaneity and ingenuity which children have naturally gets lost very soon under the whip of education, which makes well-educated conformists out of barbarous individualists with delightful differences.

Changing human behavior therefore seems to be inevitably tied up with the ethical aspects of the goals toward which human beings are pushed. Under the democratic form of government people must learn to make decisions, to think for themselves, to doubt, and to question. In most instances, the many organized forms of religion want to change human behavior in such a way that basic tenets and faith will be accepted without further thinking or doubt. It is the faith itself that is expected to bring about the change of behavior.

In a study for a gasoline company, we were asked to develop techniques which would make gas station attendants better salesmen. Our psychological interviews revealed that the majority of them had a rather negative view of their own occupation. At the same time, they felt themselves to be at the complete mercy of the mother company and to be considered unimportant by it. We could demonstrate that the company would succeed in making the gas station attendants good salesmen only if it knew how to combine a feeling of independence and creative decision making with a feeling of protection and security. We could, at the same time, point out as social scientists that ultimately this changed behavior of the gas station attendants would make them not only better salesmen for the benefit of the company, and eventually for their own benefit, but also better human beings.

Thus, another realistic technique of changing human nature consists in tackling the realistic environment and giving people the tools to cope with it. We teach our children knowledge, history, geography, and math, but unfortunately we do not teach them by means of specific lessons how to control their emotions, how to make decisions, or how to distinguish correct from incorrect information. What we ought to have is a systematic and regular test of maturity which would tell us how many prejudices our youngsters have learned to overcome—whether they are truly emerging out of fairy-tale thinking which organizes the world neatly into black and white, good and bad. Are they ready to accept grayness and chaos as a permanent condition of the world in which they live?

Of course, one of the immediate effects of such systematic training might be a radical decline in the popularity of many mass media, such as the overly simplified tabloid papers or television programs. It is reassuring, however, that in many cases this real change of human behavior, a change toward greater independence and greater maturity, is not necessarily opposed to commercial success. The more discriminating reader may require a more intelligent writer or editor, but this does not mean that he will read less—he will probably read more. He will not watch television less—he will probaby watch it more.

In a book entitled *The Dynamics of Therapy in a Controlled Relationship,* Jesse Taft talks about the mechanism of growth and change and what is involved. The book approaches the subject from the point of view of fear of the unknown, saying that growth involves change, and therefore a fear of the unknown, and that fear is the necessary part of all experience because if one is to have a new experience, he will be taking a course of action he cannot completely control since he cannot completely understand it. Therefore, it is a fearful situation.

Jesse Taft has an interesting concept of the fear of dying. She says that what we call "fear" of dying is actually *guilt for not having lived.* As the individual lives, he is constantly pulled between the desire to continue and the desire to stagnate, to stay where he is. She states that the interaction between the will to unite and the will to separate is continuous; for example, the fetus is supported in comfort and is united with the mother, and yet it feels the need to explore and to come out. Photographs of fetuses in *Life* magazine, May, 1966, show that the fetus does explore—there is a need to grow, and there is the need eventually to discontinue the relationship.

Jesse Taft's particular type of therapy, called *relationship therapy,* is based on the idea that the therapist must put the patient's interests first, giving him support and security similar to that which he enjoyed in the uterus as a fetus. She theorizes that because of uterine life, everyone has a basic desire to abandon his own ego and attach to something stronger. In this type of atmosphere, the patient gains a feeling of wholeness—of being protected by, and relating to, something that is real. He therefore feels freer to *experiment* with all his impulses, pursue them in all directions in great depth, and to better understand the ambivalence of the impulses which he experiences toward himself and other people and to the reality of the outside. He then can, it is hoped, discover what makes the outside world, other people, and himself tick. This she believes is the only way to bring about change.

Radical environmental changes, such as being forced to live in a concentration camp, having suffered a heart attack, or having survived a fire or an accident, can bring about a change in behavior. Such changes are, of course, difficult to duplicate as a therapeutic measure.

Researchers who have interviewed survivors of Hiroshima and Nagasaki report that people had difficulty in recalling details of the holocaust. However, they seemed to be more blocked by the fact that despite all the horror, they discovered within themselves the need to go on with normal human activities, such as eating or going to the bathroom. This discovery shocked them almost more than the death around them— "How could I be such a monster?" Combined with this was an understandable feeling of guilt at having been spared, when so many others around them were dead.

Reality treatment, in which people are torn radically out of their normal surroundings, could be used as a means of changing behavior, for example, letting children shift for themselves after having been dependent on their parents. Revolutions during which values and the environment change almost overnight often have radical effects on behavior. If it were not so cruel, one could almost contemplate the possibility that a physician might exaggerate the threat of a heart attack in order to induce a patient to change his ways.

In *Nationalism Is a Disease,* I suggested that for the purpose of helping in the unification of Europe, frontiers could be abandoned for a month to see what changes, if any, would occur in the respective national citizens. By means of advertising or public relations, new surroundings, a new city, and new means of transportation could be proposed to get people at least to think about a possible change of environment and to bring about a change in attitudes.

4

Removing Resistance

The most logical way to get people to change seems to be to ask them to do so. This is how the Ten Commandments have been utilized—even though they have not really worked. If we look at human history, there is as much killing, adultery, and stealing going on now as there was 5,000 years ago, if not more. Psychoanalytic techniques recognized a long time ago that you cannot ask a patient to use his willpower to get rid of his symptoms.

Let's say that we want to train someone to become interested in math. Often people are convinced that they are incapable of understanding mathematical abstractions. For often unconscious reasons, a respondent puts up a resistance. He really does not want to learn and understand math. He explains these attitudes, however, as if they were inborn, unalterable parts of his personality. The same thing is true about certain aspects of human behavior: "I am a modest person; I am embarrassed to speak in public" and "I am sorry, I just fly off the handle easily" are remarks heard quite frequently. Psychoanalysts refer to this behavior as a "character armor."

It is not the purpose of this book to describe complicated and long, drawn-out psychoanalytic techniques. But I do want to show how an understanding of deeper-lying mechanisms can help in using successful approaches in problems of communication or everyday behavior-change problems.

A politician recently asked us why a columnist consistently maligned him and reported his speeches as verbose. No matter how much material was sent to this journalist disproving his opinions with facts, he still refused to change them. Why was this so? What could be done about it? The reporter obviously needed to be right. Changing his mind about the politician would have meant admitting that he had been wrong before. He resisted changing his attitude because to do so would have destroyed his precarious equilibrium. The only way such a change could be brought about was to attack his resistance itself. A way had to be found, short of psychoanalysis, to permit him still to be right, although he now began to express a different opinion.

The solution was to permit him to feel that the politician had reformed, that the circumstances had changed, and that therefore, as a well-meaning objective reporter of history, he now could change his attitude.

Changing to a different brand or another political party is tied up with similar complicated behavior. In doing so, I inadvertently admit that the brand I used or the party or candidate I voted for represented a wrong choice on my part. The fault is largely my own for not having been intelligent enough. Switching now means additionally that I am disloyal, particularly in the political field.

We at our organization successfully advised a political candidate that fear and the voters' feeling of disloyalty might prevent a change in their voting behavior. He then devoted several of his speeches to the removal of this block rather than simply to a discussion of political platforms. He convinced his voters that by switching to his party, they were, for the first time, really loyal—loyal to his broader interests in humanity, rather than to purely partisan beliefs.

The "management" books talk about the fact that the main problem in getting people to do something new is to get them to overcome an innate resistance to change, as well as fear of criticism. The *New York Times* carried a reprint of an article which appeared about ninety years ago about a man who was arrested for getting funds for a new invention that he called the "telephone." He claimed that it could transfer voices over wire in the same way that the Morse code could be tapped over wire. The article went on to explain that anybody knew that while you could transfer dots and dashes over the wire, the human voice was impossible to get on a wire and that this man was obviously a quack. So he was locked up. The emotionality of the article led one to believe that the writer's attitude was not dictated by logic. He was frightened by the dramatic change in everyday life that such an invention would involve.

Thousands and thousands of people are willing to work in large bureaucratic companies or government offices where they do clerical or even assembly-type jobs that are very well defined. They derive a sense of security from this regularity and predictability. These people are resisting change. They do not want a job that will require them to change every month. Installing a new method of doing something through a new machine, for example, results in panic and turmoil. People resist a change in their life pattern.

I was recently asked to run a seminar for Afro-Asians, in Vienna, for the purpose of teaching them information and propaganda techniques. This seminar was partially a success; yet in many ways it was a failure. To demonstrate some of the techniques that I felt should be successfully employed, I proceeded to criticize, for example, several Ethiopian brochures designed to attract people as tourists and as investors.

Specifically, there was a folder entitled "Meet the Women of Ethiopia." The title page, however, showed a picture of the Virgin Mary; on the inside page, there was a picture of Emperor Haile Selassie, and on the succeeding nine pages members of the imperial family were portrayed. It was only on page 10 that one encountered the first Ethiopian woman. My criticism of this was not accepted, however, because the representative from Ethiopia had not learned to accept such an analysis as an objective endeavor to help him improve his country's publications. Instead of that, there was a basic resistance, which seems to exist in many young and developing countries, against being criticized in any way. I spent considerable time trying to move his resistance against criticism. It would have been more correct to let him discover for himself, by accepting a number of principles of communication, in what way his particular brochure did not correspond to these criteria.

From the communications viewpoint, the mistake he had made was quite clear. It was written from an Ethiopian viewpoint and did not take into consideration the attitude of the average foreigner, who is more accustomed to a logical presentation. After having been promised that he would meet the women of Ethiopia, he expected, indeed, to find them described in the booklet. The Ethiopians' viewpoint, however, was: "We want to tell our public that we are a Christian country and that we love our Emperor and that our Emperor has done very much for the emancipation of women." The writer of this booklet should, however, have been aware of the necessity of providing "hooks"—hooks for identification. For example, telling the story of one Ethiopian woman—how her life had changed in the last ten or twenty years—might have permitted such an emotional relationship between the reader and the writer.

The main point, however, was that to begin with, I had neglected to understand that people in developing countries (for that matter, most other people too) are usually extremely sensitive to criticism. Before they are ready to accept it, one has to give them a face-saving device and permit them to come forth with such insights themselves.

Much of the work being done by the Peace Corps or through foreign aid suffers from similar difficulties. An American expert will go into a village in Morocco or India or Nigeria and will try to change things from the way they have been done for hundreds, and sometimes thousands, of years. This is a form of factual criticism.

We at home, being modern, logical, Western, and pragmatic, achieve our results in the following way: "It is obvious that our approaches are superior—look at the difference in the standard of living that we have, compared with yours." Here, simple verbal methods of persuasion fail completely because we are dealing with a cultural barrier and resistance, which are difficult to break down from either side. The adviser struggles with the (to him) often silly and incomprehensible attitudes and habits of the more or less admittedly inferior people. The other culture group, from its side, resists the strange, foreign, and often equally silly (from its viewpoint) approaches to problems.

Wherever there are differences of levels, we are dealing with the same problem: it may be parents and children, the rich and the poor, or the management of a company and its employees. In all these instances, the individuals connected with one particular group operate and think within a given and often fairly frozen framework. Only if we break this framework and introduce a completely different manner of thinking can we hope to succeed.

In cultural adaptations such as the Peace Corps volunteers have to undertake, it has proved successful to have the volunteer, after he has made his suggestions to one or two leading groups of people in a village, step back and let the people themselves pass on this advance information as if it had been their own. Here, the Peace Corps volunteer acts only as a catalyst. This is desirable for many reasons because sooner or later he will leave and the villagers will have to carry through their innovations and reforms by themselves.

A good psychoanalyst does a similar thing. He refrains from really giving advice to his patient. He lets the patient discover for himself what the solution is. To illustrate this we might think of the patient or the member of a different group—whether culturally, incomewise, or agewise—as finding himself in a dark room with a lot of furniture. He is looking for the exit, groping to find his way, and not able to see; he hurts himself, gets panicky, and then often stands still. The adviser, the psychologist, comes in and turns the light on. The struggling and confused individual (or group) now recognizes the right way to find the exit. He has become "seeing"; he can find his own way without great difficulty. Resistance has been darkness—or our own way of looking at things. A resistance is particularly important when we are dealing with problems of prejudice.

A large supermarket chain wanted to convince its customers that it did not make an unnecessarily large profit. The first version of a slide film showed a pie chart. Then subdivisions indicated how much money was spent out of each dollar, represented by the pie chart, for food, for services, for advertising, and so on. Only a relatively small sliver of this pie was left over as actual profit. Despite the very detailed explanation of this factual story, the housewives to whom this slide film was presented did not accept it. They continuously had barriers in their minds; they felt that this was propaganda. They actively fought against being convinced by the actual figures.

We discovered that it was first necessary to remove the resistance against the absorption and acceptance of these facts. This was achieved by showing a housewife doing her shopping who, when she arrives in front of the supermarket, is greeted by a sign on the door saying that this market has been closed by government decree. She is taken aback and becomes irritated. The voice of an announcer asks her what the matter is. She complains that she cannot do her shopping. But rather than enter into an argument with the announcer, she goes off in a hurry to another supermarket. There, the same scene takes place, except that now the housewife is a little more irritated. When she discovers that a third supermarket has closed its doors, she is really upset.

At this point, the announcer also becomes somewhat indignant and asks Mrs. Brown (the shopper) what is bothering her. He tells her that if the supermarkets have been closed, this was done as a result of her own statements, which indicated that she was convinced that most of them made too much money and strangled the small businessman. Living in a democracy, the government had acted accordingly. Thereupon, Mrs. Brown states angrily that things would be impossible if everything that one said were taken literally. "I really didn't mean what I said in anger. I've gotten accustomed to doing my shopping in supermarkets." In other words, the resistance of Mrs. Brown has been broken.

The announcer then tells her that all will be forgiven and that he can understand her sentiments, and he asks her whether she would now be interested in getting the actual facts. The same facts are presented as before, but now they are readily accepted by the housewife because her almost subconscious barrier against being overwhelmed and persuaded by the information has been removed.

5

Humor as a Tool

Modern advertising and communication are making more and more use of humor. The following are some guideposts that could serve to help distinguish between good and bad use of humor in trying to change human nature.

Anything that makes you laugh, smirk, grin, or chuckle is humorous. Having stated this, we arrive immediately at a peculiar paradox. There are no humorous situations per se. For example, someone may fall down a flight of stairs, break a leg, and do it in such a peculiar way that it makes you laugh. On the other hand, you may watch the *same* scene and be shocked by the tragedy. Humor is a subtle, creative translation of almost anything that surrounds us.

E. B. White's *Subtreasury of American Humor* includes chapters with titles such as "Stories and People," "All Sorts of Dilemmas for (or against) Children," "Nonsense," "Reminiscence." What is underneath the surface of humor? One point which quickly becomes clear is that humor has "Vintage." A good part of the stories in White's book really lack humor for the modern reader. Humor has to be related to modern times. White also states, "Humorists have always made trouble pay."

Probably the most important directive on how to use humor as a communications tool is to take almost any human activity, desire, or hope and to see whether it can be turned inside out, as it were, in such a way that your own insight and tolerance of human behavior become clear. You could start with getting up and end with going to bed, and you could continue even with sleep and dreams, not to forget sex. There is hardly an aspect of human life that has not or could not become the content of a joke or humor. You can even joke about death, or maybe you have to because this is one of the methods of coping with it.

It would be preposterous to write a recipe for using and developing humor, just as it is impossible to tell someone how to paint a masterpiece or write a great novel. A good humorous treatment is almost like a miniature or an illuminated Biblical text. Great attention has to be paid to minuscule details. On the other hand, many things have to be taken out so as to permit participation of the listener or viewer.

When humor is used in communication, whatever its form may be, something happens to (and almost inside) the person with whom this humorous contact is being established. It is not just impact or retention or anything of a passive nature; there is a kind of dialogue and exchange taking place. What are these mechanisms that are produced when a good joke is told or humor is successfully utilized in bringing about change in behavior?

A joke making the rounds in Czechoslovakia permits the Czechs to get rid of their frustrations: "Did you hear that the Russians have landed on the moon?" The other Czech answers hopefully, "All of them?"

Another anecdote illustrating the function of humor as a liberating force, this time a Russian story, goes like this: An American goes across Siberia by train. At one stop he sees a beautiful naked girl taking a sunbath. He gets out, marries her, and takes her to America. Twenty years later he and his wife decide to visit the Siberian village again. Before the train gets there however, the conductor pulls all the shades down. Asked why, he explains, "We have been ordered to do this for the last twenty years, because whenever a train passes by, all the villagers come down to the station and take off their clothes." Humor works and impresses us because of such exaggeration.

A similar mechanism is involved in the well-known Alka-Seltzer commercial in which a bride has served her young husband a giant dumpling and contemplates making poached oysters or marshmallowed meatballs the next night. He takes Alka-Seltzer furtively to lessen the disastrous effects of his bride's first meal.

A joke about Italians that has been making the rounds goes like this: Two Italian laborers work way down in a shaft on some sewage pipe. They look up at the small patch of blue sky, when another man walks by above. The first laborer asks, "How come we're down here in the stinky, sweaty, sewer and Giovanni is on top in bright sunlight?"

"Why? Because he's smart," says the second laborer.

"What do you mean 'smart'?"

"Let me explain." The second laborer holds his hand against the wall of the shaft and tells the first one, "Hit me! Hit me hard! Hit my hand." He does, but at the last second the second laborer withdraws his hand, and of course the first laborer smashes his hand against the hard rock. The second laborer laughs. "See? This is what I mean when I say you gotta be smart."

A short while later both laborers get back to the top, and the first one meets another friend. He tries to repeat the same story, asking his friend, "Do you know why some of us have to work underground and others can stay on top?"

"No, I don't."

"Well, let me explain," says he. He holds his hand up against his face and says, "You see my hand? Hit me hard." He does, and we all know that happens. His face gets smashed.

Now, again, what happened in this joke? It is actually a rather crude, brutal, and unpleasant situation, but the mechanism that has been triggered in our mind that makes us laugh is tied up with the feeling "We suddenly got it." The first laborer has proved all over again that he doesn't even understand the simple definition of smartness and is basically dumb and never will get smart. So in a sense he has been right. Smart people stay on top; dumb people stay on the bottom. But in trying to give the definition of smartness, he demonstrates all over again his incapability.

Obviously, there's an additional ethnic thorn involved in this story in that it's about Italians. For example, it would not come off if it referred to Jews or some other nationalities because it would not correspond to the stereotypes that exist in connection with those ethnic groups.

I quoted these examples in order to illustrate that what we're dealing with is not so much the fact that Italians are used in the joke or that smartness had been defined in an anecdotal fashion. What is important for us to learn is that a mechanism is engendered—that something moves inside our brain that finally makes us laugh.

Depending, of course, on your background, there's a certain pride in demonstrating that "I got it; I really am smart because I recognized immediately, in a split second, that this was stupid behavior on the part of the laborer. I feel superior because I would never do a thing like that, and I also feel superior because I got the point right away." At the same time, somewhere in the deep recesses of our mind, we also recognize that at times we make comparable mistakes—not quite as crude as that, but nevertheless comparable. We're not the only ones to be that dumb. Apparently, there are enough people who commit such errors. To have this used in a joke provides us with a sort of *relief*. We burst out laughing because an unpleasant tension that has occurred to us in other situations in life has been, in an explosive manner, resolved.

In thinking about what makes a good humorous treatment, I came up with about 10 major insights which can serve as tests or guidelines for the use of humor in communication.

TEN GUIDEPOSTS FOR CORRECT USE OF HUMOR

What are these principles? Why are some uses of humor effective and others not? Why do some anecdotes and humorous situations make you laugh, while others leave you cold?

A distinction should be made between the form of humor, its content, and the psychological mechanisms. You can have humor in the *form* of cartoons, TV commercials, and even humorous sculptures. The *content* of humor could be racial, sexual, marital, etc. Entirely different are the real *psychological mechanisms* involved in humor. I present ten suggestions concerning the *application* of these mechanisms—together with the results of some research we conducted to test these rules.

1. *Humor Must First Establish a Humorous Mood*

The first insight we can develop is that humor can be almost anything as long as it is received in a humorous mood. This means that before he presents his material, the writer has to make an effort to give a signal to his reader or listener that he intends him to respond from his psychological arsenal of humor. It is the job of the creative person using humor to first create a humorous mood in which he expects the recipient of his humorous message to receive it. In a sense he has to say, "Listen to this; you will laugh."

When using mass media, you do not proceed in quite as primitive a fashion as all that. This preparation of the reader or viewer—to put him in a humorous mood—can be accomplished in many different ways. It may be just the intonation, or it may be what we call the "trigger system"—something that triggers off the right kind of mental set by setting the appropriate style. Accompanying music can be used for this.

Good anecdotes, humorous commercials and ads, and other humorous messages have the power to change moods, usually to restore good moods.

Part of this is due to the relief function that these stories have, and in anecdotes events are possible that cannot occur in real life. In a sense, many of the good commercials, whether they concern the white tornado, the 10-foot-tall washing machine, or similar things, present a mechanism similar to that found in humor because the exaggeration represents a wish fulfillment.

In the movie *A Visit to a Small Planet,* the main character, who is a visitor from another planet, simply pushes a button and flies right over all the other cars when he is caught in a traffic jam, thus avoiding any delay. When parking, he simply turns all the wheels at a 90-degree angle and rolls straight into the very narrow parking space. These situations are humorous primarily because they represent wish fulfillment—things we've all dreamed would happen and that we know very well are not likely to happen.

Many sex jokes are of a similar nature. Many humorous situations can also provide relief and establish a therapeutic effect by spelling out things that we're afraid of, exaggerating them, and thus helping us vicariously to get rid of them, to get them out of our system.

The man who is hanging wallpaper and gets entangled in it is in such a minor humorous situation. It is something all of us have experienced in some form or another—the battle with tools, with inaminate objects as our enemies, is a frequent topic of anecdotes and humorous treatment in advertising. After the anxiety has been created and relieved in humorous form, such advertising promises that if you use a particular brand of product, you will avoid such dire and unpleasant situations. This represents a successful advertising use of this dreamlike, nonrealistic mood mechanism of humor.

Maybe there should be a physiological test of the depth of breath created by good use of humor. A good joke bubbles; a bad one is flat. Laughing is closely associated with breathing. Breath and soul are also closely related. Hindu and Greek philosophy are full of examples of breath of various types being identified with different kinds of gods. The Greeks talk about some form of cosmic respiration. The Stoics, a Greek religious sect, used the word *pneuma.* It signified the breath of life. Humor in its original meaning therefore was a form of sound breathing.

Diseases were supposed to be related to air. Some of us still worry about drafts. We talk about being in a "bad humor" or in "good spirits." A good joke, in the modern sense, is a form of airing out the body, of getting rid of the bad things within you.

There is a subconscious remnant of all these things in the hunger that we have for a good joke, a good humorous situation. We may be depressed, which really means (in its original sense) breathing in a shallow fashion and feeling a weight on our bodies. We hear a joke or look at a humorous situation, and we are relieved; we are lightened. Some of the weight has been taken off us. These comparisons may seem farfetched—but they are important criteria in determining how to use humor properly in advertising.

The test I am suggesting is to ask: Does the person you are trying to reach and change feel relieved, feel lighter? Does he breathe audibly or inaudibly through laughter, or is he left as depressed as before?

Some of the German historians point out the fact that Hitler, for instance, had no sense of humor. Hitler's whole personality was a "heavy" one. He did not have enough lightness in his attitude toward life and history. The total philosophy of the Reich lacked humor. The generation gap is characterized by the fact that young people today have apparently little sense of humor. Similarly, many members of the Establishment could use more successfully a humorous attitude. TV is flooded with messages about pollution, hunger, arthritis, and handicapped people. If one wanted to respond to all these appeals, one would be quickly poverty-stricken and could not devote any time to anything else. A more lighthearted, optimistic, and humorous approach would be much more successful. Optimism and laughter lead more quickly to constructive action than *Weltschmerz*.

Humor used in modern communication is in itself a symptom of modernity—of democracy, if you will. We are surrounded by many difficulties in our everyday life. Modern communication should assume the responsibility for helping us to shoulder this burden and accept it as our lot and for teaching us to digest it and overcome it. The mood aspect of humor is therefore an extremely important modern means of therapy.

Because most communication has as its main job the changing of human behavior, even though its immediate goal may be a limited one —getting the buyer to switch from one brand to another, for example— it would be wise to make more correct use of humor. This means that the creative person must ask himself whether the humorous situation he is employing in his method has the power to *change* mood. Does it actually (and this may not be such a crazy test at all) change the breathing pattern of the people he is trying to reach?

When asked how a humorous commercial made them feel, some of our respondents made the following comments: "Pleased. You know, relaxed and happy." "Very entertained. It's a good feeling." "It puts me in a humorous mood."

Our first guidepost, then, consists not just in writing a "humorous" message but in asking yourself what power your treatment has actually to influence the mood of your viewers and listeners.

2. Humor Should Have Built-in Word-of-mouth Possibilities (Repeatability)

A good humorous situation or joke is fun to tell to *other* people. We take the credit that normally goes to the creator of the humor. If we didn't invent a joke or humorous situation ourselves, we can at least repeat it—and in that way simulate creativity. A good humorous approach, therefore, has built-in word-of-mouth possibilities, which other forms of advertising do not have to the same extent. Many people have told their friends about the Benson & Hedges commercials for the "long" cigarette.

A good joke or a good humorous message can be tested for easy repeatability. This is a legitimate test because our studies have shown that a good anecdote produces a "clicking" in the mind of the perceiver, something that we have called the "aha" experience, "I got it." At the same time, this getting of a message, this proper understanding of it, is an intrinsic element of retention and memory. If I have understood the principle, the structure, the idea behind a story, it is automatically much better anchored in my mind. I have a sort of peg to hang the message on and can reconstruct the specific content of the story more readily and more easily in the future. Therefore, whenever he is working with humor, the creative writer should ask himself whether or not his story will stand up when it is repeated by other people.

3. Humor Is a Drama with an Author and Protagonists Providing Identification

I must be able to see myself in a humorous message. Identification with the author or one of the other protagonists must be achieved. The Greeks knew that good drama has to follow certain rules. It has to contain a period of orientation—to let you know what it is all about as soon as possible. It has to have protagonists, and it has to lead to a climactic solution. A good humorous treatment of a message should be constructed in a similar fashion. In the beginning you want to know what it is all about. Are you dealing with a marital problem and weaving in margarine or Alka-Seltzer or bread? This orientation has to take place as rapidly as possible so that the reader or viewer can identify almost immediately the interest area that he has to bring into play in order to react properly to the particular message. Good anecdotes also have to have protagonists.

When a pun is simply pulled in artificially, no dramatic buildup or climax is established. We have a poor use of humor.

Perceiving the author of humor   You can usually perceive the creator of a good joke or humorous situation. A closer personal relationship is established between the viewer (or reader) and the creative person. You have the feeling that the creator had fun while thinking up and composing the humor.

We re-create the original effort. It is almost as if the artist (whether he uses television, radio, print, or any other medium) has a *direct* personal contact (dialogue) with us. It is therefore important that the "creator" wink at us in one form or another while communicating. Real humor is much more three-dimensional than a straight story.

I have stated before that the correct use of humor in messages involves the necessity for providing the creator of the message with an outlet for his own personality. One can perceive quite readily the creator behind any humorous story. There is a feeling, therefore, that the creative person took personal pride in putting the humorous message together—and this personal pride is somehow carried over. A good test for the proper use of humor is whether this identification can be perceived.

The following story provides another illustration of the pleasure in getting the point, indicating at the same time what this pleasure consists of—feeling superior: A school inspector visits a school. Before leaving he asks the students to give him the answer to one more question: "How many hairs does a horse have?" Nobody answers except one little boy. He gets up and says, "The horse has 2,560,321 hairs." The inspector is very astonished and says, "How do you know that?" The boy replies, "Well, if you don't believe it, count them." The inspector laughs and says, "I must remember this story and tell it to my colleagues." Some time later the inspector comes back to the same school and talks to the teacher of the class in which the little boy had been a pupil. The teacher asks him, "Mr. Inspector, by the way, how did this story go over when you told it to your colleagues?" The inspector says, "Gee— I couldn't tell the story because I tried and I tried and I couldn't remember the exact number of hairs the horse was supposed to have." The mechanism of this joke consists in having been smarter than the inspector, having understood the implication of his stupidity. A feeling of personal pride takes over.

4. Humor Should Establish a Distance from Our Problems (Relief)

A good suggestion for the development of humor is to step back and look at a situation almost as if it were happening on a different planet. We often say of someone, "He has a sense of humor." This remark is usually made when something embarrassing or something unpleasant has happened to someone and he still does not despair or give up. What is meant by such behavior? Psychologically speaking, it means that the person is capable of keeping a distance from his own problems. It is really a sort of defense mechanism. People who have no sense of humor usually take themselves too seriously and therefore may become the target of ridicule by others. In other words, if someone has committed a blunder, by demonstrating his sense of humor and laughing about it himself he prevents any stranger from doing it for him in a much more unpleasant fashion.

It is interesting to note that hysterical laughter is a sort of exaggerated form of the very same mechanism of a sense of humor. It is the last form of escapism and is very often the solution of deep-seated frustration. It is important, therefore, that children be taught a sense of humor at a very early age. Forcing a child to laugh about unpleasant situations is a psychological device for turning them into humorous ones. A person who takes himself too seriously usually does so because he enjoys his own suffering. A person with a sense of humor has learned that nothing lasts forever and that in the light of a large perspective, many things which at present look dark may look quite different a few months later.

As a guidepost, the creative person could describe his contemplated humorous treatment to someone else and see whether it provides relief or not. You may also want to analyze a deep-seated frustration within yourself—a nagging wife, a crying baby, or a nasty boss—and see whether you can treat it in such a way that you yourself can blow off steam. A sense of humor therefore provides a way of seeing yourself in a more protective fashion and of being less involved in your own emotional tangle.

In a peculiar sense, the communicator who is trying to solve a racial problem or carry out any other task of changing human behavior and who shows a sense of humor in his message demonstrates, first of all, that he is human and that he is not taking himself too seriously; what is most important, of course, his message becomes more believable in many instances than it would have been if he had kept a straight face throughout. Since he can laugh about himself, he is human, he is real; therefore, I also accept what he is telling me about his goal as real and believable.

To some extent, these things also apply to politics. If we could use a lighter approach in talking about some of the political and social problems that beset us, as people like Art Buchwald and Russell Baker sometimes do, we might, unlikely as it sounds, help to bring about more understanding than we do with simple, often exaggerated statements. There is no doubt that the person with a sense of humor is usually much better liked by others than a stiff and unbending one. If image and goodwill are important factors in commercial communication, AT&T, for example—or any large or, for that matter, small company— could benefit by showing itself as flexible, humorous, and human rather than stiff and unbending.

Some people exhibit a sense of humor only when they are slightly drunk. This shows that overseriousness is often due to strong inhibitions and fears. These fears come from exaggerated ideals of oneself. People without a sense of humor are usually perfectionists and cannot stand to think of themselves as imperfect and full of human weaknesses. This is an undesirable characteristic in human beings and is not much better as far as manufacturers and advertisers are concerned.

For one of our clients, a large bank in New York, we measured the reaction to humorous types of TV commercials. For instance, in one of them a bank employee cuts all the small chains which attach the pens to the desks. He turns to the public and explains that a bank cannot really call itself "friendly" if it doesn't even trust its customers with its pens. In another commercial, somebody tries to come in after three o'clock. The doorman refuses him entrance. Our young man, the representative of the bank, does let him in and argues with the doorman; again, in a humorous fashion, he explains that a bank has to understand that people sometimes are late and may have a very good reason. This is done in such a way that the public is taken into the confidence of the advertiser. It's a "tongue-in-cheek" kind of approach. A dialogue and an understanding are being established between the advertiser and the public.

Reduction of distance Humor is not only a lens that condenses reality but also a lens that can be looked through in a reverse, normally wrong fashion. Suddenly the things that threaten you appear to be far removed, and you can take a more relaxed and a more distant view of them.

Humor in its best form provides relief, and especially emotional relief. A very large number of jokes and humorous situations are of this type. Many jokes about taxes, marriage, and sex belong in this category. Good humorous messages can also help us over embarrassing situations. Commercials dealing with dandruff cures, reducing remedies, and hair dyes can all successfully employ humor because it permits talking about an embarrassing problem without causing dismay. The fact that this is possible is due to a number of psychological ingredients in such a treatment. The moment I hear my particular problem discussed publicly, even though it may be in the form of a joke, I am reassured that I am not the only one who suffers from it. This problem must be universal if it has become the topic of a joke. The situation in which somebody offers his underpants to a tax collector is humorous, although at first embarrassing. When tied up with the statement, "You took my shirt, you might as well have my underpants too," you can laugh because you see that this feeling is widespread and that you are not the only one who has it.

Another mechanism related to a large extent to this relief function of humor is tied up with the fact that humor permits you to get rid of frustration and aggression without fear of punishment. Many marital jokes belong in this category. In the commercial field, some of the margarine commercials offer a good example. One shows a man pretending that he doesn't like margarine. When he eats the bread spread with margarine anyway, remarking that he does so only because he likes breads, it permits the housewife to identify and to get rid of her aggressiveness and bitterness as far as the uninterested and contradictory typical husband is concerned.

Very often the fact that you have had something on your mind for a long time but have never stopped long enough to express it is sufficient to make it pleasant when you hear it being discussed in a humorous situation. A good joke or a good illustration of a humorous nature brings the real decisive aspect of a human event into focus.

5. Humor Should Provide the "Aha" Experience

Repeat your humorous treatment to someone else. Does it produce a "clicking" in his mind—a feeling of "I got it"?

A good anecdote has to leave the respondent with a feeling of having understood something, of having gotten something out of it. There has to be a "trigger" value. The way to measure this reaction is to actually watch for laughter or other forms of an almost explosive nature, indicating sudden understanding.

An ad for a safe says: "Is your present safe a safe or a stove?" One reads the ad and pretty rapidly gets the feeling of "Aha, I get it. My documents could burn to a crisp inside the safe." This point of getting it, of course, can also be established in a visual form. Whether or not this "aha" experience has been created could almost be suggested as a test of the correct use of humor.

A recent Czech joke goes as follows: Two friends meet in the street in Prague. "How are you?" asks the first.

"N'not s'so w'well," stutters the other man. "I l'l'lost m'my j'j'job."

"Where did you work?" asks the first friend.

"A'at th'the Czech b'b'broadcasting st'station."

"Why were you fired?"

"Y'you know h'how it is. I w'was n'not a m'm'member of th'the C'Communist party." The "aha" experience comes from the sudden recognition of the deeper meaning of the joke. Participation, leading to the solution of the riddle of the joke, is therefore an important element of a joke.

Another element of humor is a certain naïveté and surprise. A joke quoted by Freud illustrates this point: "Isn't it wonderful that nature left two holes in the fur of an animal exactly where the eyes are supposed to go?" Another good example of a joke with this surprise element is: "I am absolutely against the discussion of sex with children five years old." Pause: "It's too late."

Almost anything, of course, can become a subject for humor: race problems, sex, politics, marriage, income tax, psychiatry, work, funerals, travel, heaven, and hell. The topics of jokes and humorous situations are practically limitless; they range literally from birth to death and include all the human activities in between. As stated before, we are not interested here, however, in a superficial classification, but rather in gaining a deeper understanding of the psychological mechanism involved.

6. Humor Is Human and Tolerant

Another important rule for the creative person to recognize is that humor has to be human. Animals do not have humor. There are almost no jokes involving animals as protagonists. Humor has to be able to demonstrate that it can protect the individual against the dangers and errors of reality. It is a form of rebellion against the inevitability of our destiny, for example, having to pay income tax or the negative aspects of marriage. It is also a form of expressing sympathy, stressing the realization of the basic sameness of most human suffering: We are all in the same boat. We understand you. In a sense, the composer or the creator of humor represents the superego of mankind. If he can permit us to laugh at ourselves and the realistic situation, it is like giving us absolution. Thus, one can test and distinguish good humor from bad humor by its emotional effect. If it relieves us and gives us a feeling of having been forgiven and of having been able to look at the serious side of life in a more removed fashion, it has been good. If it increases our anxiety and fears, it has been bad.

A recent French ad for diapers shows well how such human humor can be utilized: "It is more pleasant to pee into a 'Chix' diaper" because in Chix the baby stays dry.

Many people have attempted to analyze why only humans have humor. Kant talked about the "sudden transformation of a tense expectation into nothing." Biologically, laughter may have originated as the expression of excitement and joy at the downfall of an enemy. The incongruity of life, its difficulties, and its eventual inevitable end lead to a form of *escapism* in laughter.

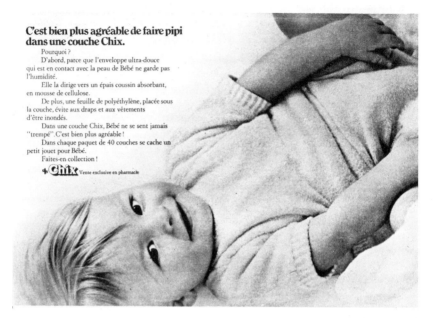

C'est bien plus agréable de faire pipi dans une couche Chix.

Pourquoi ?

D'abord, parce que l'enveloppe ultra-douce qui est en contact avec la peau de Bébé ne garde pas l'humidité.

Elle la dirige vers un épais coussin absorbant, en mousse de cellulose.

De plus, une feuille de polyéthylène, placée sous la couche, évite aux draps et aux vêtements d'être inondés.

Dans une couche Chix, Bébé ne se sent jamais "trempé". C'est bien plus agréable !

Dans chaque paquet de 40 couches se cache un petit jouet pour Bébé.

Faites-en collection !

Chix Vente exclusive en pharmacie

7. Humor Involves Condensation, Expansion, and Exaggeration

In a good humorous situation, there is a condensation of reality. It is as if a long story had been collapsed, and now it is fun to let it swell up again—to bring it back to its original size. This "swelling up" is usually done in a good joke with lightning speed—accompanied almost by some kind of "popping" action.

A good humorous story must not be too long; it must be brief. A condensed story should not take long to understand. If a lot of explanation is needed or if a lot of time elapses before the intended humor comes to light, a good part of the effect is lost. A story that takes too long to come across is either too complicated or, usually, not cut enough. Another good test is to write your story and then to cut a good part of it, until a considerable amount of participation has to be added to make it understood. Too many jokes die as a result of the mistake of over-obvious treatment.

To satirize is to comment upon something with some keenness and imagination, perhaps in a rather roundabout or indirect fashion, and sometimes savagely. As E. B. White says in *A Subtreasury of American Humor,* "almost all humor is roughly satire."

A story has been told about Mark Twain refusing a drink offered him before breakfast. He said, "I have three reasons for refusing. One, I never drink before breakfast. Two, I am a strict prohibitionist. And three, I've already had three drinks." In order to laugh at this joke, you have to translate it, re-create the real meaning behind it. We must begin to understand the exaggeration involved. At the same time, you also apply one of the criteria that I pointed out before, a feeling of the author behind it, in this case, Mark Twain.

Taking a simple fact and exaggerating it in such a way that the respondent must and can reduce it to its original meaning is a very effective form of communicating in a humorous fashion. Many recent ads and commercials that employ exaggeration are making use of this formula. The important thing, of course, is that the exaggeration has to be intrinsically correct; it must not stray from the product or service, but stay within its total framework. When reduced and trimmed back to its actual meaning, it should lead directly to the product message that was intended. A pill that promises it will make you sleep like Rip Van Winkle represents a negative example because no one really wants that long a sleep. We are really much more interested in waking up refreshed. The exaggeration would have been correct if the ad had stated that after you take the pill, you wake up with so much energy that you feel as if you are wearing seven-league boots, for example.

A recent TV commercial shows a plasterer and uses the phrase "easy to push around" to convey the idea of spreadability of cream cheese. This falls flat because it goes to too much length to state an obvious fact. Furthermore, few people really have problems spreading cream cheese.

Much has been said about subliminal methods. Although they are not as dangerous as they have been made out to be, they also are not as ineffective as others pretend. However, we do not have to look for mysterious and magic formulas for flashing messages lasting a hundredth of a second on the television screen. What we can use instead, much more effectively, is background material or something that is even more subtle, the ad behind the ad. The more associations I can develop and the more I can read into an ad, the more value in space and time and seconds the advertiser really receives. The important test, therefore, of this associative power is the possibility of re-creating the original story.

The more I can participate in a message, the more I can also be tempted to discover the nucleus of the humorous onion by peeling off layer after layer of skin. The more time I am going to spend with the message, the more value the communicator receives for his money. The creative person could test his humor according to how much time the respondent is tempted to invest in interpreting the anecdote, joke, or humorous situation—up to a point. If it takes *too* long, of course, he may lose pleasure. There are some people who take a long time to understand a joke. If that is the case and the joke has to be explained to them two or three times, a major part of the value of the humor has been lost. On the other hand, a joke can be gotten *too* quickly—before it is really finished. There is probably an optimum amount of participation that should occur. It should be rather rapid—lasting perhaps between half a second and one full second.

Freud pointed out that one of the important things about humor is that it condenses the essential elements of a particular situation. What humor does, in the psychological sense, in the mind of a person is to serve a function similar to that of a sharp magnifying glass or focusing lens. It stands to reason, therefore, that simply portraying a normal, realistic situation is not the best or most efficient way to utilize humor in advertising. What is needed is the application of an almost "psychedelic" kind of treatment to crystallize and lift out the most essential parts and put them together so that an overly sharp image is created. This does not, of course, refer simply to the optical image, but also to the well-observed little details that are utilized in putting a humorous commercial or ad together.

A cartoon uses the same kind of principle. In the typical political cartoon, some of a political personage's major facial characteristics or best-known features of dress are lifted out, often in a completely irreverent and unrealistic fashion. This condensation represents an important aesthetic element in the enjoyment of laughter and humor. It permits the onlooker, the person receiving the message, to re-create the condensed form and to go back to the original concept of the creative person. It is a form of re-creating what the artist created and pulled together in a "time-binding" way. Even journalism, to a large extent, uses such oversimplification and essentialism in order to get its message across. What, of course, is permissible and often necessary for humor in advertising can become an obnoxious distortion in political reporting. If a political jokester refers to Vice President Agnew as Tricia's baby-sitter, he pulls together in an unfair but extremely sharp and significant manner the unfortunate role that the American Vice President very often has to play.

An often-repeated joke about a salesman who is trying to sell a particularly high-priced coffin goes as follows: The buyer expresses a complaint that he has seen much cheaper coffins. The salesman says, "Yes, but have you tried to do this?" and he makes a rapid movement of his elbows, as if trying to find more space, thus explaining the price and quality differences. Without having to explain further, the essential nature of death and the futility of being interested in having elbow room in a coffin are pulled together. Although we are dealing with the topic of death, it is still a humorous story because it permits us to see an essential part of the philosophy of human life, the inevitability of death.

8. Humor Should Be Timely

The humor found in E. B. White's *Subtreasury of American Humor* and similar books is often quite dated. What I mean by that is that it is slow-moving. One has a sort of flat feeling after reading it. Is this all that there is to it?

An old joke that one has heard before creates a similar feeling of disappointment. We are less afraid to hurt today. Bob Hope shows little respect for the people who are the butts of his jokes, and thus he gives a feeling of being modern. Some jokes that apparently were very popular and successful twenty, thirty, or forty years ago fail to produce the desired effect when they are retold now.

The *form* of humor, if not the content, has changed considerably over the last decade or so. Modern humor is much sharper, more vicious, more incisive, and more rapid in its delivery. Many subjects that used to be taboo ten or fifteen years ago can now be utilized without creating any embarrassment—the Burlington TV commercial for men's over-the-calf socks, for example. Although the situation is not obscene or immoral in any sense, it is a somewhat embarrassing one, dealing subtly with men's underwear. It shows a man who is trying to get one of his socks to come down because the other one has slipped. It doesn't because it is Burlington. This is a good use of humor because several criteria are involved. It has a modern style, music, and feeling tone. At the same time it permits the contemplation of a basic human problem, reminding people not only of the sock situation but also of many other kinds of embarrassing situations that the average individual does encounter.

Modern humor has to be in line with modern style of living because if it is not, the average young individual will not feel inclined to retell the anecdote. He has to derive from it the feeling that he can obtain definite recognition and pride, almost as if *he* had been the author.

9. Humor Should Be Universal

Naturally, what appears funny to a twentieth-century European or American does not always register in a completely different society. But by and large, human motivations are the same around the world. A good test is to tell a joke in various different modern cultural surroundings and then to observe whether people understand it and laugh. If they do, they have proved conclusively that motivations are much more alike than we think. When Jack Benny says—in response to a burglar who threatens him and tells him to decide between giving his money and giving his life—"Let me have a few minutes to think about it," the joke is understood everywhere in the world. Miserliness is a universal human characteristic. Its futility in the face of death is a factor that we need to recognize, but when we are reminded of it, it becomes universally effective. Script writers should ask: "Could it, with some minor variations, show the same situation in other countries—and still get a laugh?"

Sometimes, of course, an anecdote may be unpleasant to a particular ethnic group. A joke is told about a Congolese student who returns from the United States to his native country. Going back to his cannibalistic diet, he exclaims, "This tastes better, after all, than what we ate in the Washington University cafeteria." This story may not go over well in the Congo, but in most other non-African countries people appreciate its nasty and sly humor.

Humor thrives on trouble, and mankind is full of dilemmas, difficulties, and woes. A creative person might well be advised, then, to pick a universal difficulty with a human activity related to the product field he is trying to sell—shaving, toothbrushing, even colds—and to build his theme around it. In talking to medical doctors in pharmaceutical advertising, we in our organization found that one of their universal troubles is the inability to cure the common cold. We suggested that this theme be made into a series of ads. They were and are very successful.

10. Humor Should Be on the Mark

Test the associations, the psychological ripples created by your humor. Do they lead to the intended message or away from it? We often have the feeling, when humor is used badly, that the joke has been dragged by the hair. The associations and thoughts that are being triggered do not lead directly to the essential part of the story.

Each product or service has a "soul" of its own—the very quintessence of an "idea," in the Platonic sense. Unless this idea is pulled out of its hiding place and translated into dramatic form, no real communication will take place. The basic essence of the message can come at the beginning or at the end. A good example is the commercial for Head and Shoulders, in which a young man complains about not being able to get a date with a girl. After using the dandruff remedy, he triumphantly informs his sister (who had recommended that he use it) that he got the date after all. Then, in sort of an offhand fashion, as he leaves the room se says, "And by the way, Bob had the measles," thus deflating the claim that the advertiser just made. Interesting enough this denial of the claim, creates a basic feeling of belief of the total message. The advertiser admits that Head and Shoulders may not get the young man a date. He shows, by using this punch line, that he has a sense of humor —although literally speaking he really denies his own claim. An interesting fact is that our research showed that the exact opposite takes place: His claims are really believed *for the first time.*

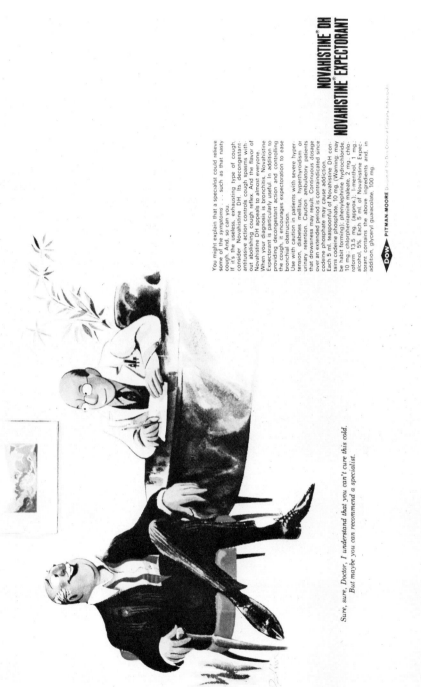

Sure, sure, Doctor, I understand that you can't cure this cold. But maybe you can recommend a specialist.

It is a pity that in many of our attempts to get a story across on an individual, national, or international level, we are learning only now to accept the power of humor as a humanizing force. Of course sometimes humor wrongly employed can backfire, as it occasionally did, for instance, in Adlai Stevenson's speeches.

While I hope I have succeeded in putting down clear-cut guidelines for the proper use of humor, I have not discussed one of the most important requirements regarding humor, which may be, at the same time, the explanation for why it is not used often enough or well enough, namely, the need for genuine creativity and the kind of sensitivity that has understanding for human weakness. No amount of rules or advice will help the creative person to use humor effectively and successfully unless he has a sense of humor (as we defined it) himself—a certain humility and basic insight into human motivations, weaknesses, fears, and hopes.

6

Helping to Crystallize
Your Opinion

SETTING THE SWITCH

Let's assume that passengers on a cruise ship are to be influenced as
far as their attitudes toward food, entertainment, short excursions, and
similar things are concerned. One way to approach the problem would
be simply to ask them for their opinions. This would not take into
consideration, however, the fact that most people are incapable of form-
ing an immediate, clear-cut reaction to events around them.

You go to a theater and are asked how you liked the show. Very
often you are at a loss as to how to give an intelligent answer. One
of your first reactions is to look around and to listen for the opinion
of someone whom you consider to be more of an expert than you. What
he says—as long as it agrees generally with your own more or less
neutral attitude—will have a very great influence on the formation of
your own opinion.

Similarly, a good guide on an excursion bus can help crystallize, to a very large extent, the opinions of the people taking the trip. When he says, "Did you enjoy the meal you just had?" or "The ruins that you visited, weren't they lovely?" the majority of people are very likely to agree, unless the experience really has been a disastrous one. Once the opinion has been crystallized in their own minds, they will pass it on as their own to other people.

We tried a similar approach in department stores. On their way out, customers were asked whether they felt they had made a good purchase and had found what they wanted. Simply because this catalyst of attitudes was provided, a sort of jelling effect took place, and the majority of the people involved agreed with the simulated or suggested positive judgment of their purchase.

This kind of crystallization of opinions takes place all day long around us. Newspapers do it by employing big or small headlines, depending on the importance of the news. The big headline appearing in the daily newspaper gives every reader a clear-cut understanding that he has to look upon this event as an extremely important one. We all have had the experience of seeing a headline on the front page of a newspaper and only then becoming aware in a full dramatic fashion that we had witnessed a really important event the day before. "Was it of that magnitude? Gee, I didn't realize; I guess it was" is often how we react. Thus we have to remember that one of the reliable techniques for bringing about a change in people's attitudes is to crystallize their opinions, rather than simply waiting for them to make up their own minds. This technique is applicable in many different situations. The wording of a menu in a restaurant, for example, may possibly even alter the actual taste experience of the dish we are eating: *Macédoine de fruits* tastes twice as good as fruit salad. Probably for this very reason most menus in the better restaurants in London are printed in French.

Any form of autosuggestion should probably be discussed in this same connection. Very often a situation can be altered radically if one simply decides to change one's attitudes. This, in turn, can be brought about by crystallizing an otherwise vague, free-floating kind of series of reactions that have not received any proper kind of labeling.

A change in trade name had been decided upon for a German supermarket. The new name had been thoroughly tested with the public, and it was time to present it to the sales staff. Showing them the name for the first time in a cold manner would have been a mistake. They would have started to criticize it primarily for the reason just mentioned—their own opinion was not formulated clearly enough. We are also dealing with another problem here. Whenever we are asked for our opinion, the danger exists that we are using the wrong types of comparisons and wrong standards. How we feel about a situation such as a change in trade name depends to a large extent on how much attachment we have for the old name and how much knowledge we have of comparable competitive situations.

We at our organization prepared a psychologically founded presentation of the trade-name change by telling the staff ahead of time what effects could be expected as a result of this new name. In a sense, we gave them a frame of reference from management's viewpoint, rather than permitting them to use their own criteria, which would have been too varied and too unreliable. We then took various types of possible solutions and differing variations of the name and demonstrated how some of them fulfilled some of the criteria and conditions that management had proposed, and we showed that none of them did this in a complete fashion. We gradually explained that the new name that had been previously chosen by management, on the basis of tests, was the only one that fulfilled a majority of conditions. Doing this, putting the problem this way, helped crystallize the public's opinion: in our case, the business associates.

An important rule, therefore, is that when you are interested in having people formulate an opinion, you should not be completely reliant on their actual views, but should consider a number of factors explained before. To repeat them in a more systematic fashion, they are the following:

1. Provide a definitely expressed and clearly stated reaction by an authority figure.

2. Give the people whose opinion you are asking a clear-cut frame of reference which they should use in order to develop their own judgment. Putting it in simple terms, liking or disliking something (whether it is the food on a cruise ship, a new trade name, or a new package design) depends to a large extent on whether or not you have concrete and sharply delineated knowledge as to what this particular phenomenon to which you are reacting is supposed to do.

3. After these precautions have been taken, get your public to state clearly what they like or dislike about the particular product or service.

4. State other people's opinions first. By making it clear that other people have appreciated a particular book or play or have found the food in a restaurant to be delightful, you can exert a strong influence on the people whose minds have not been made up yet. This is another way of describing the bandwagon effect, which is often very powerful but which, despite that, is often overlooked.

5. Give explanations when asked for opinions. In museums, modern sculptures or paintings can be presented in a cold fashion, leaving it up to the onlookers to make up their own minds. However, if proper explanations are given beforehand as to what the artist was trying to convey in his painting or why he used a particular style, color, or artistic figurement, remarkable changes can be brought about in the

public's opinion. Good museum guides (in printed or spoken form) can do this. However, such guides are extremely rare. Instead, people are left to make up their own minds, which they are often incapable of doing.

If all this sounds highly manipulative, we have to remind ourselves that education, of course, if it is properly done, should be using exactly the same kind of techniques. Presenting to a student the bare historical facts about a particular period leaves it up to him to make up his own mind to become involved, to try to identify with it, and to really understand what went on. A good teacher provides a proper explanation—a proper framework—and points out certain things to the students. He puts the accent on a historical event or the literature that he is discussing, and in a remarkable way, attitudes change.

What we are really talking about, then, is getting rid of the notion that people are always capable of making judgments or of expressing their likes and dislikes. This does not imply a disregard or lack of respect for the abilities and capacities of human beings; it is based on realism, as are most of the other points in this book.

The advertiser who dramatizes certain aspects of his products in his publicity uses exactly the same kind of techniques as the book reviewer or the art or music critic. Any good art or music appreciation course has to teach people first to see and to hear before they can form their opinions. You can listen to a piece of good music without recognizing it as such. But if you are told how to listen to music, how to recognize good music, and what to look for, your appreciation increases. The interesting and rewarding aspect of this technique is that it can train taste and discrimination. Teaching people how to appreciate wine and how to tell good wine from bad wine will add a new dimension to their lives. The same thing is true of art appreciation and culture appreciation.

While on a cruise, I observed that people were becoming bored with the Greek and Roman ruins in various Mediterranean ports of call. I recommended that a little booklet be written on what to look for in ruins and how to become an amateur archaeologist. I even went so far as to institute on board an archaeological game that would teach people how to dig for themselves. They would win little prizes; some inexpensive actual antiques were buried in a big sandpit. On later visits, ruins were not just piles of stones—they had a real meaning. I also found that reading such books as *The King Must Die,* by Mary Renault, can change people's attitudes considerably about Greece and the past. It can make a visit to the Temple of Knossos in Crete, for example, a human, dramatic event. The whole field of adult education is very strongly involved in this discussion.

7

The Third Language—
Gestures and Poses

Another way of changing behavior is to use a "third language," a nonverbal language, composed of gestures, poses, abstract designs, and symbols which can be used in combination as an effective and dramatic way of communicating emotional or intellectual concepts. It is essentially a language of the body, a dictionary of nonverbal language, and like a word dictionary it is merely a foundation.

By and large, communication continues to employ the old, traditional tried-and-true techniques, and yet we know from the many studies that we have conducted that those who have had the foresight, the courage, and the creative ability to utilize these innovative, more modern techniques have been highly successful. Many religious and political parties have successfully made use of symbols and nonverbal language. The hammer and sickle, the V sign for victory, the cross, and even the black eyepatch of Moshe Dayan are all examples.

In order to arrive at a reliable understanding and a correct new use of gestures and poses, it is important to ask ourselves first what the biological purpose of poses and gestures is. Basically, the human being, once alive, is dominated by the fundamental motivation of protection and defense of his security. By going back to the original sign language of primitive man, we can come quickest to an understanding of the meaning of the problems and topics we are trying to analyze. When exposed to danger, primitive man tried to protect himself, probably by using his arms (and his entire body, for that matter) to act as a shield or to reduce the surface exposed to the outside danger. The other biological attitude is to assuage the enemy—to open up one's arms, to increase the surface of the body, to seek contact, and thus to reassure oneself and the potential adversary that he is dealing with a friend. As far as gestures are concerned, this expresses itself in throwing open one's arms, reaching out, smiling, and making all possible movements and facial expressions that indicate a readiness to cooperate and to establish a dialogue. Probably in a condensed form all the gestures can relate either to hatred and fear on the one hand or to love, understanding, cooperation, and friendship (lack of fear) on the other.

What has happened in our modern world is that we still use the same nonverbal equipment, but in a shorthand fashion and without completely executing the original total meaning of the gesture. We still make a fist when we are angry, but we don't hit the "enemy" any longer under normal circumstances. When we are joyful we open our arms, but we do not necessarily embrace the other person; instead, we are satisfied by stretching out our arms and shaking hands.

Different cultures distinguish themselves by the degree of completion of gestures and poses. Among highly inhibited and more sophisticated twentieth-century cultures, gestures are reduced to a minimum. People in southern climates, the Latins, and the French are more inclined to carry through and come closer to the complete theatrical performance of the original, biologically purposeful behavior. Frenchmen kiss each other (even males) on both cheeks. Latin Americans are prone to hug each other. Germans, Englishmen, Scandinavians, and Americans keep their distance. They are much more miserly as far as their gesture language is concerned. Since we are concerned primarily with the "theatrical" uses of gestures in changing behavior, we have to consider cultural situations to some extent, but at the same time we can afford to go overboard in our "gesturology" or "poseology" as compared with everyday use. Even models in a message appearing in Germany can go to the same gestural extremes that Italians might in real life without our expecting that all Germans will become exaggeratedly expressive in their body movements and poses.

I have attempted to develop first a basic, overall framework for the total nonverbal gesture language. There are at least two major divisions:

1. Those gestures and poses which are inner-directed and have meaning without a partner

2. Those gestures and poses which are outer-directed and require a friend or opponent

Inner-directed poses are more frequently related to protective aspects, providing the performer with a feeling of safety and security. The outer-directed gestures are by definition more outgoing and more aggressive (not necessarily in a negative sense); they are goal-directed and have the purpose of fighting off, discouraging, encouraging, or reassuring the partner.

A word about subdivisions:

1. Among the inner-directed, protective gestures as well as among the outer-directed, more aggressive gestures are those which are of a purely cognitive, more intellectual nature and those which portray emotions.

2. All our gestures can be either inner-directed, where no partner is needed, or outer-directed, where we want to tell somebody something through body language. We can behave in a soft fashion just being alone, or we can convey to somebody else the nonverbal expression "soft." Therefore, a chart which we shall utilize for our study as an organizational technique and as background would present itself in the following way:

BIOLOGICAL ORIGINS OF POSES

INNER-DIRECTED		OUTER-DIRECTED	
PROTECTIVE		AGGRESSIVE	
EMOTIONAL	COGNITIVE	EMOTIONAL	COGNITIVE
Softness	Classic	Softness	Classic
Romantic	Quality	Romantic	Quality
Intimate	Extravagant	Intimate	Extravagant
Young	Elegant	Young	Elegant
Seductive	Conservative	Seductive	Conservative
Caressing	Decent	Caressing	Decent
Bohemian	Formal	Bohemian	Formal
Masculine		Masculine	
Feminine		Feminine	
Dynamic		Dynamic	
French		French	
German		German	
English		English	
Italian		Italian	
Comfortable		Comfortable	
Relaxed		Relaxed	

Gestures (whether bodily, facial, or digital) can be considered "signals." In their most primitive form they signal basic emotions such as fear, rage, contentment, etc. In more sophisticated forms they signal more complex emotions such as love, understanding, comfort, etc. While we call them signals, gestures are not "representational" of emotions or feelings; rather, they are (or have become) an integral part of the experience of these emotions. In fact, one of the signs of aberrant behavior is the inappropriateness of the feeling (interior) to the gesture (external acting out) or the complete repression of the acting out.

Gestures are not relegated to nonverbal expressions of emotions, however. They can, in a more sophisticated way, signal whole concepts such as danger; the coming of rain, cold, or other natural phenomena; etc. An example of gestures that signal concepts are those which we use to say "hello" and "good-bye."

Gestures are "shortcuts" to communication. They are immediately and intuitively understood in most cases. Gestures are emotionally based, grow directly out of the emotion, and occur simultaneously with the emotion or feeling. Words (language), on the other hand, while they are a kind of signal (more appropriately, a kind of symbolism), are intellectual in character. The feeling or the emotion must be "expressed" in the proper words. One must "search" for them a good deal of the time. Further, words are not necessarily spontaneous. They can be chosen "afterward." Words are often used to hide or mask what the person is really thinking or feeling. Gestures, on the other hand, most often are not used for that purpose. They can, of course, be used to lie or deceive, they can be used in a controlled way, and they can be thought out in advance and used later at the appropriate time. Actors and dancers, for example, do this. It is part of their craft. But basically the gesture is a spontaneous phenomenon which signals an immediate feeling, emotion, or need.

Gestures, then, are truly shortcuts to communication. They tell us what the person "really means" or is "really feeling," as opposed to what he is saying. By watching a person closely when he is speaking to you (his eyes, his forehead, his hands, his mouth, etc.), you can obtain a much clearer picture of what is really going on inside him.

NEW TRENDS

When we speak of the "new trends," we do not conceive of them as "moments etched in time," but rather as part of an ever-changing, ever-evolving life-style. We perceive the present time as one which is in the midst of dynamic change; values are changing, ideas are changing, and involvements and concerns are changing, so that as a result, consumers' demands of communication are also changing.

While this collection of poses is nonverbal in its fundamental aspects, we have to be aware of the fact that this total body-language is in itself moving and changing in different time periods. Thus, you have to visualize this model as being put in motion, modulating, and changing, as it were, in different ways in different time periods. Three new trends can be observed in this total structure; the basic organization, however, remains the same.

Contrast   While primitive man, when he wanted to say "I hate you," indicated his feeling in a direct fashion through his gestures of attack or threat, we are now learning that an even clearer but more sophisticated expression of this feeling can be achieved through contrast, that is, through overpoliteness and ice-cold, exaggerated friendliness. As a result, a desire or need for broad contrast in all areas of communication has arisen.

Today, for example, serious themes or statements are conveyed through the use of comedy or irony. "Black comedy," satire, farce, or slapstick may be involved. In contrast, funny or comedic ideas are handled with mock seriousness. For the most part, they seem to indicate this sharp contrast of statement. Things are underplayed or overplayed, understated or overstated. This is a successful and provocative method of making a point and making it rather strongly.

Part of the trend is the "mania" for making fun. No person, institution, tradition, or social behavior is above reproach or at least examination. From a psychological point of view, the behavior of today's youth can be seen as an aggressive acting out of this desire to make fun of the Establishment. To the advertiser this trend means, in effect, "Do not use the obvious. Do not be afraid of contrast, of the absurd, of the unexpected." The "stylized" ad can in some cases be the most effective way of telling the story.

Multiple language   Another new trend is one which is pointing toward ever more imaginative and daring techniques of communication, whether in the fine arts or in mass communication such as radio, television, and the print media. One example of this trend is the popular "mixed-media" happening, which combines the use of visual and auditory stimuli in an imaginative and often provocative and controversial way. Young people, in particular, seem to be involved with experimentation in these areas, finding new forms, styles, and techniques of expression. Borrowing the techniques of mixed media (many simultaneous sound and visual stimuli) offers a new and exciting approach to communication and makes possible the incorporation of the exaggerated pose.

There is a place for the inappropriate or exaggerated gesture or pose. It can be used for unusual dramatic strength or power where reality is purposely distorted to make a point. Expressionistic drama of the twenties and thirties and expressionistic art offer good examples. More recently, the theater of the absurd (Genet, Ionesco, Beckett, and Pinter) offers a different kind of distortion. Expressionistic drama was socially oriented. Characters were symbols of various aspects of the social system. The point of view was usually (though not always) the author's rather than the characters'. The theater of the absurd deals on a more personal level, and the distortions are generally seen through the eyes of the protagonist (or antihero, which is the modern equivalent). In this situation the gesture reigns supreme. Exaggeration and distortion (while accomplished through dialogue, lighting, set, sound, etc.) are conveyed to the audience basically through the actors' use of movement and gesture, including actual posing. Suffering humanity might writhe like snakes, capitalists might be painted like money and move in rhythm to the stock-market ticker tape, etc. The hero, in the throes of final agony, might assume a pose symbolic of Christ on the cross.

In the theater of the absurd, Ionesco's *Rhinoceros* requires the central character actually to turn into such a beast with appropriate movements, gestures, and sounds. The rhino is Ionesco's symbol of the average contemporary man: thick-skinned, unimaginative, unattractive, insensitive, unwilling to get involved, etc. In Genet's play *The Balcony* characters pretend to be what they are not, until reality and fantasy become one and the world "zooms off toward hell."

An important element of style concerns the fact that any *framework of reality or nonreality* will be accepted by the audience no matter how foreign, strange, or "unreal" as long as it is consistent within itself. Every element of the play or the picture (in this case an ad or display) must remain consistent within the style and must operate within the framework that has been established. Someone once said that the theater requires the "willing suspension of disbelief." The same could be said of communication when properly handled.

Abbreviated signal (instant poses)   While life-style as we have described it is an ever-changing phenomenon, basic human nature remains unaltered. There are certain universal and "time-binding" aspects of human nature—feelings, emotions, and basic needs—which have never changed and will never change. These can be considered the foundation on which nonverbal communication can be built. They can be appropriate for the life-style of this generation, as they have been for past generations. They are like an old house that is altered every so often—new paint, new plumbing, new wiring, new use of interior space, new interior design, etc. The basic structure, *foundation and beams,* however, remains unchanged. The unalterable allows the alterable to exist without total destruction. It also gives a sense of continuity or time-bindingness. The alterable allows the unalterable to appear flexible and adaptable to changing needs.

Still, there are some aspects of human behavior which seem to be in a constant state of evolution. One general trend over the centuries has been the use of the continually abbreviated signal. Today, that trend has been greatly accelerated. This can be viewed psychologically as modern man's lack of commitment to the gesture (making it smaller and smaller) as an expression of his lack of commitment to the emotion behind it. Yet that is not an altogether satisfactory explanation because in a subtle way the abbreviated gesture or "instant" pose stimulates participation and interaction. Take the theater (or cinema) as an example. In the late nineteenth and early twentieth centuries the concept of realism or naturalism consisted in overacting and overposturing; it was overly obvious. By our standards that style is ludicrous, unbelievable, and far too unsubtle. Modern theater and cinema are far more sophisticated. Not only is it not overdone, it is purposefully underdone. Nothing is completed. There is room for the audience to participate since they are "forced" to complete the meaning or the message.

In similar fashion, today's abbreviated gestures and instant poses serve the same purpose. While they continue to signal meanings, the fact that they have become economized allows room for the other person to fill in, to interpret, to participate. The "subtle" gesture of today (as compared with the "grand" gesture of the past) by its very lack of obviousness compels attention.

PRACTICAL APPLICATIONS

1. The use of the appropriate gesture or pose in a photograph or a display can by itself "speak" to the recipient of the message and tell the story or reveal the meaning behind the message. Often we find that while the words describe a certain mood, situation, or type of fabric or dress, the picture tells a completely different story—an inappropriate story, a conflicting story.

2. The creative man must not be concerned simply with creating a "nice" picture or a symmetrical design, but should rather understand the dynamics of gesture and pose so that he can better express the story or the meaning behind his message.

3. The pose or gesture itself can be used to express an attitude, in effect "telling" the respondent how it feels to change his behavior.

Techniques of Using Poses

Gestures and timing   We can speak of gesture or pose as the "in-between" language. It is a "bridge" between feeling, or emotion, and the spoken word. For example, the feeling of fear comes first, closely followed (perhaps just a fraction of a second separates them) by an appropriate gesture. (There are many possible gestures, but they would all involve some form of protective contraction.) Last come words: "I'm afraid," "Don't hurt me," or whatever.

There are basic rules of acting, for instance, governing the use of gestures. They are "basic" because they are psychologically correct. An actor never gestures *after* a line. To do so would be inappropriate, except perhaps in a highly stylized play. The gesture usually comes *with* the line, or if particular emphasis (dramatic emphasis) is desired, the actor may gesture before the line. "The body is behind that door," says one actor to another in a play. The actor would never say the line and then point to the door. Most likely he would point as he says the line. But if dramatic emphasis were required, the actor might point first, hesitate (the pregnant pause), and then deliver the line.

Gesture and design   The "total" design of a message is, of course, very critical. In its entirety it must tell a story. It must have a unity of purpose and meaning. It must create a "gestalt." We can ask what the basic elements are that go into making up an ad or a window display. There are (1) the objects, including people; (2) the background; (3) the lighting as it conveys moods and atmosphere; and (4) the spatial relationships. Color, too, is an integral part of the total design.

The task is to arrange the objects (including people) against the background (which must be appropriate to the total either by "blending in" or by contrasting sharply) and in relationship to one another (spatial relationship), using the appropriate lighting and color to help convey the mood. For most creative men this is elementary, even unconsciously understood. However, what is often neglected is the appropriate gesture or pose that will complete the unity and by so doing help tell the story.

Our movements and gestures are different in the dark and in the bright light, in a crowded space and in an open space, when we are happy and when we are depressed, etc. In our studies we have often seen messages in which everything has been carefully worked out to be both psychologically correct and aesthetically pleasing but in which the poses are somehow static, inappropriate, and seemingly divorced from human behavior. The models are more like statues and mannequins than living people.

Gestures and emotions   All emotions have as part of their expression certain gestures. These are reflex; that is, they are spontaneous. All artists know that visual stimuli are far more powerful than words. A gesture, a movement, or a position at the pitch of emotion can be far more powerful dramatically than anything the person might say. Even playwrights who depend on words, know this and leave room for the actor and the director to make the contribution of gesture or movement. Novelists, too, often use a particular style for highly emotional passages which forces the reader to "complete" the feeling himself. In some respects, cinema is more powerful than the stage. Why? Because in cinematic technique the word assumes subordinate importance to the visual image. Every nuance of gesture or expression can be captured by the camera, or every vista or panorama can be captured.

We think of all emotions as basic. In a sense they are; that is, they come before thought or intellectualization. They precede their concept; that is, they are experienced before they are defined. Nevertheless, there are emotions which are most primitive, some which are less primitive, and some which are quite sophisticated and complex. Further, there are emotions, such as love, which can be subdivided. There are many kinds of love: parental love, romantic love, love of country, etc. For example, ask an actress to express mother love. Her response, while individual, will undoubtedly contain elements of protection, an inward kind of thing, cherished and close. Then ask the same actress to express romantic love, and her response will probably contain elements of sharing, of giving and taking; there will be an outward kind of gesture or movement.

The psychological gesture   The actor, for instance, and also the dancer search for the appropriate psychological gestures which will help define and at the same time reveal the character they are in the process of creating. In a sense, the psychological gesture is a "summing up" of the character. If he never spoke at all (as in fact the dancer or the mime does not), these gestures would tell us a great deal about the character. They could be called "creative shortcuts" to understanding another human being.

The psychological gesture could also be called a "mannerism"; that is, it gives us insight into a character, relationship, or situation. It helps create the "aha" experience even more powerfully than words because the gesture is understood intuitively, emotionally, immediately, and even perhaps irrationally, whereas words must go through the "strainer" of the intellect before they reach the guts. For example, an actress said of a character, "She covers her mouth with her hand every time she laughs as if it might come out a cry instead." Balanchine, the great choreographer, said to one of his dancers who was interpreting a particularly vain man, "His head always turns before his body. It points the way; it indicates the direction. The head and body must almost appear to be disjoined." An actor describing a nervous character said, "He always wipes his forehead with a handkerchief, even though there is no sweat on it."

One of the most startling "psychological gestures" (and one that is universal) is the movement to the rhythm of the heartbeat. When a person is nervous, anxious, or restless or when he is involved in a stress situation, psychologists have found that the most comforting thing he can do (he does so unconsciously, of course) is to move some way in rhythm with his heartbeat.

Gestures and sensory stimulation   We have been exploring emotional or intuitive, unconscious responses and the part that gesture and pose play in creating such responses. Equally basic, but perhaps more sophisticated in concept, is the relationship between sensory perception, emotion, and gestures.

Actors, dancers, and mimes (and to a lesser degree writers, poets, and painters) are trained (or know how) to use the senses as pathways to emotions. In an attempt to evoke an emotion, recall of the emotion itself is virtually impossible. Instead, the recall of a specific event which embodied the emotion through the use of "sense memory" is the technique which is most successful. Psychologists, too, have realized this and borrowed this technique with certain modifications for use in therapy. Through exploration in depth of the sights, sounds, smells, tastes, and even textures associated with the emotionally charged event, the emotion itself can be recalled and reexperienced.

Not surprisingly, as part of this exercise, gestures and movements (whether facial or otherwise) emerge in relation to the senses. These, in turn, lead to those gestures which "signal" the emotion. Depending upon the emotion involved, the gestures might be constrictive or expansive, smooth or jerky, etc. In some cases, they become almost expressionistic as a result of the exaggerated importance the event has assumed in the mind of the individual.

PRACTICAL APPLICATIONS

1. "One picture (the right picture) is worth 10,000 words." To be modern, behavioral communication should rely less on words and more on pictures. Here, the gesture can bridge the gap between what the ad is attempting to "say" and any copy that might be necessary.

2. The gesture or the pose used in a message must be appropriate to the mood, the atmosphere, or the general feeling of the scene. The gesture must allow for an unconscious meaningful association between the picture and the copy.

3. Gesture or pose is an important element of total design. Not only does it help tell the story, but it is itself part of the total design. Gestures and poses imaginatively used can give a sense of movement, vitality, action, and life to a layout or to a display of a story.

4. Despite the complexity, the gesture, as basic as it is, can aid in making the story or the message understood. The gesture alone can be fundamental in achieving the "aha" experience, in which the reader immediately and intuitively makes contact with the meaning of the message

and understands it. Set designers for theatrical productions, for example, must be influenced by costumes—and costumes and set, in turn, influence behavior.

5. The message or the display need not be "naturalistic" or "realistic." Particularly, communication meant to appeal to the younger generation can employ "expressionistic" techniques of exaggeration that will tell the story or create the "mental rehearsal" which stimulates behavior-change possibilities.

6. Much purposeful communication and propaganda lack style, style which can in itself tell a story and create a mood or emotion. As an integral part of the style, gestures or poses that are exaggerated, distorted, and imaginative will help communicate the feeling, the mood, the "story" you want to tell.

7. In communication there is room for "symbolism" since it is at once different, dramatic, eye-catching, and meaningful. In this case the camera or the poster (which can be conceived of as a large camera eye) can effectively use exaggerated gestures and poses in combination with symbols.

8. Gestures and poses can be found which will most directly and immediately express any emotion the communicator wishes to convey. In simple terms, he can "sum up the feeling." This is a happy scene, for instance, this is security, this is a frivolous scene, this is an intimate scene, etc.

8

Encouragement

To tell someone to have courage and use his willpower sounds like a simple recommendation as far as getting him to change his customary behavior is concerned. Yet it is a rather difficult kind of assignment. One of the problems we are confronted with is that most of us have a fixed notion as to our basic psychological makeup. We are introverted, extroverted, lazy, intelligent, or creative, for example. The erroneous belief in the static and permanent nature of our psychological makeup gives us an excellent excuse not to bother with any significant efforts to bring about a remolding of our basic psychological composition. Modern research, however, shows that we are dynamic in nature—that there is a wide band of potentialities available to us. We can reach the upper or the lower limit. The way we locate our life and our abilities depends to a large extent on ourselves. At rare moments we glimpse the horizons of what we could be. Some people make this discovery when they are drunk, when they have taken LSD, or when, and this is significant, they have been complimented and encouraged to do something that they have been convinced they are not capable of doing. Leaders in wartime have been able to exhort their fellow citizens to withstand danger and difficulties beyond their normal range. Encouragement can come in many different ways. It can come from someone who has mastered a particular skill and who invites us to imitate him; it can also come from the behavior of our peer groups. If all others are capable of doing it, we too should be. Learning a foreign language in the classroom, for instance, is much easier than doing it individually. We can witness the achievements of the others and thus take courage. In a way, encouragement is a form of "psychological vitamin" that we can release into our own minds. Biologically, we are afraid of anything unusual that challenges us, and we are first inclined to reject it and to run away.

We are less concerned here with an analysis of the phenomenon of the encouragement than with the development of practical techniques. Suppose we want to teach students math. This is a difficult and, at first, unpleasant task. It is much easier for the student to say, "I am not mathematically gifted. I have always had trouble with math, and therefore I don't want to be bothered." Teaching the student the first simple lessons and then getting him to abandon his fears and showing him that he can do it is the usual approach. But one has to go beyond that. The student has to learn to recognize the hidden powers within himself. Starting with elementary school, there should be training programs on how to develop courage. This is being done to some extent in gym classes, where we are taught how to jump over hurdles. But little is being done in a psychological sense. From infancy, our children are too often brought up in a "No" atmosphere rather than one in which we say "Yes." We recently suggested to a builder that he begin to introduce a "Yes" room into homes, rather than permitting most of the rooms and living arrangements to be "No" rooms for the small child.

Programmed instruction is based to a large extent on systematic encouragement. The Berlitz method, in which you are taught that you already know quite a bit of Spanish or French, even though you have not studied it, represents similar encouragement. When prescribing a reducing diet, too many doctors concentrate on the diet itself rather than the really difficult problem—the continuous reassurance the dieter needs that he is progressing.

The training of salesmen could also be based more than it is on this aggrandizement of the ego. Sales charts for the individual participant represent such an approach. In public relations, advertising, and communication, it is often sufficient to state that a task is easy in order to get the public to participate and to make an effort to learn and to understand. Since manufacturers do not make an effort to give the self-confidence needed to master a new power tool or a new chain saw, for example, catalogues can be quite helpful. We have redesigned an operator's manual for a chain saw in which there is an appeal to people's native intelligence, reminding them that each chain saw consists of about four or five parts that are analogous to parts of the human body: the starter and spark plugs are comparable to the brain, the carburetor parallels the heart and the lungs, the cutting edge of the saw is equivalent to the teeth, and the gas tank and oil pan represent the stomach. By producing an understandable human parallel, we succeeded in creating an understanding of the basic principle involved in putting together a chain saw that is sold disassembled. We could thus prevent, to a large degree, fumbling and failures and complaints to the manufacturer.

On a recent trip to a Caribbean island I was forced to drive on the left! The warnings put in the car itself, however, read, "Don't forget to drive on the left!" I was continuously reminded. However, not a single person encouraged me by telling me that it is easy to learn to drive on the left and takes only fifteen to twenty minutes. This reassurance, more than the admonitions, would have helped to speed up the process of adaptation and to change an admittedly unimportant part of my behavior.

Many newspaper readers never bother reading the financial pages or any complicated full text of political speeches or governmental announcements. Yet it would be a simple task on the part of the modern newspaper not only to give the text of the speech or the financial news but at the same time also to precede this special section with a note of encouragement, stating and restating in one form or another, "It is not difficult to understand the financial pages." The *New York Times* has tried this approach partially in the form of a separate booklet, but does not give such encouragement regularly at the beginning of each financial section. Most people would get 20 to 30 percent more out of their daily newspaper if they were given this kind of invitation and encouragement. A good exercise would be to list the various things that up to now you have not properly understood—maybe how a computer or modern electronic device works or how a laser beam really operates.

For a department store we tried to develop a guide for men so that they could better understand the terminology used in women's fashions and eliminate once and for all this particular blind spot in their knowledge.

Another idea would be to attack other blind spots in your own arsenal of knowledge and understanding. You could simply take a daily newspaper and mark all those areas and terminologies that for many years you have never really fully grasped. This would force you to find out why you have never tackled these dark, unchartered areas and to convince yourself that your normal excuse—that you are not gifted along those lines and that nature has not properly endowed you—represents only so many false and easy rationalizations. You could then develop a plan to eliminate these unchartered areas one by one. You would start on an intellectual safari. Many of the books and instructions which you would need as guides are available, if you just looked around. It might be an idea for a publisher to develop such a series of intellectual safari books. Advertisements often make the mistake of dramatizing the advantages and values of a particular product without realizing that this is not quite enough, that what the consumer needs is encouragement to venture into an unknown field.

Interestingly enough, in some studies we found that this is the case even in higher-income groups, where there is money to buy more expensive merchandise. There is a considerable psychological and economic lag between being able to afford a product and having the courage to buy it.

Advertisers selling luxury products should be taught that many of their customers who have recently moved up into a new group are afraid of punishment if they splurge. The newly wealthy person is not very sure that his new position has been deserved and will last. He does not want to tempt the gods. If he were to spend too much, he might be thrown back to his previous low standards. The advertiser has to encourage him, reassure him, and in a way teach him the modern philosophy of economics— that only if he learns to think in more courageous terms about spending will he maintain his drive. Only if he thinks in terms of moving up in his spending will he force himself at the same time to move up in his earning capacity. In a recent ad for wallets, men were reminded of the fact that while they may dress elegantly, too often their wallets are several years old and really should be replaced.

Such an advertising approach represents an effective way of encouraging people to take action on something which is relatively unimportant but which they keep postponing. Most people make use of possibly only 50 or 60 percent of their potential. Anyone who considers this to be a pity would agree that a change in human behavior that would permit people to realize 100 percent of their possibilities for life is necessary. Unfortunately, too many religions and too many moral systems have, rather, attempted to reduce our capacity for enjoyment by surrounding us with innumerable inhibitions. Many of us have been brought up with the feeling that such full enjoyment is sinful. We are too often living under the threat of abstemiousness. Science and the development of new possibilities and new products, which have made it possible for us to get to the moon, live more comfortably, improve upon nature, eliminate more and more diseases, and lengthen our life-span, are in many ways a complete contradiction to the teachings of religion.

All such achievements are in response to the question, "Why not?" While the main purpose of many of the concepts we have been taught has been to impregnate us with a variety of warning symbols preventing us from doing what we may instinctively want to do, many of our studies, particularly those concentrating on the development of new services and commodities, start out by questioning the present form and function of things that surround us. If many people feel like putting their feet on their desks, then why not create a desk specifically designed for this purpose, saying to its owner, "Go ahead, do it," rather than making him afraid of scratching the polish. How can it be done? Easily enough, by inserting a pad of leather or plastic where the feet can rest.

Why does a house have to be stable and static rather than turning with the sun? Such a house has already been constructed. If the morning newspaper is too big and cumbersome and cannot be comfortably read, why not print one on scrolls that could be rolled up, or why not print one in a small format, as we have recently suggested to a publisher in Austria? It was then simply called die *Neue* (the New)—not much larger than a book. We have accepted many of our everyday objects without questioning whether they are still reasonable in the light of modern technological developments. We could literally start taking a fresh look around ourselves from morning to night, beginning with our beds and the way we sleep, get up, get dressed, conduct our affairs, and end up the day.

In a study for a building magazine, we in our organization analyzed the possibility of making bedrooms much more attractive than they are at present—adding fireplaces, refrigerators, and possibly a dumbwaiter leading from the kitchen into the bedroom so that breakfast could be eaten there. More studied and planned romance can be introduced with the help of the fireplace. We could even go as far as considering the possibility of having beds that could be turned around at a 360-degree angle so that one would not always have to face the same wall. You may want to look out of a window. When you wake up during the night, you may want to have a feeling of protection and coziness and face a more quiet wall. At present wall decorations such as paint or wallpaper have to be permanent. With the help of projectors you could vary the decorations, depending on your mood, by inserting different slides. It would be a good exercise to take one human activity after another and to encourage people to think about it in new and unusual terms. The way we are dressing and undressing, for example—could this be done in a more efficient fashion.

Encouragement, however, is needed not only in terms of greater convenience and functionality. We are rapidly approaching a culture in which we are beginning to do those things as a hobby which we used to do as jobs and as duty. We are discovering the possibility of a gourmet attitude toward our everyday pursuits. We have made the discovery partially as far as food and drink are concerned, but have neglected our own clothing, our own body, our everyday surroundings. L'Oréal, a cosmetics company, is now coming out with a way of decorating the body with flowers. This seems to be a somewhat related commercial adventure.

Probably one of the most important areas in which encouragement is needed, besides that of getting more pleasure out of life, is in teaching the individual in our modern democracy that he has much more power than he thinks he has. Democracy can really function only if the individual's awareness of the importance of his one vote, his one militant expression of opinion, is instilled from the early days of his schooling. We are still far away from encouraging people to live an active democratic life. We are too often satisfied with teaching them to recite the Declaration of Independence and to know the history of the country, but we have yet to develop training courses in the real exertion of their power, on which democracy depends.

9

The New Art of Flattery

Some officials of the city of Vienna complained to me that the Viennese were ungrateful for their services. No matter how many good things these officials did for them, the citizens continued to complain and were accused of being ungrateful by the officials. Identifying myself with these accused citizens, I discovered within myself a resentment against being accused and attacked continuously. If you tell someone repeatedly that he is no good, he decides at one point that he might just as well live up to this feeling or reputation. I suggested to the officials the thousand-year-old motivational technique of flattery. An ad was developed which for the first time told the people of Vienna how wonderful the administration felt they really were. (A number of practical case histories are presented in Part Two.) Only patience would enable them to accept the frequently necessary construction jobs, with the delays and discomforts that a modern city administration has to impose upon its inhabitants. This approach had never been tried before. Apparently, it worked so well that the Viennese jokingly wondered why they had to have such high-priced politicians and city council members if they themselves were so good.

A good question to ask yourself when you are trying to communicate in public or private is whether you are directly or indirectly being insulting. In terms of such direct problems as racial relations, some of our studies have shown that when liberal whites protect blacks under all circumstances, the blacks correctly interpret their attitude to be an insulting, condescending, patronizing one. Being told the truth when they are doing something wrong has proved to be acceptable to them, which further demonstrates the power of equality and constructive criticism which is *real* flattery.

In a travel brochure for St. Croix, I found a good example of such subtle flattery. The writer admitted openly that the beaches of this island were not among the best in the world but that it was the people of St. Croix of whom one could be proud. When an advertiser promises someone prestige as a result of purchasing a Cadillac or a Lincoln or increased beauty as a result of using a particular kind of cosmetic, he uses superficial flattery. However, it is important to know that the kind of flattery that was acceptable ten or twenty years ago is no longer effective. A woman feels flattered when someone else immediately notices a small effort she has made. It shows that he is observant and sensitive. Conspicuous consumption showing off to reap compliments, which used to be the byword thirty years ago, is now taboo. The *nouveaux riches* of today are characterized by the fact that they do not want to appear to be rich. They prefer quiet elegance. The recipient of a greeting card feels flattered when the person who sent it has made a special effort to pick a card that will appeal to him; he reacts to this good taste and special concern.

We suggested to a hotel association that flattery be utilized by asking the arriving guest about his special wishes and then, of course, making an effort to satisfy them. This might be an extra pillow or a harder mattress. Particularly when dealing with the public, it is important that each individual be given a feeling that he is being treated in a very special fashion. VIP rooms at the airline terminal cease to be a special privilege the moment they become available to everybody and therefore do not convey prestige any longer. Flattery is an especially important motivational technique of changing human behavior. Most of us would rather deserve the flattery; we would begin to live up to it and would change more readily than we would if we were being accused or insulted. Maybe one of the ways to speed up acceptance of different races would be to flatter, for their efforts, those people who have made (even though admittedly insufficient) attempts to accept minority groups as their equal rather than to keep on continuously accusing them of intolerance and bias.

One of the characters in a novel by Philip Wiley has attended an Asian college set up by a clique of gentlemen to teach girls, from an early age, to be artists not only in love but also in flattery. Maybe similar classes should be instituted in our schools in which the teacher not only would pass on Emily Post type of superficial manners but also would point out to the pupils how much power subtle flattery can have in bringing about a reorientation and desirable change in the person one is trying to influence. We continuously have to prove ourselves as children in school, as grown-ups, as lovers, as mothers, as cooks, as money earners. We are never quite sure of ourselves. Subtle flattery gives us more self-assurance; it is a temporary award which induces us to go on to the next step. Salesmen, too, could benefit by systematic courses in flattery.

How does one learn this technique? As I have already mentioned, it does not consist in lying and simply saying something nice about the other person. Sometimes it might be even better to make a negative remark and still have it interpreted as a compliment. One of the rules is to become observant and find out something very special about the person which may not have been too obvious to other people. Stating this observed fact gives the flattered person the feeling that he or she has been a worthwhile object of study and analysis.

Another technique of learning how to flatter is to find out what the other person is dreaming about—what his or her goals are. She may want to stay young; he may want to stay virile and not have gray hair. Guessing at these things and complimenting the person, indicating that you have noticed the achievement and fulfillment of his endeavors, is a good way to produce a positive effect.

Embellishment of existing sober facts is another form of flattery. This is very strongly the case where declarations are, psychologically speaking, flattery. Not too long ago in Washington, a bill for truth in packaging was proposed. While this is a desirable endeavor, we also have to realize that making things appear more beautiful is not necessarily anything unethical. A whole industry of a fairly large size has developed in many countries specializing in the different subtle ways of flattering the sober contents. Here we are referring to the design and artistic handling of packaging of products.

Every wardrobe represents an arsenal of flattery tools. We decide which dress or suit or tie to put on today in order to appear to our best advantage. Maybe in the not too distant future we will also have a battery of mental and psychological decoration tools and flattery equipment that we can select for a particular occasion. Actually, we do have exactly that. When we meet someone we want to impress, we reach into the available tool chest to put on a psychological jacket which will bring out the best in us and correct our weaknesses. Thus, another motivational technique in learning how to flatter is to flatter ourselves first. For every beautiful woman who is aware of her assets, there are hundreds of other women

who continually and awkwardly do those things which are the least attractive for them. This may be a wrong use of their voice, a poor way of
dressing, or unpleasant way of walking. Watching people wade into the
ocean when the water is cold and rough is unpleasant to look at. Most
of us demonstrate a lack of charm in such a situation. The human being
in this situation is like the owner of a new car who hasn't been given
an instruction manual. He often pushes the wrong buttons or does not
even know how to get the motor started. We should take an inventory
of our major potentials, assets, and weaknesses and then develop ourselves—or with the help of professional "charm schools," which are very
often unjustly maligned, we should develop each one of our positive
points and cover up or eliminate the negative ones. The use of videotape
in a self-analytical film would be particularly helpful in this respect.

I have also experimented with a so-called psychological mirror; friends
—and, possibly more fruitfully, enemies—are asked to put down what
they like or dislike about you. To see yourself as others see you is often
a painful, but very useful experience. Often an excellent way to flatter
someone is to do so in a nonverbal fashion by permitting him to get
ahead of you, by serving him first, or by listening very carefully, an art
few people have acquired. One demonstrates interest in, and appreciation
of, the other person. Modern advertising, in which subtle details are
built into the pictorial presentations which necessitate sharp observation
and sensitivity on the part of the person toward whom the ad is directed,
conveys a feeling of confidence in the intelligence of the public. This is
one of the highest forms of flattery. Overexplaining or repeating the obvious is, by the same token, a very crude (but often practiced) insult on
the part of the modern communicator.

On a recent trip to Czechoslovakia I was told that the one thing the
Communists resented more than anything else was to be underestimated.
A particularly detestable example was quoted to me concerning a Czech
visitor to Australia who was asked by an Australian, "Are you allowed
to keep your children with you, or are they taken away by the state?"
"This is exactly what we are complaining about," said my Czech friend.
"How can we hope for understanding and communication if anybody
living in a free-enterprise country, whether he admits it or not, looks
down upon us in the way a white visitor to an African country might
do." Even there I found the same kind of problem when an American
politician visiting one of the African countries distributed ball-point
pens. This created a wave of resentment because it made the local people
feel as if they had been receiving beads and glass pearls, the way one
regales the natives. Many American companies operate this way abroad,
even in Europe.

Being able to project oneself into a different culture, playing the role of someone strange to one's own upbringing, is another form of subtle flattery. In the relationship between doctor and patient, it is often extremely difficult for the physician or the psychiatrist really to understand how a person feels who has a fever or who may be worried about cancer. Much too little is being done in modern training to make the professional aware, in his doctor-patient, lawyer-client, or teacher-pupil relationships, of what really is going on in the mind of the individual with whom he is dealing. In doing some work for police organizations on the problems involved in race relations, we found that the major complaint was not physical brutality on the part of the police but, to a much larger degree, mental cruelty: "How can they ever understand how we feel? The moment we show our skin, we become overly sensitive to the fact that whatever we do is being reacted to not on the basis of normal human behavior but on the basis of our dark complexion. Sure we are touchy, but this is not really our fault. It is the job of the white policeman to learn to understand our touchiness, to become, as it were, color-blind."

In international relations, where there is often great difficulty in understanding the other person, flattery could help enormously in reducing tensions. On a recent visit to Prague, I observed an interesting display at the airport there, where a sordid series of pornographic films of strip-tease joints in Tokyo, Berlin, New York, and London was being shown. All were true enough, with the possible exception of the one about New York, and had been photographed on the spot. The conclusion to be drawn from these films was that the capitalist societies, and particularly their main cities, are degenerate and immoral. In contrast, the Communist society, where everybody works and lives in contentment, is lily-white and pure and is interested only in the happiness of mankind. What the propagandists overlooked, no matter how well trained they may have been, was, again, this motivational technique of necessary flattery. Obviously, the Western visitor, seeing these films, was in one form or another insulted. He was put in a negative frame of mind; he had to try to defend his own system, within which he lived, and at the same time had to find fault with the system this film tried to sell him. How much more intelligent it would have been had the propagandists started out by flattering the foreigner and showing him the many achievements of the free-enterprise system, the high standard of living, and the degree of freedom that he enjoyed. Then they might have told their own story. If they had been really smart, they would not even have boasted too much, but would have admitted a number of their shortcomings and asked for understanding and intelligent cooperation, pointing out their own difficulties and problems and telling the visitor how far they had already gotten and how they felt (which was their privilege); then the visitor might have felt that their system was superior, more moral, and less likely to lead to excesses.

Most of us see another culture through our own eyes and judging anything that is different and unusual as inferior. As I pointed out in my book *Nationalism Is a Disease,* many of our problems in the military and political fields come from exactly this kind of lack of understanding of the necessity for appreciating the viewpoint of the other nationality. Therefore, another important motivational technique, which is an aspect of flattery, is to try to project yourself into the other person, other culture, or other nationality and try to see things from that viewpoint. Role playing should be a daily exercise. Every good salesman needs this training program. He may have to start out by trying to imagine himself in the role of a housewife when he wants to sell vacuum cleaners or cosmetics. If he is an older person, he may have to spend half an hour trying to be a younger one, and vice versa. He may even have to go as far as imitating poses and gestures. Not only would this help him become a better communicator and salesman, but he would also enrich his own personality enormously. Thus, flattery is one of the oldest human forms of persuasion. It is part of courtship and love affairs. Man has practiced it at princely courts ever since the time of the Pharaohs, and yet it still could use a revival and a more scientific, contemporary approach.

10

The Development of Insight

Psychoanalysis and other forms of psychotherapy try to help the individual to understand himself. From early childhood we try to interpret the facial expressions of those around us—parents, siblings, and friends —and react to them. We are involved in a continuous search to understand our own motivations. We read novels, see shows, and go to the movies all, in the final analysis, because we are curious. We want to dig beneath the facade and discover the secret ingredients that make us act on the world stage in our own peculiar drama. We want to bring about a change in ourselves or in the person whose change will benefit us. We are looking for the trigger, the secret button that we can push. Insight can be a parlor game, but it is also vitally serious. The marriage may be falling apart. Parents may have lost contact with their children. The employer cannot grasp why his staff does unfathomable, incomprehensible, unpredictable things. For thousands of years, we accepted simplistic explanations. We may have guessed at the truth, but we were afraid of it. The Ibsens and the Schillers began to show us, together with Freud and other scientists, that beneath love there could be hatred. The smooth, lush, green fertile lawn of the human personality could be hollow, rotten, and cavernous underneath. The simple cause-and-effect, physical explanation of disease was shattered by the introduction of psychosomatic concepts. We have learned by now that simply to exhort someone or admonish him to stop using drugs or to behave more democratically will not work unless we also have a knowledge of the more intricate wheels and levers of which his motor is composed. We have accepted the necessity for understanding motivations, but we have not really learned to do so in a systematic fashion. Changing human behavior without understanding motivations is like trying to start a stalled car by kicking it.

How does one learn to develop insight? One could have a complete clinical knowledge of the workings of the human mind at one's disposal, similar to the mechanic's understanding of how an engine works. It is not the purpose of this book, even if it were possible, to condense this vast and often confusing body of knowledge. Instead, the aim is to provide the reader with techniques of changing behavior. Thus, one of the first prerequisites in connection with insight is simply the resolution not to interpret somebody's comportment too naïvely and too simply—to ask oneself first whether beneath the obvious explanation there could not be a more complex and deeper one. Motivational research concerns itself scientifically with the techniques that permit the advertiser or the communications expert to reach his public in such a way that he achieves his desired results. He can do so only if he learns to develop insight into his public's motivation. In the naïve empirical approach, it is characteristic to imagine that by going out and asking people why they are doing what they are doing, you are very likely to get the correct answers. Our approach consists of first setting up hypotheses as to what possibly could be likely explanations of a particular phenomenon to be investigated. Like a detective, we first develop hunches which could explain human behavior. An important rule, which by the way applies to any researcher, is to ask fundamental and often naïve and basic questions.

Why do people drive carelessly? Why do people smoke cigarettes, even though they know about the dangers? The questions to be asked first, as silly as they may sound, are: "What is an accident?" "How can it be brought about?" Obviously, it is not a deliberate attempt to kill oneself. Surely fatigue, alcoholism, and other factors may play a role. Supposedly, accident rates in England have been reduced by 20 percent recently as a result of the "breatholator" test which can measure the amount of alcohol a person has drunk. But on a more fundamental level, car accidents happen because one feels locked in, is impatient, and might have subconscious aggressive feelings. One of the hypotheses that we in our organization set up was that such impatience and aggression, if it has no other outlet, will inevitably translate itself into driving behavior which can readily lead to a fatal mishap. We suggested the installation of a separate foot pedal which could be pressed when one feels angry. Instead of "giving it" to the car by accelerating and pushing down on the gas pedal, the foot would now have a new outlet. Another idea was to install various tactile doodling devices on the steering wheel which could be fingered and played with and could thus serve to reduce impatience.

In a motivational study on women's skirts, again our approach was to ask basic questions. When did skirts start as part of the fashion in female attire? Originally, men and women wore the same type of tunic. Men going to battle found the long tunic cumbersome and shortened it. Apparently, they discovered that their exposed legs got cold in inclement weather and started to cover them—first with a sort of bandage and later on, as weaving techniques developed, with stockings. At the same time, women's skirts probably had a biological and functional purpose. They could take care of their physiological needs more easily that way and were also accessible to the dominant male. Going back a little further in our analysis, we found that in most cultures the lower parts, particularly of the female, were covered and disguised, while the upper parts, the breasts, were exposed and visible.

Almost all the things that we do and products that we use in our daily pursuits have an interesting origin and more than a superficial meaning. Understanding this symbolism and developing insight represent an important part of changing human behavior. If we are going to get Frenchmen to drink less wine than they have up to now, we have to understand what wine means to them. Robert Crichton devotes a good part of his recent best seller, *The Secret of Santa Vittoria,* to analyzing and describing what wine means to a particular group of Italians. Not only does their livelihood depend on it, but it is also almost a sacred thing to them, almost more important than life. They hide their treasure, hundreds of thousands of bottles of wine, from the conquering and invading Germans at the risk of their lives. Only if we understand in a real insightful fashion the meaning of wine to Italians can we sympathize with this behavior. This insight is a very human faculty.

There are three major types of learning. The first is instinctual learning, which with nature has usually endowed us. It is exemplified by our sudden withdrawal when we touch something hot, our reaction to pain, and our biologically meaningful responses to many other daily experiences. We reject bitter things, and we like sweet things; we react to sudden noises in a defensive fashion.

The second, more elaborate form of learning is one that we (together with other animals) are capable of—training. A good part of our so-called education, from childhood on, consists in being trained to act appropriately and in line with the demands of our culture and civilization. Toilet training, embarrassment, shame, and various forms of inhibitions all result from appropriate conditioning.

The only truly human form of learning, however, is the one based on insight, or what the psychologists call the "aha" experience, in which we suddenly understand why something is being done in a particular way or why a person reacts the way he does. In order to grasp fully the meaning of this "aha" feeling, it is necessary that we concern ourselves with how, indeed, the human mind works. We have at our disposal a whole library of structures, graphic models in two-, three-, and four-dimensional forms. In his book entitled *Displacement of Concepts,* Donald A. Schon points out that the unlearning of old ideas and the learning of new ones, which constitutes a change in human behavior, necessitates the breaking down of existing concepts. As long as these models—often in the form of straitjackets on our thinking—exist, we are incapable of, or have great difficulty in, adapting ourselves to a new situation and changing our form of reactions. Insight in the form of an "aha" experience takes place when —almost as if in a puzzle—the parts suddenly fit together differently from the way we thought they would. It is almost an audible type of clicking that takes place in our minds: "Aha, this is it. This is the explanation; well, now that I know, I'll never do this again."

Literature is taught in many schools, but more because it seems to be part of one's culture than for the real reason, which is that it helps us to acquire more insight into, and a better understanding of, our own motivations and those of other people. In a study we conducted on soap operas, we found that a major reason why 20 million American housewives listen to them day in and day out is that they are searching for lessons in living. In many creative sessions with people in advertising, I have spent hours discussing such seemingly unimportant and yet fascinating things as how people feel about dirt and cleanliness and what soap means to them. These topics were, of course, of immediate value to the advertiser, but beyond that they represent an interesting exercise in insight.

Each person should have a sort of motivational dictionary which he continually brings up to date, corrects, and uses as a training manual for motivational techniques. This book is, as a whole, conceived as such a manual, and it cannot possibly cover all variations. We could start with simple things such as our various moods: Where do they come from? What can be done to influence them or capitalize on them? What is their meaning? What is the meaning of our everyday habits? Why do we eat what we do? Why do we get up, take a shower, and get dressed the way we do?

11

Changing the Structure as a Motivational Tool

When the average person is asked to describe progress, he usually thinks of a straight ascending line. When we talk about human needs, we think of a pie chart. In both cases we're dealing with models that underlie our thinking processes. In both cases, however, the model utilized is an erroneous one. Human progress is more readily and more correctly described as a spiral development, where we come back to where we have been, but on a higher level. It proceeds along the lines of thesis, antithesis, and synthesis. Human needs are much more correctly thought of as expanding, like a balloon. With increasing satisfaction of our needs, we usually do not cut out a larger and larger slice of the pie and therefore have fewer needs, but instead "the appetite comes with the eating." Our language and our thinking patterns are full of graphic models. When these models are correct and in line with the real world and the actual structure of the events that we are dealing with, they can act as excellent guides. When, however, we have an erroneous model, we can think that we are proceeding logically and within the necessary follow-ups of the structural require-ments, but sooner or later we must end up with maladjustment. As a motivational technique for changing human nature, it is very important that we make the individual first aware of the model that he is using, the assumption that he is working with, and then check these now-conscious assumptions as to their correctness.

Restructuring our thinking   A restructuring of our emotional frame-work is all part of the same problem sphere. The Florida Celery Growers' Association asked our organization, the Institute for Motivational Re-search, to come up with new ideas to increase the consumption of celery. A motivational research study, conducted for the purpose of coming up with new ideas, showed that while on the one hand the crackling noise made when eating celery is considered to be annoying and socially non-acceptable, on the other hand it is really enjoyed. We suggested that the Florida growers use this fresh, crackling, healthy-sounding aspect of celery as a major advertising theme and that they abandon what had been tried before—inventing, to a large extent, nonexistent health and reducing aspects of celery. In other words, we recommended that they switch from the model of "wholesomeness" to one of "fun" and "hedonism" and make the fact that one cannot eat celery silently a positive aspect. We changed the structure within which the product was perceived and had been advertised.

The ability to develop models and structures for thinking is an ex-tremely important one in modern management. It also enters into national and international issues. If one is convinced of the "domino theory," which in itself is a form of three-dimensional model, then the war in Vietnam has to be won at all costs. If, however, one uses a civil war as the model for what is happening there, then it stands to reason that the United States has no special reason to continue its involvement. For a long time, the frozen-food industry permitted the model to persist in the mind of the consumer that "frozen" was the opposite of "fresh." When we found, in a motivational research study, that such a model existed, we suggested that it be destroyed by facts—those which demon-strate that most of the so-called fresh fruits and fresh vegetables are not really fresh in the sense that they reach the consumer immediately after being picked, but are at least three to four days old on the average, while frozen food, on the other hand, is picked at the highest point of ripeness and is frozen in its freshest state. Thus, according to this more correct model, frozen food is really fresher than so-called fresh food, unless we want to compare it with products the consumer picks in his own garden, which he rarely does. In media research, the erroneous assumption is often made that the size of the ad or the colors being used are primary functions of its being noticed or seen. The more correct model that has to be recognized is that ads do not appear in a vacuum—that when all the ads are full-page and in color, the small ad which appears in black and white may, because of the contrast, become much more visible than the competitive ones.

For several thousands of years, we have been trying to get the conviction accepted that the mind is stronger than the sword. This runs contrary to our physical day-to-day experience, so that we really still have had very little success finding acceptance for this world-shaking idea. Again, we are dealing with two conflicting types of structures and models. In the field of psychology, we have the same problem almost continuously. In the physical world, a person or an object cannot be here and not here at the same time; in the psychological world, however, it is very common for a person to love someone and hate him at the same time. We can have conflicting, ambivalent feelings about many things. Having been brought up within the wrong mental framework of our physical, objective world, we get utterly confused and flabbergasted when the completely different kind of organization that reigns, as far as psychological factors are concerned, has to be learned.

Freud's concept of the subconscious and the unconscious, the superego and the id, shook the world and still is considered a controversial explanation of the human personality. The majority of people cannot accept the fact that they should be unable to interpret and understand their own and other people's motivations. Hundreds of graphic representations of our thought processes and the world within which we live are possible. Very frequently utilized structures are the pendulum, the circle, the trilogy, the triangle, the square, and—going into the three-dimensional field—the cube, as is the case with chemical and atomic models, which require complicated and important structuring. Science abounds with examples which illustrate that only when the correct model is discovered can progress be made.

For many hundreds of years, the outward appearance of plants and zoological specimens was used as a basis for classification. Linne and others in the field of biology were among the first to discover that there is a difference between the outward appearance of a plant and the actual genes that will determine the next generations. A rose may be pink in appearance but contain white or red genes. The daughter generation will be determined by those genes. Two superficially white roses, paired with each other, will not necessarily produce white roses but pink or red ones.

Major problems in communication, often between different generations or between East and West, stem from the fact that each side has a completely different view of the real world, taking place within a different framework. In the field of physics, we had to learn to think of colors and sounds as electromagnetic wavelengths, and suddenly completely disparate and different sciences began to overlap, one reaching into the field of physics and one reaching into the field of chemistry. For example, this development has taken place to such an extent that we begin to talk more and more about a "unitarian" science, which is beginning to be taught in colleges, rather than about the strict subdivisions of various disciplines, as was the case for many hundreds of years. The division between physical age and psychological age, where the psychological age is the more important one, representing a more correct structure, is now being accepted.

Market research and public opinion research still operate with the classical, often completely irrelevant subdivisions of age, income, marital status, etc. We are only slowly beginning to recognize that what matters is whether you have been going up, standing still, or going down with your income and that there's a tremendous difference between three people who make, in absolute figures, the same amount of money but who use their money in a completely different fashion. The psychological segmentation of markets and the introduction of psychological typologies are of fairly recent origin.

In the sense of structure science, they represent only the replacement of wrong models with correct ones—correct in the sense of being instrumental and motivational rather than purely phenomenologically descriptive. At least part of our racial difficulty is due to the fact that for many centuries, we have been using models of the world in which dark represents "bad" and white represents "good." To a large extent, such structures have their original basis in biological facts. Night has always been threatening and dangerous. We feel safer in the light because we can defend ourselves. Being higher up permitted us to look down on other people, to prepare in case of attack. Even though most of these thought models and mental frameworks have no more meaning in our modern mechanized world, we still, in an almost animalistic fashion, hold on to them. As I pointed out in my book on nationalism, here, too, we are confronted with wrong structures: The terms "border," "frontier," "foreigner," and "loyalty" all represent, in the light of modern communications and jet travel, anomalies and outdated models for our thinking.

How can structures be developed, corrected, and checked? A good exercise is, during a discussion of political or national issue, to stop for a moment and figure out whether you have inadvertently used some kind of graphic underpinning. Sometimes just trying to organize your thoughts in the form of a drawing while you are talking can be of help. You may discover that you have been drawing triangles, squares, or circles, in order to illustrate graphically an abstract idea, thus making it more understandable.

Egypt tried to reduce its annual population growth rate by almost 3 percent. The rate of growth had been outstripping increases in agricultural productivity. The late President Nasser stated: "Everyone of you wants me to find work for his brother and children, not only for the boys, but also for the girls. How can I do this if each person has ten, twelve, eight, or seven children? Two, three, or four children are enough." In a sense, he showed that he was confronted with two arrows or graphs, one washing out the other. He tried to substitute a new framework, a new model for the one that had been in existence. The traditional attitudes, however, remain widespread among the peasantry, i.e., that children are more desirable than a greater measure of prosperity. The government has tried to introduce "antilove" songs, attempting to discourage erotic romance, and has talked about the virtues of family planning. The program has not been too successful, however, because since the Arab-Israeli war, the budget has had to be decreased. Here, again, we have an example of a model in human thinking and a value system that should have been replaced with new and more correct ones.

12

Motivating Young People

There is a psychology which is basic to *all* young people of *any* generation, and at the same time a unique element has emerged among today's youth. It is not peculiar to this country, but can be observed even in the East—in Japan, India, and so on. Special knowledge is necessary in trying to change the behavior of young people today.

ADAPTATION TO THE CONTEMPORARY ENVIRONMENT

Any era or any culture is really characterized by a way of trying to solve the particular challenges of that period and of the people living at that time and in that place. Each new generation feels that its challenges are somehow different from those faced by the preceding generation. To the older generation it often appears that the experiments being conducted by the young people merely repeat the procedures that failed to work successfully before; however, youth wants to arrive at its own conclusions instead of accepting them from their elders. The world of the younger generation *is* actually completely different from the world of the older

87

generation, and we can distinguish differences in the way the generations adapt to their environment.

THE NEW CONTEMPORARY ATTITUDES

Impatience

The contemporary style is completely different from that of other periods in our history because, for the first time, the young people are in the forefront. They are influencing the older generation more than the older generation is influencing them. The style setters are younger today—not only in the arts but also in the political arena, on the religious scene, and in the educational establishment.

What sets this generation apart from other generations is *speed:* the speed with which information is absorbed, the speed with which life experiences are chewed up and swallowed, and the speed with which decisions are made and changed. One of the new problems associated with speed is the inevitable letdown and frustration that result. Things go *too* fast! Something in your hand suddenly slips away from you. Things are even difficult to grasp because they change all the time. Just as you are getting used to something, it's gone and something else has replaced it.

A modern style in television commercials will have to use much shorter, almost split-second presentations. Color televisions, as our studies have shown, does indeed facilitate rapid perception. The print media could do much more than is the case at present to satisfy this contemporary desire for rapid solutions. Contemporary readers prefer *appeals* (and a *style* of communication) that do not require patience. Layouts of newspaper pages, even of books, could be less neat and puritanical, have more boxes as inserts, and depart from the often boring left-to-right progression of sentences. This format would make for more visual movement and excitement.

Searching for the Truth

In our attempts to unravel the difficulties of life as it presents itself today, we are confronted by a "credibility gap"—not only in political communications but also in reference to all statements by the Establishment— including advertising. Young people fear they might be brainwashed unless they defend themselves against manipulation, and they show a strong tendency to reject pat answers—whether presented in advertising or in any other form.

Some of our studies have shown that any promise of finality is definitely contrary to the contemporary spirit. The advertiser who says that "if you wear the proper hat, you will have become a man" is making an error in judging today's young people. One of the last things the modern person wants today is to be finished—to have arrived. He believes much more in the desirability of dynamic, continuous, unending opportunities and potentialities. Being dissatisfied with the status quo has become a style of living. Another aspect of contemporary "truth seeking" is the "Why not?" approach: "It has never been done that way before—but why could it not be done differently?"

These contemporary attitudes represent interesting new possibilities. Any time you have a customary appeal to prestige, progress, promotion, advancement, etc., you should ask yourself: "Is this still acceptable? Is this really desirable from the viewpoint of our young people?"

Our research for savings banks has shown that the psychology of saving has changed considerably. People no longer save for a rainy day. They don't believe that such a day will ever come. They do respond readily, however, to the proposition that saving money frees them and makes them more independent by giving them the possibility of growing and even delaying any final, definite acceptance of an occupation. If they have an occupation, they feel they can still choose a second one—such as converting a hobby into a real vocation.

Fear of Sentimentality

The appeal of "sick" greeting cards (which has now been carried over into contemporary films, novels, and other forms of mass communication) is based on the fact that young people approach their love affairs, family relations, and involvement with causes in an unusual and new form. It is now a deadly sin to be considered a romantic sentimentalist.

When they are alone with someone of the opposite sex, young people no longer say, "At last we're alone, darling." They are more likely to make a funny remark, such as "I didn't know you wore striped underpants"—or any other statement that would tend to overcome the obvious embarrassment.

Sending flowers, giving candy, and being overly solicitous—even preserving rituals of good manners—are all rejected as meaningless and superficial gestures. Young people are much more apt to ask what is really meant by a particular kind of feeling.

In a study on baby food, we found that a modern mother will be able to accept herself more readily if she is told officially that there's nothing cruel or brutal about becoming angry at her baby (at times) if he keeps waking her up in the middle of the night. Contemporary advertisers can refer to such strong feelings today with considerable permissiveness.

Emotions, sex, and romance play a considerable role in advertising—and always will—so it is important to realize that a more sophisticated modern style has to be used. Being able to mock oneself (or to laugh about romance) is a way of making things acceptable for modern people. Many people don't pose for stiff, stereotyped wedding pictures any longer; instead, we overdo romance to such an extent that it becomes ridiculous. ("Love-ins," "flower people," etc., are all symptoms of such nonromance romance.) The communicator has to be aware of these attitudes.

Humor, in the form of an exaggerated treatment of the old "standby" romantic appeals, will become more and more necessary. Too many deodorants, dentifrices, and similar products are still advertised with straight sentimental approaches, which (according to our research) gives younger people the feeling of being outdated. They are not being addressed in their own language.

Breaking through the Barriers

While we may laugh at the hippies and take a negative view of the whole psychedelic, LSD approach, we have to consider these as interesting phenomena of the contemporary world. There are a number of reasons for these developments.

We are not fascinated any longer with just plain soap or dentifrice. A modern advertiser can succeed much more readily if he invites people to try a new "bath culture"—lounging in a warm bathtub for thirty minutes to do some meditating, instead of taking a puritanical cold shower. Soap advertisers, who used to restrict themselves to cleanliness appeals, might do better today if they discussed the many problems that the modern mother has in educating her children—for example, how can she teach her son to become more familiar with his own body—to be less inhibited about it? A modern soap advertiser might suggest that mothers could encourage their sons to really *enjoy* a bath!

We are becoming aware of a basic opportunity. We are controlling our environment more and more with machines of all kinds, but control over our own bodies has been neglected up to now. We used to have to wash our bodies (and brush our hair) as a necessary duty—but now we're beginning to get interested in these bodily activities as *fun*. I don't just want to brush my teeth. I want to do it with an electric toothbrush. It adds a new dimension. It permits me to break through the regular routine of my daily life and see something completely different and new in it. Brushing my teeth electrically is a seemingly ridiculous but yet minute aspect of this LSD philosophy—of breaking through the barriers. We don't just brush our teeth; we also play with the brush. Playfulness in modern life may be a very important factor in helping us to get away from puritanical duty.

A nightclub like the Electric Circus in New York pokes fun at many of our normal activities by exaggerating them. We suddenly become aware of hitherto unnoticed aspects in as simple a thing as a wall decoration which continuously changes in front of us. We begin to question many aspects of our everyday life. (Part of our work in developing new products concerns itself with this contemporary spirit. Could we organize our desks in a completely different way? Why do we have to pull out heavy drawers? Could there be a little motor to do it instead?) The new generation is beginning to apply a playful attitude toward life, making a hobby out of it rather than a dreary necessity—and, after all, why not?

We used to produce sneezes artificially with snuff. Perhaps LSD and drugs produce a contemporary artificial itch. Some philosophers and religious leaders have tried to convince us that enjoyment of one's own body is immoral—and that people are not supposed to have fun while living. The younger generation is now beginning to question this viewpoint. The body has been created by God, they say today. Why not take advantage of all its possibilities? We are becoming "body gourmets," as we have become gourmets in food, fashion, and decoration.

What does all this mean for the modern persuader?

1. In discussing the message that you are selling, you may want to pay particular attention to the consciousness-expansion function this message may have.

2. More attention to details might be another recommendation. If you want to sell a car, you should pay more attention to the feel of the steering wheel or the way the foot pedal feels to the foot.

3. A more hedonistic emphasis in communications may become acceptable—and even required.

4. Consider the advantages of photographing a product in an unusual form—from an angle or viewpoint that has never been considered before. What would a refrigerator really look like if you were to live in it? Does the light really go out when you close the door? Maybe furniture could be photographed from above—"lying on the floor."

5. The real psychology (the *soul*) of the message could be discussed graphically and psychologically. For example, what does a desk or a pair of shoes really mean to you? We recently conducted a study (later entitled "soxology" by Du Pont, the client) which was presented to the trade (manufacturers as well as retailers) with some very positive results—increasing the sales of over-the-calf socks and introducing more colorful socks as part of the man's wardrobe. At the same time, the quality of the sock wardrobe was also increased, by replacing older socks more frequently.

"We Want to Be Different"

The generation which immediately preceded the current one has been labeled the "silent generation." During that era we witnessed the beginnings of the political, economic, and cultural rise of the Communist nations, the strains of the cold war, the threat of nuclear holocaust, the crushed Hungarian revolt, the Korean police action, and the beginnings of the civil rights movement—grass-roots involvement *and* political legislation. And yet that generation was curiously silent, complacent, and uninvolved, except for a very small minority. Between that time and now, a scant fifteen years, the tables have turned with a vengeance. Today's youth are making themselves heard, seen, and felt in almost every area of local, national, and international affairs. Today's youth could be described as restless, irreverent, savagely curious, outspoken, confused, and yet somehow determined. In short, they are involved.

That there was to be something different about this generation was evident from the emergence of the "beatniks." The influence of the younger generation has continued to snowball ever since. It is difficult to find advertising which does not at least try to cater directly or indirectly to youth —and there is little question that the "life-style" of the entire population has been affected by the younger generation.

Those who are young "have it made," and those who are not young are exhorted to become so by advertising. It is demanded of us to become part of the "Pepsi generation," to feel young behind the wheel of our automobile, to put the accent on youth in styles and fashions, and so on. Youth are also an influence because they are making noise. There is activity, action, energy. And while the older generation struggles with the day-to-day problems of getting ahead or just surviving, the younger generation is talking about love, brotherhood, understanding, peace, individual conscience, etc. They talk about these things with such conviction, and to such extremes, that at times they seem to go beyond the bounds of democracy and to border on anarchy. It would appear as if nothing is sacred—none of the institutions, traditions, beliefs, dogmas, standards, or even methods.

There are extremes among today's youth: those who are very active and rebellious, at one end, and those who are completely cut off, ineffectual, and uninvolved, at the other. In the middle, however, is the vast majority who do not belong to either extreme. There is really nothing new here. The startling difference, however, is the degree of influence that the small groups at both extremes exert on the vast majority of their peers today. Those who are not actively rebellious (do not demonstrate, burn draft cards, picket, etc.) are nevertheless involved with the same issues: personal freedoms and liberties, individual conscience, brotherhood, peace, understanding, love, etc. Few between the ages of thirteen and twenty-six completely escape the restless seeking of this generation. Even those who seem to be following a rather sane, sensible, and constructive course in their lives are concerned and involved to a degree with the "anti-Establishment" movement.

Even though the hippie movement seems to be dying out, the germ of its legacy continues to thrive. Those on the "inside" seem to feel that the trend will continue, although the direction might change.

A young woman who is "in" says:

> The hippie movement is dead! They started it all, but it is dead. The hippies were young intellectuals who were vitally concerned with the hypocrisies of the Establishment. They genuinely sought to bring a new meaning to love, brotherhood, and understanding, and they wanted to make every human being responsible, not only for himself, but for the rest of the world. That sincere but small hippie movement is dead.
>
> These dirty, filthy, young losers at Haight-Ashbury and the East Village are not really the true hippie movement. They are the outsiders, the hangers-on, the displaced people of their generation who have no sense of responsibility about their own lives and have simply incorporated all the negative aspects: the drugs, the communal living, the dirt, the sloppiness. They call themselves hippies, but they are not the true hippies by any means.
>
> Maybe that's just part of the whole thing. Maybe we have to go through this kind of stage before we can get down to the nitty-gritty and really deal with problems in a responsible way—which is what the true hippies really wanted.

A young male college student comments:

> I don't think this country is ever going to be the same again. Complacency is out; involvement is in. We're carrying the banner forward, and I think that we'll continue to carry it for a long time.

In response to a question about future affiliation with the Establishment, this same respondent replied:

> No, I don't think that's going to happen. I think that the experiences of these young people who have demonstrated, marched, been in jail, etc., are going to leave permanent scars on them. I don't think they are going to change. They aren't going to be successful, but they are going to make it a little easier for the next generation, and perhaps that generation a little easier for the next, and so on—until there is some kind of sanity in this crazy, mixed-up world.

A co-ed from a Middle Western university made this observation:

> What we're really talking about here is responsibility. Older people always call us irresponsible because we seem to do things suddenly and without notice. We are quixotic, it's true, and we sometimes think with our hearts rather than with our heads, but that's not being irresponsible. What we're trying to do is bring a sense of real responsibility, not phony responsibility, to the world.
>
> How can you be out there in Vietnam killing innocent people and call that responsible? How can you pay lip service to civil rights and call that

responsible? How can the older generation preach one thing and do another and call this responsible? How can parents pretend to love their children when they don't really give a damn about them—and call that responsible? What we're talking about here is *real* responsibility. The evils of the world are many and hideous. If you compile them, it staggers the imagination.

The social engineer can learn from these attitudes that he has to reassure his potential young respondents that his products and services will permit them to act out their desire to be different. Even in selling margarine to a young housewife, the advertiser may have to stress the fact that this is today's margarine. It should, if possible, suggest completely different concepts: Packaged in a different shape, it should also be used in a different way. Different flavors should also be considered—perhaps herbs, garlic, or onions could be added, for example.

Communicators certainly need to take a look at almost all products from the same viewpoint. In what way could they be presented (or remodeled) in a completely different and new fashion?

"We Want to Be Our Own Masters"

Youth are unique in having so many opportunities to gasp so much information—and to assimilate it, either accepting or rejecting it. Modern devices for information retrieval *and* mass media of communication *and* instruments for information processing *and* the greatest degree of mobility ever experienced *and* decades of economic prosperity—all these things have given today's youth the ammunition to rebel against the world inherited from their parents.

The basic aspirations of youth are centered around social and political issues. Their major concerns are humanistic, but they are also intensely preoccupied with finding values for themselves—especially regarding love, understanding, etc. Young people are not involved in economic or military aspects of the world because they regard them as contrary to the "simple humanity" at whose feet they worship. At the same time, they say they are rebelling chiefly against corruption and evil minds.

To the psychologist, an element of hostility is clearly present—a hostility directed toward the older generation. Many young people feel that seniority is unjustifiably rewarded; they feel uncomfortable and out of place in the world as it exists today. While a few want to run away, and some others are complacent enough to accept the world as it is, the majority of young people are really concerned about trying to arrange some meaningful change that will benefit them in the future—and also now, if possible.

What do today's youth really want? Is it so different from what the older generation wanted when it was the younger generation? Are contemporary aspirations permanent, or will they change as the young people mature? Before we try to answer, let us first take a look at the aspirations which are voiced today.

A high school student tells us:

> I don't want to be like my parents. That's for sure. I can't respect them for just sitting back and doing nothing, for devoting their lives to just doing nothing.

A twenty-year-old girl comments:

> We are very different from our parents. We want different things. We are more honest. We are more concerned. We care more about love and beauty. We have to find out what it means to be alive.
>
> It has to be more than just worrying about making a living and getting ahead and keeping up with the neighbors and sitting and watching television and the not talking and not knowing and not doing and not caring, and just kind of waiting around to die.
>
> I don't think that people of my generation want that kind of life, and I don't think we are going to settle for it. I think that's the main difference between us.

A girl in junior high school says:

> I'm not that much different from my mom. Of course, she's pretty cool. We get along pretty well, considering—but I want to get married and have children, and I guess I want pretty much the same things that she wants. Maybe the way *we* differ is just in being a little bit more honest with ourselves.

A young boy says:

> Take my old man. I wish you would! He doesn't understand me at all.
>
> He never seems to have *time* for me. I think the last time we talked was when I was about ten. If I ever have children, I wouldn't want to bring them up the way he brought me up.
>
> My parents are all right in their own way, but there is no way that we can reach each other. Who cares about money? It's nice to have, but it can't become everything to you, so that nothing else seems to matter.
>
> I think for one thing I would be much stricter with my children. I wouldn't let them get away with anything. That's the only way you know that they care: If they don't let you get away with things.

A college student observes:

> Look at it this way. This is a revolution. Kind of like the Founding Fathers. It's a revolution to try to make the Constitution a meaningful document.
>
> There is a difference between what we aspire to and what our parents aspired to. Of course, they didn't have all the advantages that we have. For most of them I guess it was a struggle from the beginning, and success became a very important personal matter.

We, on the other hand, feel that there are things which have been neglected for generations. We are the conscience of the world. We are saying: Take a look beneath the surface, and let's see what's *really* going on. Let's change what's wrong. Let's change the injustices and the inequalities and try to make the pursuit of life, liberty, and happiness possible for everyone.

It goes back to the Greek "Know thyself." That's the beginning point. You have to know yourself. You have to be true to yourself. You have to like yourself. That's the secret. When you can achieve this, you can be free in your own mind and heart and be concerned about the welfare of others and about making this a world in which it is safe and pleasant to live.

This generation can best be characterized by the word "search." I mean search for the self. We are trying to understand what we are all about and who we are—what our limitations are, what our advantages are, what our possibilities are. We are trying to do this in such a way that it will enable us to understand other people as well.

That's why there is so much anti-Americanism in the old sense of the word. Nationalism is a dirty word among young people generally because these artificial boundaries no longer suit the temper of the time. People are people. Although their ways of life may differ, their languages differ, and their customs differ, beneath all that we are all human beings. We are all striving somehow to understand what life is all about and how it can be meaningful.

I know this sounds kind of intellectual, but it's really what I feel. We don't want to take things for granted. We don't want to simply accept the old things because they are "tried and true," so to speak. We want to search in a profound way and try to bring together all the desires, drives, and needs that people have felt from time immemorial—and make them realities. It's as simple as that.

We are only beginning to scratch the surface by examining our own motives, and by questioning what is really important in life. I don't see that this necessarily has to conflict with progress or science or technology. It depends on how you use those tools—in the same way, I suppose, as it depends on *how* you use weapons of war. It depends on your attitude toward them and on your basic understanding of life.

Many of the problems which we face seem insurmountable in the face of the great debris of misinformation and miscalculation that has piled up over the centuries. It's going to be a slow, painful digging-out process, shovelful by shovelful. We have to make changes which are vital and necessary if man is to survive and if man is to go forward as a conscious, rational animal.

What differentiates *this* generation from other generations is that it is really a *revolution*, and it's not simply tongue-in-cheek. It's a dedicated effort on the part of many of us. Unfortunately the press and the other mass media always seem to focus on what's going to sell: the dirt and the filth. I don't think that is really representative of this generation at all. I think that's a very small minority.

Most of us firmly believe in what we are trying to do. Some of the methods may be questionable, but in a revolution or war of this kind—even though we hope it's a bloodless one or as bloodless as possible—you are going to make mistakes, and trip and fall. I think we have to be aware of that.

Now, to continue our analysis. Today's youth have their real roots in existentialism—that is, that sense of responsibility which dictates that one is responsible not only to and for himself but also to and for all humanity. Beginning with Kierkegaard and continuing through Sartre to Camus, the philosophy of existentialism has become a vital force in contemporary society.

There will probably continue to be demonstrations on the part of young people against the injustices of our society. I also foresee the possibility that the leadership of these demonstrations will become more responsible and mature—and that the objectives will be better defined. Those young people who are now, for instance, between the ages of nineteen and twenty-six will continue to make their influence felt as they go out into the world—and they will carry with them the seeds of this contemporary rebellion. Some of these people will be the nucleus of the leadership that will affect younger groups taking part in various demonstrations. This continuing desire to participate and to correct the wrongs may not really reach its full fruition for another decade—if then—by which time the teen-agers of today will be young adults entering into responsible positions in American life. If they can maintain this dedication to creating a better, safer, saner, more rational world, theirs may be a valuable contribution to the future of this country.

How will adults react to rebellions on the part of youth today and in the future? Flexibility and understanding may lead to encouraging results, but hostility—or even ambivalence—could result in rebellions that take a different shape: more destructive, aggressive, and militant than before.

The communicator who is trying to speak the contemporary language should stress some kind of psychological "do-it-yourself" prescription. In the field of men's fashion, for example, I have recommended that young people be told that they don't have to play roles via their clothes, but can be themselves. They can be the masters of their own destiny—at least externally. We should ask young people to help one another in cutting down on drug use, rather than preaching to them from above (see the section on youth and drugs in Part 2). Such a new appeal, to cite another example, might pertain to the car that does not represent the manufacturer but is flexible enough to permit a young person to express himself. This is a kind of promise that could be applied to almost every goal promoted today.

Rejection of Materialism

Success, monetary gain, and possessions were once the principal aspirations that motivated generations of Americans. As a large part of the population has achieved these goals to varying degrees, they have now declined in significance. Youth is trying to discover new values. We have enough to eat, shelter, and the basic necessities of life—where do we go from here? A major proportion of the "dropouts" in this generation come from middle-class homes.

Even among the black youth, who have not yet reached the feeling of satiation, material achievements are no longer the principal goal. We are witnessing a rejection of materialism for its own sake and a basic distrust of the traditions regarding property. There is a desire on the part of all youth to return to the essential elements of human existence—to get down to the "nitty-gritty," as the younger generation likes to call it.

An important redefinition of our real contemporary world may be necessary. Many of our studies have shown that, particularly in the United States, we are getting closer to an antimaterialistic society. We're involved, for technological and economic reasons, in a "throw-away" society. Now much more depends on what the material products are to be used for: A new car can mean discovery, travel, and an exploration of new possibilities in our lives—it is less and less something to show off in front of the Joneses. The same is true of books, music, and other aspects of culture. You don't just collect a big library, without ever reading a book; sales of paperbacks have increased considerably, and often they are even thrown out after having been read.

From the modern communicator's viewpoint, an educational job may have to be done with youth. You could point out to them that you are in agreement with their philosophy—that material possessions are not the all-important factor and that it is the *use* to which you put material things that really matters. Too often, in our advertising approaches, we still stress the old-fashioned pride in possession itself, rather than the pleasure and enrichment of experience that our possessions can give us.

CONTEMPORARY STYLE

Young people use a unique language, of course. It had its birth during the 1940s, among jazz musicians, but it has since been modified and extended so that there is also a very different vocabulary today. Youth speak of material things in a language which represents their *lingua franca*, understood by nearly everybody within their age group—"pad," "bread," and "speed." Inner states are described using such terms as "turned on," "tuned in," "dropping out," "put down," "up tight," "swinging," and "groovy." They also talk about "freaking out" and "blowing your cool." This is the language of young people.

The music of today's young people evolved from "jive" and "rock 'n' roll" and has now evolved into "folk rock" and "soul music," with lyrics that have a contemporary significance because they deal with psychology and war, with hatred and bigotry, with killing and love, with sex and "making it"—in short, with personal and social problems.

Changes continue. Indian music, as well as Indian philosophy, has recently emerged on the contemporary scene, with still more concern about involvement in this world. The music is haunting, and the melodies are very intricate, in regard to tonality and scale.

In literature (including poetry, news reports, etc.) there is also a contemporary style. The present trend is away from realistic naturalism, toward a more personal style, which is often difficult to follow and is based in some instances on the absurd—and on subtlety and incongruity.

In the visual arts, everyone is now familiar with "op art" and "pop art" as well as with new forms of sculpture and architecture and more experimentation with sound and light—including color. The contemporary mixed media (a kind of artistic drug taking) lean toward bombardment of the senses, which gives contemporary people a "high" without actually taking drugs. The new styles in film are also very personal and "expressionistic" or "individualistic"—also dealing with the incongruous and the absurd, as a way of depicting personal reactions to the paradoxes of modern times.

In fashion there is the "peacock revolution" for men—fur coats, ruffles, colorful jackets and shirts, and so on. The modern young woman lives in minis, midis, maxis, pantsuits, hot pants. Among both sexes there is a greater sense of individuality, of dressing to please oneself, as well as an appreciation of color and beauty.

Another aspect of contemporary style is greater sexual freedom. Young people do not regard this experimentation as a breakdown in morality, but as contemporary frankness about the sexual drives which had previously been considered taboo. They are apt to regard the "old-fashioned" sexual mores as hypocritical rather than virtuous—partly because they now consider women to be "liberated," by birth-control devices and pills, so that sexual freedom is no longer the province of men alone. The young woman of today feels she has acquired greater freedom of expression, and she values this right as much as men have valued it for generations.

What does the contemporary style mean to the communicator?

1. Techniques, to be more meaningful to most young people, might place even greater emphasis on speed and sensation—and they could also contain a larger dose of honesty.

2. Humor, particularly wry humor, will probably become more common in advertising directed toward young people; for example, advertisers will not be so afraid to make fun of their products.

3. Messages which tell a story, while at the same time maintaining an air of detachment, will probably be another effective way of reaching young people.

4. Production techniques will also continue to change, thereby reaching the "now" generation more effectively. They will use "psychedelic" art and multimedia techniques, for example. Young people "pick things up faster." Their world moves quickly.

5. Color will become more important. The contemporary world *is* colorful; cars are being painted all kinds of colors, for example. Perhaps the use of color is one way of counteracting what today's youth consider to be an ineffectual world.

6. Young people are quick to see paradoxes—and the unexpected, the brushstroke of chance. What seems disconnected or discordant to the older generation somehow makes sense to them. They perceive sense in nonsense. They don't see life as a gift-wrapped package, but as a continuum where there is no beginning, middle, or end.

FUTURE TRENDS

A graduate student at an Eastern university makes this prediction:

> I think in the future young people are going to exert more of an influence over their own lives than they have ever done before. We're beginning to see the signs of this already. The old idea of accepting what is laid out for you as necessarily proper or necessarily in your best interest, simply because that's the way it's always been done, isn't going to exist any longer.
>
> Young people are going to have some say in how they are taught and what they are taught. They are going to have some say in the economic and political future of this country and of the world, and for better or for worse, this is how I think it's going to be. Personally, I would hope that it's in a more temperate form than we've been seeing recently, although probably the physical act of sit-ins and demonstrations and all that is important in the beginning of a movement—you have to have a certain amount of fanatic devotion to a movement in order to get it off the ground, in order to shake the stupid complacency of the vast majority of people.
>
> Once that's been done, and I think that's being done right now, generally history has shown us that the movement itself becomes less militant and less destructive, and while I would certainly hope that this progress does not die down or die out, does not dissolve or become absorbed by the Establishment, I would hope that youth can make their feelings and their sentiments known—make their influences felt with less hostility and aggression. But as I said, for better or for worse, this is what's going to happen, and it's got to be an accepted fact.

What we can probably expect to see, then, in the next decade is the continuing growth of the influence of young people on all areas of society. Most likely, the movement will become less aggressive and less hostile, but nevertheless we are probably on the brink of a new era—an era of "jeunesse" which is going to force us to reexamine old values and which is going to usher in a period of increased personal freedom.

We may witness a renaissance of religious fervor—not, perhaps, the Establishment religions, but something more closely attuned to what many religious establishments professed at their origins. There will probably be greater cultural and political flexibility and mobility—and the economy will continue to be influenced strongly by the youth markets.

I foresee the possibility of a trend toward continuous questioning—and rebellion against the Establishment—but the trend is becoming more a positive and less a negative phenomenon, with a growing concern for the mechanics of somehow investing the Establishment with these new ideas and new approaches. Our analysis of the present situation and of its probable effect on the near future shows that there is disillusionment with the *form* which the rebellion has taken so far—as much of a disillusionment with *that* as there previously was with the Establishment and the adult world. In other words, we are observing a "psychological backlash" which is beginning to make itself felt among young people. For example, drug use among today's youth is slowly on the way out—at least the *thrill* aspect and the "hand-in-the-cookie-jar" aspect. The use of drugs may well be continued mainly among the hard-core group of users who actually depend on the drug for their survival—much as some people depend on alcohol to fulfill similar needs.

The various experiments in communal living, and the total divorce from the greater society in respect to dress, grooming, etc., will probably disappear too. Although many youngsters (especially teen-agers) seem to be flocking toward this kind of life—running away from home, deserting their families, escaping from reality, and avoiding the problems of living —this trend is probably at the high-water mark now and will slowly begin to recede over the next five or ten years. Many of these kids now become disillusioned rather quickly.

One positive result might be noted: The teen-ager is often seen for the first time by his parents as an individual with adult needs and requirements that the parents have avoided recognizing. Now, teen-agers are no longer simply asking, but are demanding. In the process, these teen-agers are beginning to find their way back to their families and their communities. Although the destructive aspects of this present rebellion will probably disappear, some positive and constructive aspects may survive. As one writer has pointed out: "Inexorably and inevitably they all turn thirty!"

13

Charting the Future as a Motivational Force

Suppose you were sure that within one month you were not going to be alive any longer. Would you change your way of life? Each minute and each hour would take on a completely different significance. Many philosophers have claimed that if we were more frequently reminded of our mortality, we would very quickly cease doing many foolish and wasteful things. For a very long time we live under the illusion of having eternal life. Often we become aware of the necessity of carefully controlling what we eat, what we drink, and how much exercise we get only when it is almost too late, after we have reached fifty or sixty. Living only for the present is a characteristic of children and immature people. Trend analysis—realizing where we are going—is a powerful force for bringing about change in behavior. Before making a decision, we should chart all the consequences two, five, and ten years from now.

Reading more and more frequently about the demise of people in one's own age group can have a decided influence on one's philosophy. One does not always have to think of death, however. Some philosophers claim that one should live only for today; Carnegie spoke of "living in day-tight compartments" and not worrying about tomorrow. I consider this dangerous and wrong. Many of the annoying, silly, and embarrassing things that account for a good part of our aggravations could be avoided with a little more long-range planning. Even biologically nature seems to plan ahead. Psychologists have analyzed the total life-span of famous people and have often found that geniuses like Mozart, who died at a very early age, progress through all life's phases much more rapidly than the ordinary person.

It is during the period from age twenty-eight or twenty-nine to perhaps age forty-five or forty-eight that most people settle on their life's work. They get to know what they are after and what they want out of life. They have concentrated on a specific profession or occupation. After this period, there is another transitional span which may last up to about age sixty-two or sixty-five; then there is the beginning of old age. During the last thirty or forty years, however, these stages in the average life have been occurring later and probably will be even more delayed in the future. We can assume, therefore, that a person of about sixty might find himself to be only middle-aged and that old age may not really start until after seventy-five.

People often complain that they have no time for vacations. Suddenly they become aware that half or three-quarters of their life has gone, and they then start on a frantic chase to get as much out of life as possible. In a study for an international company dealing with food products for older people, we found that, contrary to what one might normally expect, older people do not restrict their diets. Just the opposite is true. They buy more expensive, quality-type food, often becoming belated gourmets. They want to get as much out of their food as possible, something that we have called "the insistence on nucleus—the kernel of food values." Similar developments take place as far as their attitude toward other products is concerned. Sports cars are often bought when people are fairly young, and then again after the age of forty-five or fifty. Of course, this phenomenon is due partly to economic factors. People who do not yet have the responsibility of a family can often afford a relatively expensive sports car, as can those who have accumulated enough wealth over the years to permit such an extravagance.

Semanticists talk about time-binding as an important ability of the human being in contrast to animals. While it may be true that man is basically a "naked ape," as the zoologist Desmond Morris has claimed in his book, he has quite a number of faculties that no animal has, as Morris also points out. The most striking one is his ability to plan ahead. As a technique for changing human nature, it is very frequently neglected.

Again, as has been pointed out in previous chapters, the problem really starts as early as elementary school, or even kindergarten. Appropriate courses should be instituted to teach even the young child to plan ahead and to make him realize that what he does or does not do may have repercussions in a week or a month or even later.

The orthodox psychoanalysts, of course, claim that most of our childhood experiences have a decided influence on our entire life. Today's parents, or modern parents of the future, might consider the possibility of keeping a "psychological diary" for their children which could help in their later analytical understanding and could show the parents and the children how important planning is in influencing human behavior. People used to maintain family almanacs, but these recorded only the events as they were taking place. What I am recommending is a dynamic kind of almanac for one family or the individual in which aspirations and plans for the future could be noted. This would give us the chance to find out how often we changed our minds and to what extent we have come closer to our stated goals. It would be a navigational chart for life; it would be a form of time-binding. Seeing present things in relation to the past and the future is, of course, also an extremely vital exercise in better interpreting and understanding daily political events. Dr. Crane Brinton, of Harvard University, is the author of a book entitled *Anatomy of a Revolution*. This book is an example of a dynamic interpretive attitude toward human history. Dr. Brinton talks about the phases that revolutions pass through, using the analogy of the course of a fever in the human organism.

Sometimes overall company names have to be determined. Often even a large company makes the mistake of getting stuck with a name that provides too small an umbrella for possible future expansion and diversification. In a sense, such enterprises have failed to do any long-range planning. One of the difficulties in looking ahead in an intelligent fashion is that too often we use frameworks and modes of thinking that have been in force in the past and are valid for the present. We simply project these into the future without realizing that frequently the expansion of a particular facility changes the total outlook. When people are shown new types of packaging or urban renewal developments which might take place in the next ten or fifteen years, their first reaction may be a negative one. They would almost prefer to stay with the old, often uncomfortable but conveniently familiar surroundings. In testing future developments, therefore, it is important that the laboratory procedure have built-in devices that permit people to experience ahead of time what the new surroundings will mean. We in our organization suggest, usually, that the experiment be repeated three or four times to provide a warming-up period. Only after this has been done can the respondents' true reactions be registered. Another approach which is recommended is that the subject be permitted to explore the new situation in a step-by-step fashion, to go, as it were, through the phases of all the three-dimensional implications that will be involved once they are in the new milieu. Not long ago, we tested how people would react to a 200-mile-an-hour train. The subjects' first attitude was a rather negative and fearful one. After seeing a film which portrayed how this train would operate, people calmed down and began to appreciate all the advantages that would result. By letting them go into the train, sit down, and take the ride—all, of course, in a fictitious, imaginary way—we finally broke down their basic consternation, and they came to the conclusion that this new kind of train would be a considerable success.

In my study of Europe and eventually a world without nationalistic boundaries, my interviews showed that people were not so much afraid of the political implications, which really meant very little in the life of the average citizen, but were worried about everyone having to speak the same language, having to salute a foreign flag, and becoming uniform and losing their individual differences. Any intelligent thought, however, demonstrates that first of all we have, to a very large extent, a uniformity. Most people within the Western world, and more and more also behind the Iron Curtain and in new African countries, drink more or less the same beverages at cocktail parties; they dress more or less the same way, with variations depending on climatic conditions. In western Samoa dignitaries wear white shirts and black ties modified only by a lavalava, a colorful rectangular cloth worn like a skirt or kilt.

In the United States, for example, the nonexistence of passport requirements between states has not necessarily resulted in the widely feared and wrongly proclaimed uniformity, but in a new emergence of very many regional differences. Certainly the differences that make the individual character and personality would only be enhanced rather than diminished by the disappearance of external, often silly and unimportant distinctions. In many of the jobs that our organization has done in different countries, one of the comments we have heard most frequently is, "We are different." This can be driven to such an extent, particularly in Europe, that the people in the northern part of Germany consider themselves radically different from those living in Bavaria. Those living in the northern part of Munich feel that they are different from those living in the southern part. In his book *Hawaii*, James Michener describes how many long and bloody battles were fought in China between the mountain people and the valley people. They belonged to the same race, were the same color, and spoke the same language. However, one group lived in the mountains, and the other in the valley, and it was considered sinful for a valley girl to fall in love with and marry a mountain boy.

An excellent radio commercial in the field of racial tolerance was used in the United States. Two people are speaking in excited voices about the fact that blacks have moved into a hitherto white apartment house. "What happened—what happened," asks one man. The other one, in a very upset voice, says, "Nothing," which is a brief and heavily significant answer. In our planning of the future, we would have to include the reassurance that many of the things that we are fearful of, and therefore don't even want to contemplate, may, in reality, be quite different from what we imagine them to be like.

At a moment when East and West are caught in a tremendous power struggle, we cannot visualize a world in which truthful coexistence with open borders could exist. We forget too often that it has been a relatively short time since many countries became united. Germany, until the year 1870, and maybe even later than that, did not even represent a national unity. Factions, regional groups, and the kings and dukes fought tooth and nail the idea of being absorbed in a larger national unity.

In the course of doing some consulting work for a major politician, we pointed out, on the basis of our studies, that political communication has changed radically over the last thirty years or so. The kind of language and rhetoric that a politician might have learned when he entered the field of politics is no longer acceptable or understood—particularly by the younger generation. The same thing holds true as far as ministers, priests, and rabbis are concerned, who often feel that the moment they enter their professional religious field they have to adapt an oily, unctious style of speech. They would be much better off, in communicating with the modern world, if they rid themselves of this often hypocritical attitude.

An international organization concerned with the fact that more and more men are not wearing hats engaged us to find out how this trend could be combated, or at least slowed down. The organization stressed the fact that they had used such slogans as "Get ahead with a hat" and "The hat makes the man." Our studies showed that getting ahead, in a superficial fashion, is a thing of the past and exactly the thing that people do not want anymore. They want to have their personality developed in a continuous fashion. Therefore, they do not want to wear hats that will indicate that they have reached their goals. At our recommendation, the dynamic hat, the hat that permits you to keep on developing, was introduced.

14

Demonstrating Absurdity

Another motivational technique which can be used successfully in getting people to change their approach and bring them closer to a desired personality goal is to let them develop their own ideas but encourage them to carry them through in all their consequences until all details have become dramatically clear. Many times, such a test leads to a reinforcement of the original goal and decision. In many other cases, however, the exact opposite is true. The person who has been given a free rein in his pursuits, often without having to use up a lot of energy to defend himself in his progress, discovers that what he thought he wanted is not at all his desired achievement. The purpose of many discussion programs on TV and radio, and also of private discussions, is often to change somebody's mind, to make him do things differently. A method not frequently enough used is not to stop the antagonist, but to agree with him and let him discover by himself, either in a verbal or a three-dimensional fashion, that what he has been pursuing is really absurd. Many people dream about eventual retirement, for example. If they could take a kind of trial retirement first, they might discover that this is one dream that they wanted only in their minds—that when they experience it in a tangible, three-dimensional fashion, they really don't want it.

Some time ago, our goal was to help a radio and TV network convince people that the real problem of the atom bomb and nuclear war could be solved only through a universal federal government and an understanding that wars with a clear-cut winner are not feasible any longer. Going back through history, one could find many examples demonstrating the value of military solutions and many others demonstrating the opposite. Recently, as a result of the Arab-Israeli war, many people have unfortunately come to think that wars, particularly if they are of only a six-day duration, are indeed shortcuts and can solve complicated situations that do not seem easily resolved. In order to bring about this change of attitude toward nuclear war, we could have demonstrated what the atom bomb did in Hiroshima and Nagasaki. When we tested such a newsreel, we saw that people's reactions represented simply various forms of escapism: "If only we had dropped the bomb sooner, the war against Japan would have ended sooner." "If we had had the atom bomb, maybe the war against Hitler would never have been necessary." Even recently some authors have suggested that when the United States was the only power possessing the bomb, it could have exerted a sort of beneficial blackmail against the Russians, threatening them with annihilation unless they opened their closed society and made it an open, free one. Our goal is not so much to present a definite solution of one type or another, but to force people to think the issue through for themselves in an independent fashion.

Instead of presenting our newsreel, we developed a one-hour program entitled "Operation Crossroads," and we took all the possible solutions and developed them in such a way that their absurdity became clear. For example, one of the possible ways out of the atomic dilemma, it was suggested, was to drop bombs on Russia and force Russia to surrender. This idea was rejected not because it was cruel or impossible but because of what became clear when it was carried on to its absurd conclusion. We asked the person representing and defending this idea how he would go about it. "I would occupy Russia, in the same way that Germany was occupied," he answered. "Do you know how many people would be required to do that?" we asked. He admitted that he did not know. We called in a general who said, "I can answer that for you. It took 2 million people to take care of Germany—it would take about 10 million people to control the Russian territory effectively."

"What would then happen to our labor force?" the man asked.

"That I do not know. It was your idea to drop the bomb on Russia and to occupy the country afterward, not mine," said the general.

Thus at least one idea was developed in such a way that the person

suggesting it as a solution became aware of its absurdity and impossibility
—even aside from the attitude of the rest of the world, the American
allies, and other people concerned with the hegemony which would be
established for the United States. We took six or seven various forms of
suggested solutions, each of which was impossible, and demonstrated that
when carried out, they would lead to an irrational development that
would not really solve the problem. Tests showed that this kind of approach changed more opinions on the solution of the nuclear bomb problem than a simple newsreel presentation frightening and warning people
about the danger of a nuclear war.

Recently, Art Buchwald described an imaginary scene in one of his
columns. On coming home, the children, particularly the daughter, ask
the mother whether their clothes have been ironed, whether dinner is
ready, and whether the mother has performed the other tasks that children normally expect from their parents. It turns out that nothing has
been done—no meal has been prepared, and the house is in disorder.
The mother simply declares that she has accepted the hippie philosophy,
which the daughter had strongly professed to believe in. The daughter is
consternated and then replies, "Well, if you are a hippie, then I can't
be one; one of us has to take care of the house." Maybe this little anecdote should be expanded on a larger scale to the country as a whole. You
can drop out and declare yourself not concerned only if the rest of the
population keeps on plugging ahead and following apparently silly pursuits of regularity and work and discipline.

A frequent topic of discussion among many people is their supposed
desire to "get out of the rat race." They make it appear to be true that
they are caught—that there is nothing they can do about solving this
problem. A properly trained psychiatrist, if one were needed in such a
case, would permit the person to carry out his apparent wishes—would
let him discover for himself that he really never wanted to get out of the
rat race and that he actually enjoys it very much.

Some time ago, I treated a patient who continuously repeated that he
hated people and really loved being a hermit and living alone. The
therapy prescribed was a relatively simple one—that for about three
weeks he should, indeed, live completely alone, not see anybody, and not
talk to anyone. It didn't even take a full week before the patient called
up and admitted sheepishly that he never realized the consequences of
his desires, that he really needed people and was even more miserable
without them than with them.

On an international scale, it would also be interesting to conceive of
a world in which the Communist threat had completely disappeared—
either the East had adopted the ways of the West, or the West had become
socialistic. By carrying this idea out to its extreme, we would probably

discover that we would have to find substitutes for an enemy, even if it were nothing else but a football or baseball team clad in different colors. We are dreaming about paradise, eternal peace, or continuous, permanent spring on a South Pacific island. All these ideals have never been carried through in a systematic fashion. If they had been, millions of people would have discovered that they had been pursuing fallacious and absurd dreams that they really do not want. A great deal of unhappiness that exists in individual lives would be eliminated if we began to realize that what we say we want is often quite different from what we really want.

Authors and script writers are continuously looking for new topics. People's wishes and their dream worlds would provide a fascinating and almost limitless series of titles and topics. More and more countries are awaiting a time when people will no longer go hungry, when an affluent society will be more and more a reality, and when gadgets and material possessions will abound. We are now discovering, to our dismay and puzzled surprise, that we're still not happy, that there was more fun in dreaming and working toward these goals than in actually reaching them. A millionaire, for example, may long for the days when everything was fresh and desirable and when he had to struggle to make a living—this now appears to him as the happiest period of his life.

Demonstrating absurdity is an effective form of reality therapy. No amount of verbal conviction will do as much good as letting the subject experience for himself what the particular situation he is dreaming about is really like. In a sense, it is like calling somebody's bluff. At my advice, the city of Vienna tried an interesting experiment. Almost every boy in Vienna, as in almost every other city, dreamed of being a fireman. When it was discovered that many of the city's fire engines, particularly on weekends, were not fully occupied, fathers were invited to bring their sons, and also their daughters, to ride around the plaza of the city hall in real, honest-to-goodness, full-sized fire engines. The firemen, many of whom were parents themselves, had tremendous fun. So did the families, and the whole thing came off excellently as a public relations gesture. However, the children also became aware of the many negative aspects of such a profession—how quickly it became boring, dull, hard work.

Not long ago, a writer had the chance to fulfill one of his dreams on a TV program—to play as a member of the Philharmonic in New York under the leadership of Leonard Bernstein. He soon realized that he would not want to do it permanently—he had learned to be a percussionist.

It might be marvelous if we all had the chance to act out our Walter Mitty dreams in a three-dimensional form, to find out once and for all whether they are absurd, whether we really like them when we are faced with them in full reality, and whether, indeed, we would want to pursue them further. The school of tomorrow might well have special classes in which pupils would be encouraged to engage in such wild flights of fantasy in an uninhibited fashion, as long as they did not result in any direct antisocial experiences. Certainly, in terms of appreciating literature and understanding our own motivations and those of other people, such acting out and tangible confrontation with often absurd wishes would have a wholesome effect and would deepen our tolerance and respect for unusual pursuits. Even on governmental or international levels, the many unripe and dangerous ideas put forth in books, articles, and oratory would die an early death if we once learned to play the game of permitting the originator of these ideas to translate them, in a protected and limited fashion, into reality or at least to think them through.

15

Why Be Afraid of "Fun"?

Dr. Robert S. de Ropp, in his book *The Master Game,* states that one of the most effective ways of approaching life and bringing about change in human behavior is to look upon life as a series of games. The master game is the one in which we try to become more aware of ourselves. Our new generation is challenging the puritanical approach to life and the complete devotion to the achievement of goals as a viable life philosophy.

Our motivational research shows that instead of doing many things in a sober way, we're beginning to take a "hobby" approach to life. We used to go fishing to make a living. We needed the fish for food. Now we fish as a hobby. We used to wash our bodies and brush our hair as a duty. We are now doing it for pleasure, for fun. Carving a turkey or chopping wood may be a chore, but when we do it with an electric carving knife or a chain saw, it's a hobby; it's fun. Ice cream is basically milk or cream; freezing it suddenly gives it a whole new aspect. We are witnessing a basic desire to expand our consciousness, a sort of LSD philosophy. It represents a new form of motivating human behavior. Why just brush your hair normally? If you use an electric brush, you might do it more often, and you might brush differently. The electric toothbrush represents a similar example. Basically, we can brush our teeth in the usual way. But the same activity that we are taught to carry out in a sober, almost duty-bound fashion suddenly is translated into fun. A very minimal spark of pleasure is added to brushing your teeth, so that when you get up in the morning, you don't just do it because Mom told you to. Suddenly it's a little bit of fun.

Playfulness may be a very important factor that would help us get rid of the puritanical, duty-bound approach to life. In other words, if I work because it is fun or if I make it fun to study, it's more pleasant. We're resisting this because somehow we're still afraid that anything that is fun is not quite permitted. Even reading a book in paperback form or electronically may be part of fun in education. CBS is already experimenting with a gadget that would permit you to put a book on film and project it through your television screen. In the future, the doors in our homes might work electronically; each time you closed or opened a door, it would be fun. Could your desk be organized in a different way? Could a well be built into your desk that would pop up with all your pencils in it when you pushed a button? The electric pencil sharpener is a similar thing. In other words, it's a play world, which shows that we probably have gotten over the purely utilitarian, serious control of our environment. We can afford to approach it more lightly.

The original purpose of sex was procreation—a very sober biological function. For quite a long time now we've known that playfulness in sex can make it more fun. Occupying yourself occasionally with your own body in a playful way is probably antibiological or superbiological. It is one of the methods used in encounter groups, in which people learn to get rid of their hang-ups about themselves and other people. They learn to touch one another to establish more emotional contact. Feeding your body is one thing; eating gourmet food is a playful approach. Brushing your hair or cleaning your body is in itself a utilitarian activity, but by caressing your body while doing so, you can squeeze out the last possible ounce of pleasure from the experience. Encouraging people to make a hobby out of the necessities of life rather than a duty may well be one of the most effective motivational tools we have at our disposal.

Here we're going back to what the Greeks knew 2,000 years ago—that life is to be enjoyed. We need to develop a "tickle" society, in which we can produce artificially some bodily or intellectual "itch." Christianity to a large extent—and some other religions, too—has told us that this self-indulgent, erotic, ticklish view of one's life and one's own body is not permitted—that it is immoral. We are now discovering that this whole concept may be wrong. We're becoming more sophisticated; we're becoming gourmets in terms of our lives and our bodies, not just our

palates. Some people might consider this to be the beginning of degeneration. I don't subscribe to that. Enjoying life more, getting more out of it,
can be a better motivator than fear. Puritanism was just another form of
self-indulgence.

We in our organization recently analyzed people who reduce. We found
an interesting relationship between sadism, sex, and losing weight. Reducing—depriving yourself, withholding pleasure, and punishing yourself—is another form of masochism, self-love, and narcissism. It is a form
of self-flagellation. We are only now beginning to discover that it may be
much more intelligent not to deny oneself pleasure. An ascetic person is
more obscene, if you come right down to it, than an openly hedonistic
one. In Maugham's story *Miss Thompson* (on which the play *Rain* is
based), the same thought is expressed: A minister who threatens hellfire
and damnation and thunders against mortal sin is himself overcome with
lust.

Fun is a form of growing and maturing. We are learning to control our
own instincts better than we could before. We're less afraid of letting go.
Of course, some people can't take it and become guilt-ridden, but the
majority of people are beginning to relax. I can go into hitherto forbidden areas; I can tickle myself between my toes; I can massage my hair
with an electric brush; I can overheat my body and then cool it in ice-
cold water after a sauna and discover a new form of exhilaration—a less
dangerous one than alcohol produces. In a sauna you suddenly see
another part of yourself; you discover a new part of your consciousness.
It's exhilarating and frightening at the same time.

Discovering that we are allowed to do something previously forbidden,
like bathing in the nude, has a lot to do with our sense of security. We
don't have to prove our morality any longer by sticking to customary
ways. We can afford to enjoy ourselves. The discovery of fun as a motivator occurred about ten years ago. Probably various factors have come
together—new drugs, and perhaps dissatisfaction with ordinary, everyday
life. Maybe it just took that long for some of the puritanical concepts to
thin out and wear off. It's simple: We've tried everything else; we are
discovering the future, like learning about new solar systems or reaching
the moon. Well, the year 2,000 is coming within our reach, and it was not
possible before.

Probably three or four factors have brought about this new approach:
increased financial security, technological advances, a change in morals,
and a heightened psychological desire for discovery. It's not much different from a scientific discovery. Just as we have discovered cures for
many of the illnesses that plague us, now we are discovering new psychological forces within ourselves. There now exists a whole new area in
which we're trying to make life-laboratory experiments for the purpose of

developing, inventing, and discovering new pleasures. Maybe a "pleasure laboratory" ought to be set up someday in which we would control untamed nature more and more. We're not afraid of nature any longer: we have the birth-control pill, the antiwrinkle pill, tranquilizers, the whole field of psychopharmacology, and the organ transplants. We're fooling around where we did not dare to before. Now, if we can replace a heart or create life in a test tube, although in a very primitive form, we can also try to change our outlook on life. It's an area of our existence that, technologically, we have not dared to touch up to now. We have been conquering distance; we have been conquering darkness; we have learned to fly; and we are chemically influencing all kinds of things. We have lightened our daily chores by means of technology, but we have not dared to tamper with the more "godlike," basic aspects of nature—particularly our own minds and bodies. Now we see the possibility of this, and because we see the possibility, we'll do it. We might create life artificially and begin seriously to combat death as an inevitable biological phenomenon.

Part Two

Application of Motivational Techniques to Current Problems

APPLICATION OF MOTIVATIONAL TECHNIQUES TO CONCRETE CASE HISTORIES

In the second half of this book we shall apply the various motivational techniques of influencing and changing human behavior to a wide variety of situations.

There are probably tens of thousands of problems connected with our daily life, our political goals, and matters of national and international importance. I have selected only those areas which offer meaningful examples that can be utilized to demonstrate or clarify a basic principle.

16

Motivating for Social Progress

SELLING SOCIAL PROGRESS? LIKE SELLING PRODUCTS

Many large corporations and individual business leaders are becoming aware of their obligations to society as a whole. They want to contribute to plans and programs that can be helpful in changing human behavior for the better. The difficulty is that too many well-meaning efforts are handicapped by snobbish, intellectually aloof attitudes. Recommendations are haughtily communicated only among peers, or people reiterate sermons when instead they should use their intelligence *pragmatically*. That is, we should not just complain about our problems, but offer sensible ways of solving them. Here are a few ways that pragmatic intelligence can be put into actual practice:

1. Profit from past experience. Compile an encyclopedia, a storehouse in book form or committed to computers, of those techniques which have worked in the past in solving human problems. (Even lawyers now have

a computerized system for calling forth previous court decisions to help them solve problems.)

2. Face problems with the realization that human behavior can be changed only if corollary corrections are made. People are afraid of change; thus one necessary accompanying technique is *encouragement.*

3. Reduce large, complex problems such as birth control, racial imbalance, juvenile delinquency, and the like to simplified, comprehensible, *step-by-step* procedures. People can grasp the concept that a 1,000-mile trip begins with just one step.

4. Don't be squeamish about applying techniques that have proved successful in switching people, say, from old-fashioned soap to modern detergents, from fresh to frozen foods, or from natural to synthetic textiles. After all, what is the purpose of education if it is not to open minds, to invite exploration, and to encourage people to try new ways of making life physically and aesthetically satisfying?

Corporations, business groups, or individuals who sincerely wish to contribute to remedying the world's ills should realize that what is needed is a technological arsenal of applied intelligence—and they should take steps toward furnishing that arsenal with the most practical weapons available.

GETTING PEOPLE TO GIVE

Needed: Tougher Thinking about "Sweet Charity"

Most thinking about raising and dispensing money—whether for charity organizations or social welfare operations—is unrealistic. Either we are too one-sided—"How do we get that guy to make a contribution?"—or we are too likely to preach conventional axioms about duty. We also assume that recipients of "charity" are sure to be made happy, while actually the unskillfully given contribution can easily backfire and have negative results. Whether the goal is feeding starving children overseas, conquering disease, or improving the lot of blacks in the ghetto, policy makers should consider the following human motivations in giving and receiving.

The "disease" of poverty. Many people subconsciously fear that poverty will contaminate them. The act of giving (making oneself a little bit poorer) reminds one that, with a little bad luck, he might be as badly off as those to whom the contribution is made. Fund-raising appeals should help to calm this secret fear of involvement—and, if possible, switch the emphasis from "charity" to "smart business." In our work for the United Jewish Appeal, to combat the idea of Israel as a "bottomless pit," we suggested promoting aid as an intelligent investment. Similarly, whites might be less fearful of helping blacks financially if they thought of such help as building a potential market for business.

Fear of embarrassment. This also inhibits giving. In everyday life, people are afraid of overtipping or undertipping. This same fear of not behaving properly also applies to fund raising: "Am I acting too ungenerously?" "Are I being too easy a mark?" "How can I decide how much to give and to whom?"

"Psychological taxes." Fund raisers should point out that giving helps relieve guilt feelings. Tell people they've done some good—and now deserve to go out and enjoy themselves. Or, if they've had some good luck that doesn't seem to have been earned, a contribution will allay that guilt feeling. If you've paid your "taxes," destiny may leave you alone for a while.

Giving goes both ways. The donor is dissatisfied if he doesn't receive something too. What the donor really wants is approval—or self-approval, really. If he's not told that he's a great guy or if he isn't given some concrete symbol of his generosity, he may not give again. For instance, we found that pictures of happy children ("Win the gift of these children's smiles") are more effective in soliciting aid than pictures of starving, miserable ones. In another project, we found that men are less likely to contribute blood than women because they associate this with a loss of virility. Our advice was to use promotion showing the "loss" being restored: the donor surrounded by beautiful girls.

Competitive giving. It's possible that giving, just like having an impressive job title or buying big houses and boats, could be promoted as a way of competing and earning prestige.

The charity "backlash." Receiving help, although pleasant, also has negative effects. In a way, the recipient has been picked out as a needy person, one who is incapable and hasn't been able to earn his own way. When minority groups complain about not having enough dignity, simply giving them money isn't the answer. The real need is to show the recipient how this money can be used to build—to show him that it is "seed money," so to speak—and to demonstrate to him that he has been selected because he's most capable of making progress.

"From a friend." Although a gift is supposed to be an expression of love, too often it appears to come from a large, impersonal, "nonlove" sort of organization. "Personalities" or symbols are needed to establish contact between giver and receiver.

17

Communicating Better

WHY 80 PERCENT OF COMMUNICATIONS MISS THEIR GOAL

The means of communications are developing far faster than the uses of them. Recent studies we have made in the broadcasting field reveal the following areas of opportunity to improve communications:

1. *Creation of an "Aha" Experience.* The form and content of a message should be designed to bring an audience response, something akin to "Yes, that's right—aha, I understand."

2. *The Role of Style.* Style is related to uniqueness. Not only must the communicator have something to say, but he must also use a unique method to deliver it. Style is subtle, and yet it's real. It is the "gestalt," the configuration of communications.

3. *Participation.* The key to good communications is to give your audience a chance to "fill in" missing parts. When they do, they become involved, interested, and open to persuasion.

4. *Increase the Use of Symbolism.* Symbols were once primitive means of communications. Today their use has come back. The good ones are a

form of "below-the-belt" communication—where an almost visceral contact is established. Instead of talking about power, we could use a symbol such as a tiger to make the other person "feel" the power.

5. *Discovery of the "Inner Jones."* The Joneses don't live here any more. The modern consumer is more concerned with himself, and with how to express his own individuality and personality. Communicators must take into consideration this "inner Jones." They will have to understand better this new, possibly rather unexpected aspect of the respondent whom they are trying to reach.

HUMAN NEEDS AND THEIR TRENDS

There is a French proverb which says that you cannot ever bypass your predecessor by following in his footsteps. The marketing and communications fields are closely tied up with progress. In order to assure progress, they have to break down barriers, start their own revolutions, and point the way ahead. The faster your car goes, the farther you have to look ahead to prepare your steering maneuvers. If your car is going 40 miles an hour, it might be sufficient to look a few hundred yards ahead. If you are driving at 100 miles an hour, you have to double or triple your foresight. The same thing applies to marketing communications and research.

How are human needs going to change? Shall we have to use a different language, different appeals, and different products to reach the market of the future? The answer lies in understanding the emotions, fears, and hopes of the citizen of the "brave new world."

Are human needs changing? I think so. The following points are not based on soothsaying. They are the result of research, of dialectical developments, and of observable trends. I think these predictions are sound.

Human Needs Are Plastic

Many ill-informed people worry that with the increase of available goods, we're going to run out of human needs and human wants. Most of our planning and thinking leans for its correctness on the proper use of thought models. In our studies we have often found that when advertising people and manufacturers start speculating about psychological facts, they make a basic mistake; they think, for instance, of human motivations, needs, and wants in terms of a flat pie chart. They speculate that if I have satisfied the need for visual forms of entertainment through television, for example, I have cut out a major section of this pie chart. There is only so much left for movies, home projection, looking at slides, and similar visual entertainment. It sounds logical, but it is a wrong concept.

Human motivations are much better thought of in terms of an ever-expanding rubber balloon which practically never bursts. Once our desire for visual satisfaction has been aroused, it does not become satisfied; rather, we keep on expanding and wanting more visual entertainment. Appetite comes with eating. Many industries have wrongly and prematurely foreseen their decline because they were misguided by the flat pie-chart concept. The home movie projection industry started to boom rather than to decline with the advent of television. The phonograph record industry had its real beginning with the advent of radio. Many of the products which exist today did not exist ten years ago.

As human needs for the basic necessities of daily life are being satisfied, we are discovering that we have more and more freedom, more and more leisure time, and more and more disposable income for the satisfaction of wants. We travel more; we become more interested in the so-called inner luxuries. We want more beautiful things. We want things which are very far removed from the necessities but which have become necessary in order to make our modern life fuller. Some of them are material goods; others are of a more spiritual nature. Sometimes new wants are created by changing the original purpose of a pursuit. Guns were used first for survival and then for sport and for hunting. Now it is very likely that a tremendous future lies ahead for gun clubs, which will compete with bowling clubs and tennis clubs and which will have the social get-together as a main purpose. Printing as a hobby was recently reported to be on the increase; more women do canning today than ten years ago, and more sew their own dresses.

Ten years from now, many new needs will exist. To satisfy them, new services and new products will have to be created. What specific new needs or variations of old needs can we safely predict?

Desire for Individuality

More and more, modern advertisers will have to accept and recognize a growing need revolt against mass society. "I want to be different, and I am different" is the conviction which the consumer is increasingly beginning to develop. If you talk to him about the millions of other people who use your product, you may be insulting him. It will become increasingly difficult to hold more than 30 to 35 percent of a market with one brand. The so-called mass market will dissolve itself into a market of psychological groups.

Many of our market research studies still make distinctions that date back to the early days of the census: breakdowns according to age, income, and other demographic factors. We in our organization have introduced more and more truly dynamic classification systems into our motivational research studies. For example, three people belonging to the $10,000-a-year income group may actually be members of distinctly different groups: five years ago one may have earned $5,000; another, $15,000; and the third, the same amount he is earning today. We propose that these three different individuals, motivationally speaking, belong to completely different groups. What the person does with the money he earns is much more important than the exact amount he earns. Such a dynamic factor can be introduced into almost all demographic classifications.

However, we have to go beyond even that. In some work with doctors we found that distinguishing between various types of doctors, such as conservative, progressive, possessive, patient-oriented, profit-oriented, etc., permitted a much more pinpointed form of advertising and sales approach. Many psychological classifications permit the ascertainment of syndromes. A person who uses laxatives is also very likely to use three or four other proprietary drugs. His basic syndome may be one of hypochondriasis. Gadget consciousness is another one of these syndromes. If you want to sell a garbage-disposal unit, you are better off seeking out people who have electric can openers and electric carving knives than paying too much attention to income, age, or marital status. Psychological segmentation of the market depends on the eventual establishment of a psychological type of census. But this is one of the barriers that will have to be broken down in the future. It is a revolution in marketing and communications which is just around the corner.

The Aesthetic Revolution

Style consciousness and aesthetic appreciation have been increasing continuously, not only because of the influence of movies, books, plays, and the field of interior and exterior decoration, also, but to a large extent, because of the influence of advertising itself. The public is becoming more and more demanding. It wants good-looking things. It wants more sophisticated things. Style and aesthetics are to a very large degree an element of the level of the presentation. If you compare the Shakespearean or modern Broadway play with a soap opera, you will discover that the contents are often very much alike. It may be a "whodunit," or a marital triangle may be involved. The main difference lies in the way the material is presented. The soap opera makes the situation obvious; it is as if the person sitting next to you at the movies or in the theater were to nudge you and explain to you what was going to happen: "Just watch— he is going to kiss her." "Just watch—he is going to kill her." Of course, this robs the onlooker of a good part of his pleasure.

If we were to analyze these differences in style levels, we would find that they are based on the degree of participation permitted the public. The obvious story presented in an obvious style begins to fall flat and will not impress the citizen of 1970 or 1975 any longer. It does not show that the artist has been creative or has condensed in any way what he has observed and experienced. Part of the aesthetic pleasure lies in the opportunity to re-create the original effort of the artist. Showing a perfect cake in an ad is not nearly as effective as showing it in a more human, more imperfect (possibly crumbly) fashion, permitting the reader to add his own ideas and associations. The word "recreation"—fun—is derived from "re-create," "to create again." Fun comes from adding your own creative efforts in order to understand the original intention of the artist. "Aha, I get it; I understand it" is the basic, essential element of the psychology of esthetics. People are becoming more and more demanding as far as beauty and aesthetics are concerned.

An international paper company making facial tissue neglected to perceive this early enough and insisted on advertising the practicality of its product, an aspect that everybody else was taking for granted. A competitor, on the other hand, was stressing the fact that the advertising message came off with the cellophane wrapper and was offering the public a choice of different designs. In this way he was able to command an important segment of the market for himself. His product was not superior; it was simply more beautifully packaged.

Beauty will become more and more important in modern packaging. The housewife of today and tomorrow will want to be able to open her cupboard and be impressed with the aesthetic quality of the products she has bought. She will be able to put them on the table if she wants to. All this will present a tremendous challenge for the modern package designer. More and more beauty will have to be introduced into our stores as well.

Another aspect of this increased need for beauty is the eventual downfall of stereotypes. Stereotyped presentations are a major sin committed by the communicator. "Let us choose a model for our ads which will be acceptable to everybody," we say. "Let us tell our story in such a way that it will not offend any segment of the public." This would be like a novelist starting his book in the following way:

> It was a typical Middle Western town. Main Street looked like any other Main Street. All the trees were planted the same way. Suddenly there was a revolver shot which sounded like any other revolver shot. . . .

A lot of advertising is written that way. The really good novelist—and he does not have to have too much literary talent—will do the exact opposite. He will describe a scene in a very unusual and nonstereotyped fashion. He might say, for instance:

> This was a town that looked like no other town. Main Street had elms missing on the left-hand side. Several city gardeners had tried to plant new ones, but they had always died. There was a rumor that a body was buried

underneath these trees and that this was what made them die. The steeple was also very peculiar; it was crooked as a result of some misconstruction, some miscalculation by the town architect. The revolver shot was like no other shot. . . .

The interesting aspect of the last example is that it is much easier to identify oneself with such an unusual, very specific description than with a generalized, stereotyped one. When I hear this town described, I think of my own town, which has its own singular features that cannot be found —at least so I imagine—anywhere else.

In communication we are concerned with the law of identification. Identification, it so happens, is more easily produced when real, concrete, singular items are presented than when stereotypes are used. The aesthetic revolution I am talking about would have to learn to take these factors into consideration.

The Distribution Revolution

The distribution patterns of the future will have to satisfy human, not technical, needs. Our stores, our displays, and the interior arrangement of supermarkets and drugstores may become completely different from what they are today. We are still organizing things in technological terms: food stores, shoe stores, clothing stores, furniture stores. The individual of the future—and this future is beginning to materialize already—will think much more in terms of his own needs. We may have stores keyed to, and designed for, particular moods—there may be a store where I can buy all those things which will help me get rid of a psychological depression. This may be much more than just a liquor store. Another outlet might concern itself with offering people all the merchandise that is suited for a vacation. Again, I can foresee the possibility of a store whose designation will be "so you feel like splurging . . ." rather than "clothing for sale."

The gas station of the future will do much more than dispense gas and oil; this function will become a minor one. It may take on the aspect of the general store, in which providing gas and oil is simply an incidental service. Our Institute has started to develop such innovations in some South African and European gas stations. Hotels of the future may have special sections where the traveler can keep a suit, some shirts, and a few personal belongings, so that the hotel would come closer to being a part of his home rather than a completely strange place. Displays in supermarkets and sections of supermarkets may be arranged completely differently from the way they are now. Instead of having all the items used at breakfast in different parts of the store, they may be all grouped together in one section. Maybe there will be special departments for men and others where children can shop.

We Must Learn to Break Down National Barriers

More and more companies are beginning to think internationally. French, German, and Italian companies are for the first time developing European brands. The fear of neglecting national characteristics still exists, and yet the answer must lie in international forms of marketing, advertising, and brand development. No loss of desirable differences has to occur.

French cheeses can be sold all over the world, but do not have to become American or German cheeses. In a study for a company making Tyrolean Loden, our advice was to retain the label of origin but to make this Loden available to all Europeans. While French perfume has seemed to be the undisputed leader up to now, it will be possible in the near future to introduce Spanish perfume, as is already the case, for instance, with Tabu, which is manufactured in Barcelona.

American companies have to learn to abandon their isolationist attitudes and to adjust themselves to different markets. On the other hand, foreign exporters coming into the American market have to learn to recognize that no loss of identity is involved in trying to combine their own brand characteristics with the requirements of the American market.

International soft drinks are just around the corner. Human needs will become more diversified and sophisticated. We shall want to travel all over the globe—at least via the products we consume every day.

In a study conducted in South Africa, we tried to distinguish between various tribes as beer consumers: the Zulus, the Bantus, the Xosas. In reality, our dividing line became much more valid when we let it run horizontally and compared the emancipated Zulu with the young European and the young Bantu. Tribal and even color barriers began to fall. We found that all young people belonging to the same generation, regardless of tribe and color, resembled one another much more than the young Zulu resembled the old Zulu.

In a recent survey of the toy market we found that a whole social group, the senior citizens, represents a market ready to be tapped for toys and games, a fact that has been largely overlooked up to now. These people have time on their hands, are sociable, and want something to do. More sophisticated types of toys and games could be developed for this specific market.

In an analysis of heavy beer drinkers, we found that the stereotype of the heavyset, somewhat older manual laborer is false and has to be replaced by a psychologically more correct classification. Heavy beer drinking often goes together with problems in coping with life. The heavy drinker wants a liquid with "body." This basic frustration with life's problems, which is often at the core of heavy beer drinking, exists as much among young people as it does among middle-aged or heavyset persons, if not more. Many marketing men make the mistake of thinking about their public as static, instead of accepting the fact that it changes continuously.

In a study for a German detergent company in Spain, we found that although it was true that the Spanish housewife had been accustomed to buying cheap detergents, a concentration of the dynamic factors of this market and the social change taking place dictated a completely different kind of strategy. We found that the low-income housewife has a great appreciation for linen and is concerned about its preservation and that she was basically dissatisfied with the detergents that were on the market. We recommended to the German detergent company that they introduce a high-priced detergent and, at the same time, that they recognize this high regard that the Spanish housewife has for her treasure—her linen. The resulting slogan, "Marry your linen to Persil" (the name of the brand), turned out to be one of the most successful advertising campaigns in a long time.

A study for the candy industry demonstrated that to think only of children or women as candy eaters is a narrow, outdated viewpoint, particularly in light of the current anticigarette campaign. The old slogan "Reach for a Lucky instead of a sweet" could easily be reversed. Many men, if offered candy in a masculine fashion, could be convinced to use it as a source of energy as well as a substitute for cigarettes. The barrier which is still permitted to exist but which will have to be broken down in the future is the one of thinking of markets in terms of immovable, basically static social stratifications.

Modern marketing has to be aware of the coming classless society— classless in a much truer sense than has been the case even behind the Iron Curtain. We are facing a continuing trend toward internationality and social change in the symbolic and social value of many products and services.

More Direct Communication—Frankness

Advertisers are still inclined to think and talk in terms of themselves. Pharmaceutical companies blow their own horn, not realizing that they are antagonizing the physician, who thinks at least as highly of himself as he does of the research activities of the huge drug company. In some recent work with pharmacists we found that they are highly resentful of being regarded as tradesmen and businessmen rather than as professionals, in comparison with physicians.

Communications in the marketing and advertising field and also in the political field still suffer from the relative inability of the communicator to break down his own ego barrier and to put himself into the role of the recipient of the message. How does he perceive things? What does he understand? Asking ourselves these questions often shows us that the clever, apparently forceful sales message falls completely flat as far as the recipient is concerned. For example, an advertiser shows beautiful babies in order to sell his baby food. Our studies show that the average mother is jealous of this beautiful baby because her own baby does not look one bit like him. Furthermore, what she is really interested in is saving time on feeding—getting through with her "mother love" in half the time. Her motivations are not at all those which the advertiser presumes exist. We have to learn to understand how people really experience products.

We have established a "behavioral theater," in which we ask people to act out many things, sometimes going as far as to ask them to "be" a product: "You are a cake; you are a shampoo." This is similar to the games played by children, who will easily take on the role of a choo-choo train, a truck, or a plane. Such direct, nonverbal communication will probably take place more and more in modern advertising. The tiger used by Esso and other brands, and the white tornado used by Ajax all point in the direction of the need for us to revise our thinking on how best to communicate our messages. Breaking down the logical, superficial viewpoint and permitting the emotions which are experienced by the recipient of the message to be the controlling factor will increasingly become a necessity.

Antifatalism: A New Need

Our organization has been asked to serve as consultant to, and to participate in some of the problems of, the Job Corps, which is part of the President's antipoverty program. About forty thousand youngsters, many of them school dropouts, have to be trained to become employable. One of the occupations they are supposed to be trained for is that of salesman. The normal diagnostic type of research approach would consist in finding out first what makes a good salesman. In our discussions in Washington we were told that research accumulated up to now points to the fact that such qualities as empathy, friendliness, ability to understand adversities, etc., are simply accepted as known factors. Our job from now on, we were told, was to *train* these people in a goal-directed fashion to become friendlier, to develop more empathy, and so on. I would like to suggest that this is a very healthy and pragmatic attitude toward many problems. Too many social studies which are being conducted simply prove the obvious. The distinction between diagnostic research and blueprints for action and therapy resulting from it is often an artificial one. Modern society has waited too long for solutions; it has become impatient. The need for answers and action in many areas will increase. Minority groups are not willing to wait any longer.

Only if the research is designed from the beginning in such a way as to produce pragmatic end results can it be fruitful. But this goal-directedness has to be introduced right at the start. Programmed instruction and teaching machines are wonderful new learning devices, but they require a preamble of appropriate motivations. Telling salesmen to be friendly to customers and to accept the fact that the customer is always right, even when done with the help of carefully prepared frames of easily digested lessons, does not always produce desired results if the motivation of the salesman has not been properly controlled.

We portray the interrelationship between management, salesman, and customer on the thought model of a triangle, where management is on top, the customer is on one side, and the salesman is on the other. The normal type of training program often results in the creation of an artificial barrier between management and the salesman. Management is perceived by the salesman to be on the side of the customer if it proclaims that the client is always right. Instead, we try to divide the triangle in a completely different fashion by putting management on the side of the salesman and, if necessary at times, making fun of the customer. A new motivated training approach and goal-directed research study resulted, for instance, in the development of booklets on the five most obnoxious types of customers in a particular department store. Management thus succeeded in laughing with the salesmen about their joint enemy, as it were, thus creating the feeling in the salesman that management stood on his side rather than on the side of the outsider, the customer.

In a training program for gas station attendants, our goal was to get the attendant to pay more attention to the customer. Instead of telling this to him directly in an authoritative fashion, we suggested that he become an automotive Sherlock Holmes—he had to observe certain things such as the dust on the fenders, the mileage, and the kind of people in the car. He then had to ask a number of specific questions of the motorist. On the basis of his observations he would arrive at the possibility of guessing how long the motorist had been driving, how good a driver he was, where he came from, etc. If he guessed correctly, he would receive a high score as an automotive Sherlock Holmes. Obviously, we were not interested in his score; rather, the trick behind all this was to develop an attitude on the part of the attendant which forced him to pay attention to the customer—to do all those things which he previously had to be told to do in an authoritative and dictatorial manner, which resulted in arousing his inborn resistance.

More and more communication with a good orientation will become necessary.

The Discovery of the "Inner Jones"

We worry a lot about our increasingly materialistic society. In reality, we are approaching the exact opposite, and as is often the case, when we seem to approach the extreme of one phenomenon, its antithesis is often just around the bend. Having satisfied, to a very large extent, many of our material needs, we are now ready to contemplate other wants. Having bought two or three television sets or two or three cars, we now discover that we're still not satisfied.

The American, in particular, is one of the first to discover or rediscover that life is not complete unless it contains a goodly portion of unnecessary things, luxury items. In the course of this development, we are beginning to look at ourselves much more than we ever have before. We seem to be less intent upon impressing the Joneses, our neighbors, and we begin to worry about satisfying the *"inner* Jones." We are becoming aware that we have a soul, that we have a right to express our individuality, that we want to be different, and that being different is one of the basic aspects of humanity. What we are witnessing, therefore, is the reassuring spectacle of American society, which has been accused of being almost wholly materialistic and product-oriented, discovering culture (in the form of art, literature, etc.) in its basic, original meaning. Culture is turning upside down, churning up, cultivating. It is the exact opposite of superficial covering up, plastering, and painting. This country is probably among the first to discover mass culture and to consume culture on a truly democratic basis. When we admire the ancient Greeks, we often forget that their admirable culture was based on a prerequisite of slavery, that the real culture of Greece belonged to a very small clique of aristocrats, while the level of the common Greek was far below that of our factory worker.

Human progress does not proceed along a straight ascending line. Instead, it can be best portrayed in the form of a spiral. We are dealing with thesis, antithesis, and synthesis. Individualism is the thesis. We then developed a mass society, and on our next turn of the spiral we rediscovered individuality, but on a higher level, thus synthesizing or combining our primitive individualism and the discoveries of the mass society.

Our so-called materialistic mass society is on the verge of bringing about another revolution, possibly the most encouraging and most important one of our time. American art is beginning to be recognized all over the world. Many of the modern composers are Americans. Without sounding chauvinistic, it is probably correct to say that New York at least rivals, if it has not surpassed, many of the cultural centers of Europe. This culture—although it is available to, and coveted by, millions of people—is one that reaches deeper than ever before. It is based on a desire to mold one's mind, to go back to the cause of our strength. Maybe we are slowly beginning to realize that we have not been driven out of paradise but driven into it—that knowledge, realization of one's potentialities, and continuous growth are really the basic elements of life. Biologically, we are doomed to decline in strength. As the existentialists say, we start dying on the day we are born; but being human beings, we have the power and beauty to become a little bit bigger, a little bit better, and a little bit deeper and more cultured in the true sense every day we live, so that if we have conducted our life properly, we should be worth more spiritually on the last day of our sojourn on this earth than we were the day before. What we are beginning to learn is that life does not offer as its goal a kind of cowlike contentment and happiness, but rather constructive discontent.

The security we have been seeking, as long as it is a static one in which we try to barricade ourselves against the onslaughts of life's difficulties and problems, is an illusory one. There are no platforms which we can reach and upon which we can safely and undisturbedly pass our time away. They don't exist on a South Pacific island or anywhere else. Instead, real security is a dynamic state, wherein we accept the fact of continuous change, progress, and growth. Maybe the major revolution of the next decade and the new changing needs will reflect the acceptance of this new philosophy. We are beginning to accept it and are doing so more and more. We are beginning to liberate ourselves from the shackles of inhibitions, superstitions, and medieval thinking. The man that I foresee is one who will be truly free and will have a belief in his own strength mixed with new humility, but who at the same time has begun to see himself as a master of his own destiny, rejecting fatalism in any of its forms. This revolution, the discovery of the "inner Jones," will be a major one for marketing and advertising people to recognize and incorporate into their thinking and strategy.

HOW TO RECRUIT AND KEEP GOOD PERSONNEL

Today's labor shortages here and nearly everywhere in the world call for more positive and productive recruitment advertising. The conventional appeals of salary, company stature and size, and locality are relatively poor motivations. New techniques are needed. These are often subtle, go deep into reasons not often directly expressed, and have much to do with satisfaction of ego. The following is a summary of some of the basic motivations that have been found to be successful in recruiting new personnel, and keeping them.

1. *Ego Involvement.* Call it a "partnership feeling," a sense of participation. This can express itself in open communications, in profit sharing, and in a personal interest on the part of management in all employees.

2. *Role Playing.* A promise of changing roles—letting employees do different jobs—can bring out surprising new interest in the whole company. This prevents boredom.

3. *Automation.* Workers should not be given tasks that could or should be done by machines or devices.

4. *The "As If" Approach.*   It is possible to make personnel behave "as if" they were, for example, "friendly," "courteous," etc., by helping them first to maintain an illusion of the trait; signs, greetings, badges, etc., can be used. Eventually, they live up to the illusion and find it more fun and stimulating.

5. *Increase Personnel's Interest in the Job.*   Often, pointing out the importance of each task and its role in the overall success of the company can boost interest. When the significance is understood, the work is more enjoyable.

6. *Size Is Not Everything.*   Small, new companies can often offer greater future promise for employees; they can "grow" with progress. Management can convey this feeling by being dynamic and by helping individuals grow through training.

7. *Management from the Bottom Up.*   Reverse the chain of responsibility. Pass the buck *up* instead of down the line. It improves morale and efficiency. Blame should be placed with the better-qualified, more highly paid superior.

8. *Sociometric Charts.*   Actually getting people's names down on a map or chart helps them understand their role and their job. It increases pride.

9. *Employees Are Individuals.*   Don't let an employee feel that he is an automaton in a mechanical labyrinth. Stress his uniqueness and differences. Give him a chance to be himself.

HOW NEWSPAPERS CAN OFFER MORE TO THEIR READERS

Our studies of newspaper show that as people become better educated and more sophisticated, they expect more from their newspapers. Our studies show that people want newspapers to give them more *depth of understanding* of what goes on in the rest of the world. They do not want simply to be informed. One also senses that in an era of change, newspapers have remained much the same—or may even be growing outmoded as new electronic and visual media are constantly demanding our attention. How can newspapers do a better job for their readers?

1. *Use Stronger "Identification Hooks."*   There is a strong, unfulfilled desire for personal and human identification with events and the people behind them. Too many newspapers have not learned the art of the novelist and dramatist. They present news as abstract historical events rather than as reports of human activities. Colorful details can often be powerful "identification hooks" (for example, at President Kennedy's funeral, little John saluting the coffin). Such details may not have histori-

cal significance, but they are bridges that help the reader understand in depth.

2. *Readers Seek Order Out of Chaos.* To many readers, the real world is too complicated. They want the newspaper to bring it into clear focus. Some newspapers overdo this. They oversimplify. Others leave the world too unstructured. The balance might be found by paying more attention to the communication process itself, that is, by considering the newspaper a sort of optical lens that can reveal the overall significance, while at the same time showing close-ups of details that are often more emotional and human.

3. *Newspapers as Contemporary History.* Again, newspapers could borrow from creators of fiction. The novelist knows that his reader is more interested in the hero or the characters in his book than in its broad historical significance. Moviemakers know this too. Audiences can better understand the story if it is interpreted to them through the roles of "real" and identifiable people. They can imagine themselves taking part.

4. *New Visual Interpretations of News.* Most people think in simple visual terms. (Even the most educated person, when asked to describe a spiral staircase, will make a circular movement with his hand.) What are visual symbols that would help make meaningful the war in Vietnam, our foreign aid policy, the civil rights movement, the country's economic health, etc.? For almost any important event, a quick visual equivalent or "mental model" would aid in fast comprehension; think how much the Dow-Jones averages communicate to investors. This mental model might be some translation of the "systems model"—a three-dimensional visualization not only of all important elements in a situation but also of the progress, or lack of it, in various areas.

5. *Can Newspaper Formats Be Improved?* Many newspaper managements feel that any changes in format are upsetting to the reader. Yet there are many aspects that could be improved—stories that are continued in odd places throughout the paper; the hard-to-fold, large paper, which is difficult to read in trains and buses; and typefaces and graphics that are much the same as they were fifty years ago. All these may be improved in future newspapers.

YOUTH AND DRUGS

We obviously need law enforcement to curtail drug abuse, but what we need much more urgently is a better and psychologically more correct form of communication and a less naïve approach to the whole problem of drug addiction. To tell a youngster to stop taking drugs or not to start taking them is of little avail if all he sees is the excitement that drug use has created. In some cases youngsters are often first made aware of the widespread use of drugs and have their curiosity aroused to try them too by the people who warn against drug use. In a way, therefore, newscasters become almost "psychological pushers." The more they are threatened, youngsters tell us, the more thrill they get out of it. They have found a remedy for coping with the problems of the modern world. As a result of mass communications, the youngster is much more aware of such problems than his parents were. He is resentful because we, the adults, try to take this one last—in his mind—successful tool away from him. Simply admonishing him to give up drugs is like taking a crutch away from a weak person who has been leaning on it because he is not able to walk without it and is afraid of falling.

We portray the drug addict as the villain—and the message bearer as the clean, holy person. The youngster knows otherwise. The same person who has the nerve to tell him to get off drugs smokes himself to death and thinks nothing of having three martinis before lunch. We have to take a good, brutal look at what is taking place now in the field of communications and the awakening of social consciousness.

In addition to headaches, cavities, stomach disorders, and dandruff, we now have discovered drug addiction, litter problems, pornography, pollution, lung cancer, criminality, commuter dissatisfaction, and consumerism. The total amount of money and talent that various groups expend on these problems must be considerable. Never has more money and talent gone down the drain. We are harsh in our criticism of an ad for detergents or dandruff remedies. We check to find out whether it does do the job. Does it really sell the product? When we are dealing with racism, violence, drug abuse, or environmental control, however, we feel so good about finally having said or done something that we forget to question the practicality and real effectiveness of all these worthwhile attempts at controlling and improving our lot on this land and on this globe.

We should realize that repeating commandments of various kinds has not really gotten us very far. It is time we concerned ourselves with the techniques of implementation. We have to try to find out what will make a person obey a command and what will not. In whatever clever form it practiced, admonition is one of the poorest methods of getting people to mend their ways. We are much too concerned with the "what" and the "how" of the communication rather than with its goal and effectiveness.

Our organization, the Institute for Motivational Research, recently conducted a pilot study checking into the reaction of the public to the avalanche of antipollution, birth control, and antismoking messages that have been streaming in on them. Between 80 and 90 percent of these messages are almost completely useless. One of the most prevalent reactions we have found was that of increasing escapism. When a drug addict is told about the potential danger of taking drugs, a factor which makes this message almost useless is that the real drug user enjoys what he is doing and has reasons which he feels are more important than the possibility of endangering his health or being sent to jail.

How does one communicate then?

1. *Produce Identification.*   We have to begin by understanding fully the person who commits the crime or misdemeanor. We have to put ourselves on the side of the person that we are trying to reach. You can't convince anybody who smokes cigarettes to stop doing so by portraying a guy on TV who is racked by coughing spells. The smoker knows darn well that this is not the case as far as he is concerned. The average youngster who smokes pot has fun doing it. As radical as it may sound, if we want to reach him, we have to imply that we too appreciate what he is trying to get out of drugs, maybe even by admitting that we, the guys from the Establishment, are not so far removed from bad habits and bad things.

If you want to do something about pilfering, you are better off admitting that almost everybody is a potential thief by showing, for example, that we all occasionally like to take a towel from a hotel or, when we receive wrong change in our favor, at least hesitate before returning the money to the cashier. We have to talk as potential villains to those who might become real villains. Furthermore, by using authoritative language, talking from the top down, we automatically introduce a barrier—one that prevents the youngster from listening to us. We should admit that we are as fallible as he is. We should also admit that we are equally weak, thus establishing a better rapport than we would by preaching from our platform of superiority. We should use more youngsters talking to other youngsters without their appearing to defend the Establishment.

2. *Provide a "Psychological Methadone."*   One of the few effective methods for getting people to stop using heroin is to provide them with a cheap and less harmful substitute, methadone. Youngsters take drugs because they lack excitement, because they are bored, or because they have no real goals except to tear down what is around them. What they are really trying to tell us is that they are hungry for heroes, hungry for excitement. Why don't we make an effort to introduce more excitement into schools—to introduce "happenings" that will be a form of psychological methadone?

We should start analyzing ways of providing young people with a trip, getting them high, without the use of drugs. Without realizing it, we are probably suffering from real and unexpected effects of the affluent society. Drug use is now particularly popular among middle-class students. While the previous generation had to struggle to make a living, we have now reached the point where despite some poverty, material things are more commonly available and accessible. Hunger is not as much a threat as it was before. We need new goals for an affluent society. When we speak to young people about unemployment, old age, or the need to earn a living, for example, our warnings fall on deaf ears. They very often use the atom bomb as an excuse, but in reality, in my opinion, it is boredom with the security all of us have been told is the goal of life. We could set up groups for mind expansion, theatrical groups, creativity courses, and discovery clubs that would make youngsters constructively discontended. As hedonistic and unpuritanical as it may sound, every school day, every boy scout meeting, and every church meeting should be a new exciting experience, rather than a boring, goody-goody duty. We need courses in emotional subjects, in how to make decisions, and in how to control fear. Factual knowledge is not enough.

3. *Actions Instead of Well-meaning Messages.* We have found that very often the adult, and even more so the young listener, who is bombarded by hundreds of messages and admonitions mistakes the messages for the accomplished action, even if he admits that drug use is bad. "Something is finally being done. Why should I get involved?" He wants to go where the real action is. Very few announcements of this sort, however, show the public what to do outside of marketing contributions. We also often have a feeling of impotence. How much can our physical or monetary contribution really mean? Much more frequently radio and TV programs, ads, and public messages should present individuals who have actually produced desirable changes through a number of specific activities they have set in motion themselves—no matter how weak they thought themselves to be. Young people want to be Davids who can slay Goliath. By exaggerating or even realistically showing the enormity of the problem, we very often produce the opposite effect from the one intended.

In our work for the American Heritage Foundation, we found that it is wrong to emphasize the fact that relatively few Americans participate in national elections. The public reacts to such a negative statement with the feeling that they are better off staying with the majority of nonvoters. We tried, with success, to create a psychologically positive bandwagon through the use of numerous small ads showing still another person who has pledged to vote this time. We have to make it chic to go off drugs and show a steady stream of successful abstainers who were turned on by turning off, rather than creating an atmosphere implying that everybody is taking drugs these days.

4. *Let the Youngsters Do It Themselves.* Young people frequently complain about a paternalistic attitude on the part of grown-ups, who have no right to feel superior, judging by the mess they themselves have made of their own lives and their world. Some young people have discovered drugs as their own "thing." "Here we go again," they say. "Now

they are trying to take that away from us, too." I would suggest using the same modern management techniques of participation that are applied in big corporations, rather than psychological authoritarianism. Don't preach, don't talk down, don't warn, don't cajole. Come to understand young people and ask them to help themselves.

In a way, many youngsters feel like Portnoys—they don't want to be crushed by parental love. In human history we have witnessed various forms of emancipation. The feudalism of race is crumbling, and so is the feudalism of age. One way, if not the most effective way, of making youngsters more responsible is to give them more responsibility. They are trying to communicate with us, but they don't know how. They haven't had any lessons in effective communication, so they are looking for their own way, which we—and they, too, deep down—consider to be the wrong way. The generation gap is only a communications gap. It is futile to reach out and try to make the young like us, and vice versa. What we need is equality—what we need is new channels. How many newspapers have sections in which young people can express themselves? How many corporations have a twenty-year-old top manager? Why not have encounter groups between old and young? Let's invent new forms of pressure groups for the young, not just for the oil industry. We might even have a Secretary of Youth in Washington.

5. *Make Good Behavior Fun.*   In a world where the mass media offer primarily fun and enjoyment, it is difficult to convince young people to expend their energies fighting such things as drug abuse, pollution, cancer, overpopulation, or riots. We are letting unpleasantness compete with enjoyment and pleasure. In reality, most activities of this sort, although their content may be unpleasant, can give one a potentially high degree of pleasure, if only they are properly presented. They can provide the very things that youth are looking for, giving them a feeling of achieving something and helping them to get rid of their feelings of alienation, isolation, and lack of purpose. We grown-ups have to start getting rid of our own hang-ups—the attitude that anything that is fun is by definition sinful and bad. A cleaner world, a nondrug world, has to be presented as what it actually is—a more fun world. *As long as the real action is in hell, heaven has a poor chance.*

We need to study in a fresh and frank fashion what youngsters get out of drugs. If they tell us it gives them a kick or a thrill, we have to double the competitive appeals that we can offer. We have to keep on showing them that they have not even begun to realize the potentialities that exist in this world. Unfortunately, most of the young people I have talked to have a general feeling of pessimism as a result of their sudden upsurge of awareness of the many problems that await solutions. They react with a sort of gigantic shrugging of their shoulders, an almost sadistic, passive waiting and wishing for the collapse and downfall of the world we live in. Many messages dealing with the problems we face are themselves permeated by this philosophy. Biologists, philosophers, and public leaders apparently love to wallow in predictions of doom. Unfortunately, it is often easier to get glory and publicity by predicting the end of the world than by trying to figure out how to preserve it.

No task, no matter how skillfully approached, can ever be accomplished without a good dose of optimism. Optimism is simply good therapy and not just corny whitewash. Life is a game and a gamble. Las Vegas and Monte Carlo would have disappeared a long time ago if people were convinced that nobody wins, and so would ambition and work. Games and aims go together. When I stop having aims, I stop playing.

Drug addiction is only one of the many problems facing us. Few of them will be solved, however, if we keep on accusing one another of negligence, stupidity, and incapability. What we need is to make a new landing on the planet earth—to look upon it as if we had just gotten here, as if it were a new discovery. It is full of imperfections, but it is the only place we have. Let us stop being naïve sermonizers and use our modern means of communications in a really modern way, getting down to the nitty-gritty of slow and painful persuasion and motivation of "real" imperfect people. Instead of being voluntary or involuntary drug pushers, let's become pushers of some of the oldest (and newest) values in life: excitement, fun, and constructive discontent. They are the real superdrugs.

WHAT TO DO WHEN PEOPLE WON'T EAT, OR WON'T EAT THE FOOD YOU WANT THEM TO EAT

This problem has recently disturbed several basic food industries—dairy products, lamb, fish, and some fruits and vegetables. Our studies usually show that nothing is particularly wrong with the flavor or quality of these foods. The trouble is, rather, with the industry. They fail to promote the food's best features or to correct basic misunderstandings and negative attitudes toward the product. We found, for example, that women wouldn't buy lamb for their families because it was considered a weaker, less virile food than other meats. Only when we began to masculinize the image and to describe cuts of lamb in more exciting terms did we begin to succeed. Another example is fish. The recommendations we made recently to increase fish consumption might apply to other problem-food industries as well.

We recommended promoting fish as a man's food, featuring big, powerful game fish such as swordfish in ads and fish "steaks" for an aura of strength. We suggested surrounding the product with the appetite appeal of hearty vegetables and beer or ale and eliminating dainty, feminine connotations in serving dishes or settings. Fish should also be promoted as a well-known, popular food—putting "fish and chips," say, in the same category as corned beef and cabbage. New serving methods and occasions for eating fish were suggested: barbecued fish, fish for breakfast (the British eat kippers, after all), fish appetizers, and fishburgers. Another suggestion was to create new "fun" outlets for fish: fish stands at county fairs, fish bars and cafeterias, tanks filled with live fish in supermarkets, more fish for school lunches. We recommended that fish be labeled appropriately. Meat comes with United States government labels of "prime" and "choice"; women might feel more comfortable about buying fish with such reassuring words to aid their judgment. We suggested playing down the negative aspects of fish (bones, believed difficulty of preparation) and playing up its glamour and excitement: the ocean (symbolic of life and sex), the wide variety of flavors (perhaps a flavor chart describing, in mouth-watering terms, tastes of the different kinds of fish), exotic preparations, perhaps a "fish of the month" promotion, and the color and beauty of fish. Fish is also extremely low in calories—a "seven-day fish diet" could be promoted. A multitude of approaches are possible for fish and other underconsumed foods. A little imagination, a sense of sales promotion, and the right human motivations are what's needed—and, often, a little spice.

18

Combating Racial and National Prejudices

WHAT'S REALLY BEHIND THE RACE RIOTS?

Crowded and dirty slums, lack of jobs, the aftereffects of slavery—all these are brought forth as explanations of recent race riots. But they are only superficial explanations. I suggest that there is one basic cause, in the social and psychological sense: the clash between a sober, goal-directed culture and an easygoing, fatalistic culture.

Most Westerners, regardless of their political ideology, have been brought up to believe that hard work is a virtue and that leisure is a sin. We fail to realize that our puritan philosophy is merely a philosophy— not a built-in feature of humanity or a necessity for all human beings. Many other cultures are more nonutilitarian in outlook, more concerned with the enjoyment of life. Our Western culture fights hard to resist the attractions of "la dolce vita" or of beachcombing in the South Pacific. Complicating this conflict today between white "achievement" beliefs and black "enjoyment" concepts are the effects of American affluence.

Americans foresee the necessity for working less and the prospect of having more leisure time—and it frightens them. A real cultural change—which the "hippies" temporarily symbolized—in which monetary rewards and hard work are beginning to lose their importance is taking place.

What the black dreads most—enough to snipe and loot—is the threat of surrendering his outlook. He does not want to become integrated into the rat race. He does not want to become saddled with the white man's philosophy because it has dawned on him that the white man himself has become dissatisfied with his puritan ethic.

Solving the problem   On one hand, the blacks must be reassured that their basic differences are going to be maintained. And the white community must not feel that any change is a threat—must understand that the United States of the future will not be white, puritan, and unemotional. In the not too distant future, the United States will be a much more colorful society—in every sense of the word.

Americans' desire for independence and dedication to hard work and getting ahead have undoubtedly helped some of us to become rich and powerful. We are suddenly discovering, however, that there are millions of citizens who feel that they are the responsibility of the total community, who refuse (or so we think) to take care of themselves. They offer such excuses as "We were slaves," "We were mistreated," "We didn't have your chances." There is some truth in this, but it is also as if your son said, "It is easy for you, Dad. You are disciplined in your work habits; you were trained to work hard, but I am different." To simply agree and say, "All right, I'll make things easier for you" might only perpetuate the very symptom which has appeared. Marshall Plan aid worked only because it was used by Europeans to help themselves. Today Europeans don't like to be reminded that they needed our help. They have convinced themselves that Americans helped only because they needed Europe as a market. In the same way, we should tell blacks that we help them to help ourselves.

Instead of trying to convince the white American to "reward" the rioters by pouring more money in the "black inferno," we can try three approaches:

1. Modify our competitive philosophy by developing communal activities—joint black-white activities that could benefit the whole community.

2. Treat blacks as new immigrants, helping them to get going on their own. Perhaps we could send teacher corps into the slums to show blacks that the rest of the community wants to have a better black neighborhood.

3. Help blacks achieve a sense of dignity. The only way one acquires dignity is by discovering that one is capable of solving one's own problems by peaceful means.

American blacks are perhaps only now beginning to feel the need for identity. They are undergoing the same struggles recently encountered in Nigeria, Ghana, etc. These identity crises are not logical or reasonable—but they are necessary nevertheless. The Congo may have been better off under Belgian rule, but the Congolese had to find themselves. Most people need an identity—no matter how miserable the economic results may be. Perhaps such struggles are temporary. In some formerly French colonies in Africa, for instance, the old "masters" have been called back to help in building the new nations.

We can hope that in the future, American blacks will be able to display their unique culture as proud, dignified American citizens. Such an evolution could stimulate the widespread acceptance of a more relaxed and human interpretation of American values. This will be a desirable substitute for the present situation, in which the black is chiefly a recipient of handouts designed to "solve" social ills. Money is not going to solve the evil of race riots—unless the handouts can be transformed into the outstretched hand that joins with the black and encourages him to grapple with his own problems.

PARTICIPATING IN COMMUNITY ACTIVITY

As we talk more and more about a participating kind of democracy, particularly as far as young people are concerned, the problem arises as to what can be done to motivate people to show more interest.

People give all kinds of reasons for not participating. Very often, however, these reasons are nothing but rationalizations. They have no time. They don't want to get involved emotionally. They are not sure whether they can really contribute or not. We have experimented with an "excuse eliminator," which confronts people with the real explanation of their behavior. We could have a chart, where after having stated our obvious explanation for our failure in the first column, we are being challenged by questions such as these in subsequent columns: "You said you have no time. Is this absolutely true? Could it possibly be an excuse?" These columns would most likely contain the answers closest to the truth.

We were asked to help people to get along better with their Mexican neighbors. Very often they talked in generalities. We therefore asked them specifically what were really some of the bad experiences that they had had with the Mexicans. The majority of people could not remember any. When we asked what good experiences they had had, they did not remember too many either. We pointed out that this was due to a large extent to their really indifferent attitude and that they had to change it into a more positive one. Furthermore, in ads and other forms of communications, we asked, "Well, if you had bad experiences, what were the causes? Maybe they were just coincidence. Were they really due to the basic bad nature of Mexicans?" We developed, further, a sort of psycho-therapeutic approach. We asked, for example, "Could you have repeated these generalizations because it helped you get rid of your own frustrations?" "Was it just the thing to do?" "Did you want to appear to be smart and with it?"

Another attempt to bring about better understanding, and therefore more willingness to cooperate, consisted of asking people to project themselves into situations that were not too well known to them—for instance, having to live on a small amount of income or being jealous of someone with a better-paying job. We asked, "How many physical fights have you been in personally, and if you have been in any, what were the reasons?" Then we switched from attempting to get people to identify with situations that were strange to them to trying to promote a better understanding of what the unknown ethnic group of Mexicans meant to them.

Another approach was to ask people to suggest solutions to their neighborhood problems. This method is very often productive because it forces the citizen to carry through his own ideas to their very absurd conclusion: "Ask all the Mexicans or blacks to leave"; "Kill them all"; "Send them back to Africa or Mexico." Usually the end result is that the person comes to the realization that there is only one possible way of resolving the problem—by helping educate his neighbors so that all can live a more pleasant life.

Another approach we used was to ask respondents who they thought could bring about the improvement of human relations with minority groups. The obvious answer was "the government" or "a committee," but by carrying the argument through, we forced people to arrive at the conclusion that they had to be responsible for the situation and had brought it about themselves. They could not simply pass on the solution of the problem to other people. Developing this approach further, we asked people what could influence them to participate more in community affairs. The checklist we used included questions such as, "If a friend took you along to one of the meetings, would you go?" "If you were paid for it, would you go?" "If it were at a different location, would you go?" "If it were held at a different time, would you go?" The purpose of this checklist was to point out that none of these reasons really applied and that nothing was really stopping them.

Summarizing, we developed about seven major principles:

1. Accept the law of inevitability. There is nothing you can do about undesirable neighbors except make friends with them and educate them.

2. Paint the future. Show what your city could look like if racial relations were improved, depicting a somewhat idealized but still realistic enough situation.

3. Create identification. Have your friends call you a "nigger" or a "spic," for example, for a whole day and see how you react. Or, better yet, pick out a negative aspect of your personality, not related to racial problems, and ask people to make insulting remarks to you about it. This exercise is intended to show you that prejudice would make you aggressive too.

4. Show photographs of slum neighborhoods. How well behaved would you be, how nice would you be, if you had to live here all your life?

5. Try to reach your so-called undesirable neighbors halfway. You both might be surprised, and they may be willing to meet you halfway.

6. Don't waste a lot of time and effort building up fences and protecting yourself. It's easier to take down the fence than to build it up. Once it is up, it has to be maintained. It never really is safe.

7. Remember that teamwork pays better dividends than hatred. Hatred is a poor investment. Carry this idea through to all its logical consequences.

REMOVING PSYCHOLOGICAL BLINDNESS

We are living in a world full of barriers. It is difficult for a man to understand exactly how a woman feels, and vice versa. We speak about the generation gap. Do Europeans really understand Americans? Do Italians know exactly how Germans feel? Many of our racial problems start with the difficulty of understanding the thoughts and emotions of different groups. Role playing is one of the methods recommended for dealing with this problem, and yet we have to go beyond that. We have to develop the courage that is necessary to play somebody else's role for any length of time. We should start in school with regular lessons of shedding our own identity, even if it is only for fifteen minutes or half an hour, and assuming that of a different group. For the success of such an exercise, it is necessary to understand first more fully what prevents us from carrying through these mental gymnastics.

As is often the case when we talk about changing human behavior, we are confronted with fear—in this case, the fear of losing our identity. We suffer from an almost infantile anxiety that we may not be able to become ourselves again. Sometimes it is helpful to start simply by imitating the gestures used by people belonging to another group or to wear the clothes they normally wear. In an experiment intended to help Peace Corps volunteers adapt to a different culture, they were asked to wear jellabas for a certain length of time. These are an important part of Arab wearing apparel, together with slippers. Immediately the young Americans gained a much better understanding—in an indirect, three-dimensional fashion

—of the Arabs' shuffling gait and of their inability to move too rapidly. Many of their ideas, mostly of a negative nature, about the peculiar way the Arabs walk disappeared, since they discovered themselves that this is due to a large extent to the clothing they wear.

William Styron's book, *The Confessions of Nat Turner,* contains many insights which could help a white person better understand the mentality of the black man. Blacks, says the hero, are trained to pay attention to the intonation of a white man's voice and not just hear what he is saying, which is similar to what a dog apparently must learn to do. This rather brutal insight causes an almost audible clicking to take place in the mind of the reader. He suddenly understands one aspect of being a black man in a white community.

Salesmen often have the job of bridging the gap between themselves and the customer. By adapting some of the customer's gestures and imagining his worries and fears, the salesman can get closer to him in an almost direct, nonverbal fashion. Watching members of different ethnic groups on TV—an Italian politician, for example—and observing their mannerisms and trying to copy the way they move their arms or their facial muscles can bring one a little closer to successful role playing and removing psychological blindness. A friend of mine once stated that while carrying two cameras around his neck, dangling down on his chest, he had for a fleeting moment a better understanding of what it would feel like to be a woman, at least in the physical sense. Lying down on the floor and looking at everything from the perspective of a 3-foot-high child can be another interesting experience. Suddenly one begins to understand how frightening and threatening the enormous size of an adult must be to a small child. Even experiencing such a simple change of the horizon is a good exercise.

Playing waiter for as short a time as half an hour can change one's attitude. It's a little bit like the joke about two people who work in the clothing industry. One is trying to describe a third person by the way he parts his hair, his friendly manner, and other characteristics. He does not succeed until he says, "Don't you remember? Short size 42." Then the other realizes who is it. Professional groups have their own vocabulary and way of looking at things. When trying to remove our psychological blindness, it is often helpful to learn this vocabulary. Most successful psychiatrists know that learning to speak the language of their neurotic or psychotic patients is a prerequisite to establishing contact with them. It is often the case that an apparently completely disoriented, psychotic person still has a rather intelligent and logical system which is meaningful within itself—the only thing wrong with it is that very often the basis on which this logical structure has been constructed is false and out of tune with the real world. By the way, many national and international decisions suffer frequently from a similar inability on the part of statesmen or politicians to learn the meaning of the language and the grammar used by the opposing group.

U.S.A.—NO TOURISTS' PARADISE

The United States government and public hope desperately that European tourists will flock here in record numbers to relieve our balance-of-payments crisis. But "Visit the U.S.A." won't succeed if Americans don't understand the real reasons why European tourists stay away. "Too expensive"—the typical European response—is only a superficial reason. Although obviously airlines' rate reductions should prove salutary, promotion must take into consideration deeper inhibitions.

Fear of tomorrow   Europeans don't want to see here what they fear will be their own status in the future. The average Frenchman wants to think of his wife as a docile creature, busy shining his shoes and stirring the beef stock on the back of the stove. The United States represents the probably inevitable future, in which there will be career women, canned soup, and instant coffee. There is the same feeling about sleek American cars (wedged into traffic jams), housing developments, etc. America is tomorrow's newspaper—full of "bad news."

Inferiority feelings   Europeans also don't want to have to admit that in the United States, many things are more efficient, more comfortable, and better run. They may go for American cowboy movies, expressions, and rock 'n' roll while at home. Coming here is something else.

Disorientation   Typical American promotion stresses such attractions as the "Wild West," scenic and historic sites, skyscrapers, etc. It doesn't help to dispel what really confuses the potential European traveler: United States egalitarianism and "poor service," possibly no understanding of English, and even lack of knowledge of what clothes to bring and what kind of food to expect. Other countries have put their people and businesses to work to welcome tourists: Jamaica, Spain, and even France, with a "smile" campaign a few years ago. But the European tourist here finds no organized welcome. There is a tremendous gap that all kinds of American companies and government groups should fill. The following are a few examples of what might be done:

1. Tell Europeans what to expect in terms of American social structure: Waiters will be less servile; taxi drivers will start long conversations. Travel literature put out by hotels, airlines, and others could prepare Europeans for this more casual way of life.

2. Provide more everyday, down-to-earth information on how to get along in the United States. American restaurant associations might provide such help as menu translations, tips on tipping, and guides to typi-

cally "American" eating places. Phone companies should place special multilingual instructions in phone booths. Banks also should provide signs in several languages with instructions on changing money, etc. Hotel lobbies or other facilities might be established as foreign tourist "welcome centers," where visitors could rest their feet and obtain maps. American Express offices in Europe are natural gathering places where Americans abroad cash checks, receive mail, and meet compatriots; there should be "European Express" offices here. Department stores could make shopping easier for Europeans by establishing international fashion symbols; sizes, for example, are totally different in various countries. Such measures (up to and including telling Europeans how to find rest rooms in American cities) would provide the genuine feeling of welcome that is now lacking.

3. Admit that a few things are wrong with the United States. People from other countries are so braced to hear bragging about the "American way of life" that it would be excellent public relations to discuss some problems: slums, racial problems, even the New York subways. European audiences would then be more receptive to the interesting, appealing things that would make a visit here worthwhile.

HOW TO COMBAT THE "WRONG IDEAS" ABOUT AMERICA

Similar ideas could be used to combat the preconceived notions that people from other countries have about Americans—that we are conformists and materialists; don't have good taste; are uncultured; lack individuality; are superficial in values; make shoddy, mass-produced products; live in houses that all look alike; drive typical "Detroit" automobiles; eat bland, tasteless food; are careless in moral behavior; are rude and discourteous; have too much money and pay too much for things; overtip; give poor service; etc., etc.

Is it all true? In a few cases, yes. In most, no. Yet this is the way millions of people abroad judge us. This is the "image" foreigners have of America and American products and services. Unfortunately, it is not a matter to treat lightly, for nearly every American company—directly or indirectly—has a stake in people and markets overseas and also in the growing tourist trade to our shores. The *myths* about America should be exploded. Efforts should be made by companies and industries to correct the wrong impressions, to erase the misconceptions, and to replace the wrong ideas with right ideas, such as the following:

1. *Americans Are Far from Conformists.* Today this country is the most revolutionary nation in the world. We are more individualistic and more outwardly expressive of individual likes, dislikes, tastes, and prefer-

ences than any other nation. As manufacturers have discovered, hardly any product in America can be mass-marketed today.

2. *Americans Do Not Prefer Bland, Tasteless, Unsophisticated Products.* In our present affluent economy we eat, drink, and enjoy a wide variety of products that are exotic by anyone's standards. We have popular gourmet foods, ethnic foods, fine cheeses, wines, and desserts which rival the good things in life in any country.

3. *America Is Far from "Uncultured."* Our literacy and educational levels are the highest in the world. And it follows that a larger percentage of our population appreciates good music, literature, theater, and films than is the case in other countries where these interests are more often confined to a small number of upper-class people.

4. *The "Materialistic" Label Is Exaggerated.* We are a nation that uses and enjoys many products. This is due, however, to our stage of economic development. We are no longer an agricultural society or an industrial society. We have reached a postindustrial age wherein the average American family can afford discretionary spending of more than 35 percent of its income. Obviously, this means wider ownership of goods and more use of services. Moreover, Americans have moved well out of the bondage of living which required people to spend most of their lifetimes practicing thrift and conservatism.

5. *Americans Are Mobile.* To many foreigners this appears as rootlessness, a restless shifting and traveling which they attribute to a weakening of family and home ties. But again this is simply a manifestation of a maturing society in which the means and the freedom to be mobile are available to a larger number of people.

6. *American Communications Are Faster and Reach More People.* Again, this accounts for the swiftness of change in our fashions and fads, which foreigners misunderstand for fickleness and superficiality. It is neither. It is simply that we can avail ourselves of more information more quickly and, if we prefer, do something about it faster.

What if there were an "American image kit." This is purely an invention of our own. But it might be an answer. For example, a group of companies selling products or services abroad might band together to produce a portfolio of prospects abroad. Such a kit might contain photographs of the "true" American suburban home, the typical middle-income city apartment, and the average American family—its interests, hobbies, and life-style. The kit might also contain brochures and booklets. For example, an auto company could show that it produces not a "standard" car but forty or fifty different models in different colors and shapes. A department store booklet could show the variety of items for sale and some of the bargain prices. A home furnishings company could show the range of furniture from modern to traditional and the room settings

Americans prefer. Textile companies could show samples of modern fabrics in some useful form (a scarf, handkerchiefs, etc.). A hotel chain could include literature on its major hostelries showing room interiors, restaurants, services, etc. A gas station chain could show the multitude of services it offers to motorists.

A further step could be an actual "pack" of products. This should contain only items typical of American good taste and ingenuity that would surprise and enlighten prejudiced foreigners—for example, fashion-smart cosmetic or toiletry items; delicious foods not usually thought of in connection with this country, such as cheeses, pastries, soups, jams and jellies, and wine (if feasible); small, useful gadgets; tobacco products; a hot shaving cream; a new laundry product; a soap or bath product; fine candy; a new soft drink in a can; canned cocktail mix; etc. Such a pack might even be marketed at airline terminals as the ideal present to take to friends abroad. It might come in different sizes and at prices ranging from about $8.50 to $24.50. The concept is that each package is an ambassador of goodwill, a myth exploder, a prejudice fighter. Of course, it would obviously present opportunities for the participating companies to promote their wares and their goodwill.

PSYCHOLOGICAL EXPORT: A NEW NEED

American exports have to be competitive in price, quality, and performance; but what about psychological competition? Often overlooked, psychological competition is becoming more and more important today—and may become of the utmost importance in the future.

What is meant by psychological competition as applied to exports? Let us consider some examples. Abroad (even in Europe) people rarely see an American restaurant—although it is easy to find Japanese, Korean, Italian, French, or German restaurants in virtually every European capital. Consequently, people living abroad may be acquainted with foreign food styles, but they are *not* too familiar with American-style food. This lack of awareness (of an American style) is a barrier to American food exports. To offset this psychological competition, we would need to create *distinctly American style* in food—*and* in fashion and other types of exports as well. In brief, to compete psychologically, the United States has to become more aggressive in stressing its style and its uniqueness.

In his best-selling book *Le Défi Américain* (The American Challenge), the French Author Jean-Jacques Servan-Schreiber points out that the United States not only is developing superior technical "know-how" but also is becoming a cultural leader—in modern art, architecture, and many other areas.

For decades, Americans have been accused of being "conformists." This was probably never true, and it *certainly* is not true today. Compared with the typical European, the average American is really an individualist —but the American has failed to speak out in his own behalf. Instead, he has permitted these prejudices to exist. Expatriates contribute to the propagation of this myth of conformity. In reality, however, Americans are innovators—which gives them a tremendous advantage, not only in technical areas, but also in the field of fashion. For example, American shoes not only are good-looking but also combine comfort, style, and practicality. These advantages are the result of innovation, combined with another important facet of the American way of life: the pragmatic, experimental "Why not?" attitude.

There are other false ideas about the United States which need "debunking." For example, we should attack the misguided notion that the United States is just a materialistic society. (The exact opposite happens to be true.) Compared with people in other countries, the average American is much less attached to material possessions. He lives in a "throwaway" civilization. Unfortunately, the term "throw-away" still has a negative connotation—but retention of useless and outdated products is clearly detrimental, and the American talent for *discarding* such products is worthy of appropriate publicity.

Not enough has been done to dispel the misconception that all American cities are identical ("carbon copies") and dull. Tremendous changes are really taking place everywhere in the United States—often giving each city more individuality—but people abroad remain largely ignorant of this fact. They don't know that imaginative projects like New York's Lincoln Center have many advantages over their foreign counterparts. While many European cities have become too functional and cold (in a poor imitation of an American trend that began in 1945), the newest American projects benefit from the very revolutionary discovery of the utility of "unnecessary" things. For example, an American urban plaza contains not only "useless" trees but "useless" statues as well!

Human development can best be understood if we think of a spiral instead of a straight line. Americans *began* as individualists. Later the United States became a society dominated by mass production, but the *latest* development is a synthesis between individualism and mass living, as America continues to move ahead.

It has been recommended that the American exporter try to adapt himself to foreign markets—but it is equally important to realize that the foreigner will appreciate American *uniqueness!* Up to now, foreigners have complained about the lack of uniqueness in American styles. We are criticized for being too eager to please and for "playing the chameleon."

In my role as host to many foreign visitors, I have made it a practice, for example, to serve American (instead of French or German) wines. I also serve frozen cakes or pies—although I usually pretend (at first) that these are homemade by my wife. Guests always accept my story about homemade baked goods—and they experience a shock (and even disbelief) when they are later shown the container in which the frozen cake or pie was packaged—American style.

Here is another example, from the field of fashion: "Made in the United States" is really superior to "Made in Britain." For instance, the cut of slacks and pants made in England does not compare with that of superbly fitting American slacks. The lightweight *materials* (used in men's clothing produced in the United States) are also appreciated abroad. To my knowledge, no American manufacturer has yet dared to advertise that these are typically American virtues.

Another example can be cited in regard to furniture. American designs are practical, lightweight, and psychologically mobile. Young people almost everywhere appreciate these qualities. The American manufacturer nevertheless feels inclined to use the word "continental" to praise his American designs—despite the recent popularity of Early American styles in continental Europe!

Even hotels in the United States are apt to overlook pictures that portray the American scene. Instead, there are countless paintings or etchings of Montmartre, Spanish landscapes, or Italian scenes. Any visitor from abroad could easily arrive at the conclusion that there really isn't any *American* style of life!

I would suggest that major American industries become more aware of psychological export—which is really an extension of America's justifiable pride in its unique achievements.

To provide foreigners with a "face-saving" device which would permit them to *change* their opinion about things American, it might be advisable to consider a new term such as the *"new* American style," the *"modern* American style," or even the *"young* American style." We could be magnanimous enough to suggest to foreigners: "You *may* have been right until now, *but* things are changing—and we want *you* to be the *first* to know!"

If American exports are to find even more acceptance abroad, the American exporter will need to radiate more self-assurance (without arrogance or boastfulness). First, however, he will have to convince himself that he *really* has something to offer beyond competitive prices and quality. Only then will there be a major step forward, toward greater confidence in America's export wares. The ultimate result should be greater acceptance of America's products by customers abroad.

In today's world, many values are becoming more and more international. True internationality, however, does *not* require anonymity; for example, Volkswagen is an international product, and yet *everybody* knows that it originates in Germany. American products *can* and *should* contribute more to the variety and beauty of modern life. However, their American origins should *not* be hidden. Let us provide buyers of American exports with the opportunity to *feel* that they are enjoying the wide choice of products and services offered by "one world." Instead of feeling overwhelmed by economic "Yankee imperialism," your customers and prospects will be flattered by the attention you pay to them.

YOUR SEVEN BIG MISTAKES AT SALES MEETINGS ABROAD

When you stage a sales meeting in a foreign country with a "This worked for us in the United States, so it will work here" approach, you run into trouble. Trying to apply American solutions to foreign problems is likely to jeopardize the success of the meeting and future meetings and also the acceptance of your entire company.

If your own past experience doesn't seem relevant in the foreign country, what can you do about this before you arrive? If you study the simple cultural and psychological differences between yourself and the foreign attendees, the meeting is on the road to success. The following seven major points about foreigners and foreign meetings can help the meeting planner in this regard:

1. The first and probably the most important thing for a meeting planner to do is to get rid of any national misconceptions and stereotypes about foreigners he might have.

2. Everyone wants to be different. Europeans, especially, are becoming conscious of national differences, regional differences, and even local differences. This wish to retain their identity leads to mistaken stereotypes, often started by the citizens of the various locales themselves. One such stereotype, is that Germans are the most industrious and efficient people in Western Europe. In reality, the French and Italians are more industrious and efficient than the Germans, while the German people are often more easygoing. "Foreigners are always late" is another erroneous stereotype. At one time this might have been true, but not anymore. Foreigners exposed to English and American habits have become time-conscious, just as we are. In fact, they will stress being on time by being early. In doing this, they are proving that they are trying to meet us halfway, and we should do the same. One way of meeting foreigners halfway is first to probe all stereotypes and misconceptions in depth before accepting or rejecting them.

3. Remember that Europeans are more concerned with hierarchy at meetings and not with equality. If, for example, the president of the company or any other high officers are present, a foreign audience expects

them to be treated better and with more respect than the rest of the audience. The seating arrangement at the meeting is important. Remember to put company executives in the front or best seats in the house during all sessions. When officers are present, the atmosphere should be austere. Foreigners are very "Emily Post conscious," so etiquette should be followed to the letter at all meetings, but especially when executives are there.

4. Avoid a certain brashness. Brashness manifests itself in several ways, for example, calling a man by his first name too soon. Foreigners take great offense at this, since in their own countries they demand to be called by their full titles. If, for example, a German is a doctor, architect, and engineer, he likes to be called Herr Doctor Architect or Herr Doctor Engineer.

Another kind of familiarity at which foreigners take offense is backslapping. An "Americanism" at a session spoiled one company's international sales meeting. The meeting started with "wake-up" martial music, as meetings usually did in the United States. One German voiced the opinion of the group by saying, "This is familiar. It's not much different from what we had under Hitler."

5. Remember at foreign meetings to avoid the American condescending attitude. Americans have been suffering under the illusion that foreigners believe that American products, ideas, and people are the best in the world. This superiority complex alienates foreigners and causes a rejection of anything American. Our studies on the American condescending attitude show that foreigners get the impression that they are finally invited to enjoy the benefits of American life. Their reaction, particularly now, is that Americans can keep their benefits. With the world situation as it is now, Americans should change their condescending attitude to the underdog approach. There would be fewer "Yankee Go Home" signs if we did.

6. Avoid overly dramatized pragmatism at a meeting in a foreign country. First, it is necessary to point out that foreigners have a perverse feeling about salesmanship. In Europe, "a real gentleman is not a salesman, and selling is not an honorable profession." The American planner confronted with this problem should find some way to cover up the fact that he is selling at the meeting. He should emphasize the service qualities of the men, the company, and the product and play down the selling aspects. One way to play down selling is to use a "cultural" approach. Foreigners may or may not be more cultured than Americans, but the point is that they think they are. At a meeting you should include cultural points whenever possible. To quote writers or philosophers or give the history of the company or its products is not considered out of place in foreign countries and will put at ease an audience that is made uncomfortable by regimented efficiency.

7. Another point for a meeting planner to remember concerns humor and its use with a foreign audience. Jokes told to a foreign audience should be less subtle than those told in the States, since they lose something in translation. Foreigners are best at understanding political jokes, and they greatly appreciate those directed against the United States. The main reason for this is that such jokes alleviate any feelings of inferiority on the part of the audience. One kind of joke that should never be used is a dirty or off-color joke. Europeans especially are very puritanical and don't feel that a meeting is the place for such stories and jokes.

Foreigners, on the whole, are more organized than Americans as far as little details go. They expect Americans to be even more organized. This all stems back to their feelings about their own inferiority and American superiority. They criticize Americans, but subconsciously they admire us.

19

Bridging
the Generation Gap

On the one hand, advertising shows us beautiful young models swinging to rock rhythms, cavorting on beaches, and holding hands on dates. On the other, news media present a picture of youth in terms of student riots, hippies, and "communal" living. Neither picture probably really represents today's young population—the target of so many mass-marketing strategies, designed to sell everything from acne aids to automobiles, and of retailing efforts on almost every level, from department stores to franchise food chains. We must, however, strive to break past the stereotyped presentation of youth and recognize that the so-called disruptive element does represent general attitudes which must be understood. Young people may indeed be spoiled, ungrateful, unreasonable, conforming, and "copycat" in areas from revolts on campus to jewelry fads, but "unreasonable" motivations are also marketing facts.

On the basis of recent interviews with youth, I have isolated a group of psychological elements of significance:

Emancipation and action   Today's young person has a longer period of dependence—with greater financial and social freedom than in previous generations. The satisfaction of action as proof of "virility" (as young elks seasonally battle with old bucks) and personal worth is one influence in "disruptive" behavior. So is the desire for "equality"—the feeling that they are individuals with importance equal to that of adults. Age doesn't automatically call for respect or justify condescension to youth. Adults are perceived as irrational themselves—too concerned with maintaining security and not concerned enough with "understanding" young people.

Antigoals   Young people—perhaps because of the security implicit in affluence—reject such ideas as "working toward" something or "getting ahead" by means of a predetermined series of events leading to a goal (from training program to junior executive to senior executive, for example). In their clothing, for instance, young people resist the feeling of having "arrived": The gray flannel business suit is not the thing. The development of the "whole person" and of "identity" is important, while high salaries and status defined by career are less attractive. Student rebels, in fact, see the entire adult value system as something not to be altered but torn down completely.

Achievement is less impressive   Things that interest or boggle adults in terms of technological achievement from moon ships to freeze-dried coffee don't affect young people in the same way. Through personal experience, travel, and television, today's young person has a much larger "taken-for-granted" area than any old man of thirty.

Fear of compromise   Young people have a deep-seated fear that they will eventually succumb to the group pressure exerted by the Establishment. Compromise is considered unclean, a betrayal that makes any "new era" impossible.

The soft side   Young people are not, however, quite so tough and cool as their outward actions might indicate. They are obviously highly visually oriented and hedonistic in terms of self-decoration. While *Che* is said to be top campus reading material, so is frankly sentimental, sensuous poetry. There also appears to be an element of nostalgia for ages past (way before their parents' generation), when there were stronger heroes.

Communicators who want to reach youth must now apply fresh thinking—almost the same methods that cultural anthropologists use when dealing with strange societies. The following points should be kept in mind:

1. Playing on teen-age fads will be increasingly dangerous. Often the use of teen-age idioms, dress, and musical fads serves only to convince the ad writer that he himself is still young. The obvious hazard is jumping

into a fad too late. Worse, it may only make the advertiser look silly or condescending; e.g., Betty Crocker shouldn't wear a miniskirt.

2. Talk to young people as adults. "Youth" talk may only be perceived as talking down. It may be better at times not even to use teen-type models. The young person wants recognition as a complete, valuable individual.

3. Don't talk to youth as a group. Your product may really be a great thing for kids and no one else. But kids don't like to be categorized as an age group. It's far better to position products for individual kinds of tastes.

4. Do your own thing. Perhaps advertisers—and other adults—have been trying too hard to please the younger generation. The strongest position may be to state your case and explain your values, with more of a "take-it-or-leave-it" attitude.

5. Advertisers might profit by developing ways to help the young identity-seeking person better understand his own motivations and his strong and weak points. Products could be promoted as aids in self-analysis.

6. Do it yourself. The young person is looking for badges of adulthood —the driver's license is just one—that give him the sense of being an effective "someone." Advertisers may consider how products can help to develop creativity and capability. There could, for example, be a renaissance of sewing, cooking, or even chicken raising.

7. Don't hang appeals too much on newness, technological achievement, and the like. "Why did you take so long to develop this new product?" is the likely response to such an approach.

20

Making People Do Things That Are Good for Them

PUT THE SEX APPEAL IN HEALTH

All products and services involving health exist in a much more competitive environment than many people seem to realize. Vitamin pills, iron-enriched cereal, weight-loss aids, exercise equipment, dietary supplements and just plain nourishing food, germ killers, and cavity preventers must compete not only with products of the same kind but also with the wider universive of sweet, fattening, beautifying, and pleasure-inducing ones. Every warning to stop smoking, cut down on eating, or have a medical or eye examination competes with the desire for indolence, escape, and hedonism. In short, health is apt to be boring. And consumers resist health appeals for complex, nonrational reasons. Many current campaigns, in fact, may be building up "antihealth" resistance.

Our studies show that health-product appeals tend to play right into a variety of consumer fears, such as the following.

Fear of embarrassment   This is often stronger than fear of sickness. No one likes to show undue anxiety or to appear foolish or silly, as when we consult the doctor about a problem, only to be told, "It's nothing." Preventing vitamin deficiency or visiting the doctor for a yearly checkup sounds perfectly sensible to people—but they also don't want to be considered "overcareful."

Fear of contamination   To many people, any contact with health-oriented things—hospitals, pills—should be avoided. They may be "catching."

Fear of old age   Many health problems and ills are associated with growing old. Young people, it's reasoned, don't have to worry about their hearts, lungs, weight, blood, or energy level. Merely doing something about any of these problems is an admission that one is no longer young.

Fear of lack of willpower   One reason why people don't make even an effort to do the "sensible" thing is that they don't believe they are capable of change. It's really a fear of failure. "How can I give up candy when I have to buy it for the children?" "I'm really too lazy to exercise every day."

Fear of loss of freedom   In a study on automobile seat belts, we found that a number of people feel that the belt represents a sort of tentacle reaching for the driver out of the car body, depriving one of freedom and possibly imprisoning the body inside the car if an accident takes place. Many people who "know" that they should cut down on cholesterol or indigestible foods or that they should use a dentifrice to prevent cavities won't do these things—they "can't live that way." Health seems to imply regimen and lack of enjoyment of a full life.

Fear of too many authority figures   Many health appeals stir up all sorts of guilt feelings. The white-coated health authority appears cold and parental, telling the person he should have done so-and-so or he wouldn't be so badly off now. There's too much scolding and unpleasantness. Health figures are also associated with the Establishment; negligence, with the real swingers.

How can "health" advertisers expand their markets and compete with the allures of sinful, less sensible living more effectively?

1. Gutsier language is needed. "Health" itself is a static, relatively meaningless word. No "healthy" person ever says he is. "I feel on top of the world" or "I'm rarin' to go" is more typical. Advertisers must translate their product benefits into ideas that are more meaningful to consumers. For example, we advised one organization promoting early eye examinations to point out that the right glasses make for more successful girl watching.

2. Use a sense of humor to show you understand people's irrational fears. Point out that staying away from the doctor won't really keep a

person well or that buying vitamin pills doesn't indicate that he's an "overworried," prissy sort of person.

3. Associate preventive actions and products with youth. Perhaps the whole concept of health should be identified with "youth preservation," the idea that it's foolish to run away from the longer, sexier life that modern medicine can provide.

4. Give people the courage not so much to succeed, but to fail. Modern doctors even include a sort of splurge in reducing programs. The consumer or patient needs to have his confidence built up—and to understand that no one's perfect or can remain up tight all the time.

5. Promote the idea that taking care of oneself isn't selfish, silly, or threatening to one's freedom. It is, rather, a means of staying in control of one's fate.

6. Use a less "antiseptic" approach and fewer Establishment figures. More fun is needed. Clinics, perhaps, should have more of an Electric Circus atmosphere. Teen-agers or suave jet-setters, for example, might promote weight control, eye care, etc., better than doctors. Too much of health has an old-fashioned, moralistic, dull image.

PLANNED PARENTHOOD

We were asked to help in motivating big companies to become interested in planned parenthood. The technique that was being used was to show photographs of major political leaders, accompanied by their pronouncements on the dangers of the population explosion. Our study showed that this was the wrong approach. The manager, the large company, and people who might contribute money and real effort are motivated by entirely different forces. Here are a number of the specific recommendations that we made:

1. Present the problem in managerial terms. A product—in this case, children—is produced and at the other end of the production line is being destroyed because there is no room for it. From a managerial viewpoint, this is wasteful. We asked the managers within the framework of their identification to help and to lend their managerial know-how.

2. Don't present planned parenthood as a hopeless cause. This is a poor motivational approach—nobody likes to participate in hopeless causes. Showing the progress that has already been made and discussing the various methods that have been tried and have worked in various countries, including such classic ones as paying Indian men to be sterilized and doing it in a kind of offhand fashion at railroad stations, would indicate that the problem can be solved.

3. Present planned parenthood and birth control as a management problem. This makes it socially (and prestigewise) acceptable.

4. Give the executive a sense of power by pointing out to him how big a role his advice, money, and other contributions can play in the determination of the future of the country and the world.

5. Influence the mental set. By that I mean admit in ads, films, and public statements that "Yes, we understand you. At first you feel ridiculous getting interested in a problem like that, but it shows real heroism, real courage, not to be influenced by such silly considerations."

6. Present planned parenthood as a more complicated and even more exciting project than a trip to the moon: "How would you like to go to a different kind of moon—the moon of social, psychological, and political problems?"

7. Present overpopulation as a problem of negligence and stupidity. Most intelligent people react vigorously when they become aware of the possibility of continuing a mistake just on the basis of stupidity.

21

Obeying Recommendations

HOW TO GET PEOPLE TO FOLLOW RECOMMENDATIONS

Poor recommendations discourage people from trying out a vast variety of ideas. All too frequently the drawing up of recommendations is underrated, relegated to unimportant employees, and underresearched. Yet instructions that are confusing or sound too difficult can discourage change right from the beginning. And all too few people realize that intriguing, comprehensible, and motivationally oriented recommendations can have the positive effect of encouraging change.

The need for social engineers to better understand how to develop "how to" material is growing. It certainly exists in the area of many new habits that we want people to develop or new skills that we want them to learn. How can we keep instructions from turning off action—or from irritating and angering people? The basic mistake is that most instructions are written from the viewpoint of the instructor—not the consumer, the pupil—and do not take into consideration modern concepts of communication and education. The following are a few instructions for successful instruction writing:

1. Flag the "pupil's" attention to the instructions in the first place. Many people start to spread paint, put together furniture, or plug in an appliance, confident that they know how to do the job, and then encounter trouble or confusion. Say right at the start, "You'll be much happier in the long run if you take two minutes now to read this."

2. Take a hint from recipe writing and clearly state all the materials and tools that are needed before starting the job. Nothing is more annoying than to be halfway through and discover you have the wrong tool.

3. Start the reader out with the "big picture." Most instructions go step by step—but the reader has no idea where he is going or why. Good instructions should translate into meaningful terms the basic principles of the total task. Then the consumer won't just be going through mechanical steps; but he will really know what he is doing. For example, as mentioned earlier in the book, we recently developed directions that described a chain saw in terms of its "stomach," "muscles," etc.

4. Use concepts of programmed learning. This means dividing a task into easily learned portions, checking at each stage for correctness. Reward should also be involved: "You're doing fine," "Halfway through now," etc. The physical layout could reflect this programming, with each stage presented on separate sheets or cards to make the task look less formidable.

5. Use mind reading. The instructor should understand the novice well enough to know what errors he is most likely to fall into. Look ahead and catch him before he makes the error: "I know what you're tempted to do."

6. Don't use technical or trade expressions without making sure that the average person has heard of them. "Spackling," "pilling," "tweeters," etc., may be everyday terms to the manufacturer, but not to the new user.

22

Motivating Communities

HOW TO MOTIVATE COMMUNITIES TO CONSIDER TRANSPORTATION PROBLEMS THEIR OWN

The 1970s may become the decade of the *active* majority. The American people are beginning to get tired of continual warnings about pollution, breakdown in transportation systems, etc. We may soon reach the point at which the average individual will begin to realize that unless *he really does something himself*, nothing much is going to happen. How can we develop this awareness so that it reaches a "boiling point" and can be channeled in *constructive* ways?

1. Dramatize communications that have led to effective results—for example, messages intended to involve local, state, and national legislators that did bring about changes pertaining to capital improvements and operating expenses.

2. Expose the inhibitions which exist among the people of the community and which act as barriers to the solution of transportation bottlenecks. For example, is there a feeling of frustration? ("We have tried all

kinds of things, but nothing has really worked.") Do they resign themselves to failure in advance?

3. Introduce continuity. Past activities may not have been systematic enough. Perhaps the traveling public was inclined to give up easily because there was no way of being continuously involved, such as wearing buttons to demonstrate their dissatisfaction.

4. Don't rely on ordinary appeals to government. These have not been very successful—so far—because the government is dependent on the appropriation of funds. In the final analysis, the traveling public has to motivate all the people who hold the purse strings. One of the new possibilities might be the "positive ultimatum"—a commitment that within six months (or some other time period) there will be a specified improvement in operations.

5. Get the transportation users to agree to pay more for six months before the improvements are completed—with the fare increase to be put into escrow. If no real improvement has taken place after six months, the mass transportation system would have to return the money! This could be an example of a modern form of pragmatic participative democracy. Trying such an experiment would project travel research and pilot projects into a completely different sphere. Transportation could become an adventure in social engineering rather than a frustrating "necessary evil." Carrying this approach a little further, commuters themselves could do certain things (perhaps help keep the railroad stations cleaner) by cooperating in many little ways—and at the same time could expect a reciprocal positive response from the mass transportation system. After a six-month period, an evaluation could be made of this mutual-aid project.

6. View the problem as we do in underdeveloped countries. We could look on the mass transportation system as being parallel to a highly inadequate, old-fashioned, dilapidated transportation system in India or Nigeria, for example. The question would be: "What can we do, considering the 'native' power structure and economic and psychological attitudes?" One end result might be to give people a feeling that it is *their* transportation system—not the enemy's. This experiment could set a fascinating precedent for getting American citizens to participate in coping with many of the other problems of today. Up to now, despite our profession of democratic beliefs, an attitude of "let George do it" prevails —which has led in many instances to a battle in which two groups put pressure on each other group, and blame each other, with a final result of zero.

A recent article in the *Wall Street Journal* reported on the unhappiness of youth in Sweden. The young people are unhappy because they are not allowed to participate; everything is being done *for* them. As long as passengers are only passive beneficiaries of a well-functioning transportation system, the likelihood exists (judging by the Swedish experience) that they still will not be happy. Clean physical facilities and vehicles that run on time may not be enough.

Sometimes we refer to a motivational "law of inevitability": If no miracle is going to occur, people may consider *practical* measures after all. The law of inevitability says that if you have an undesirable neighbor, for example, and you cannot wish him away or kill him, you finally realize that there is no other way to get a *desirable* neighbor except to *help* him to *become* one. Much of this project may very well consist of finding out what can be done to convert people from a passive stage of awareness to constructive action.

DOWNTOWN'S BIGGEST NEED—PSYCHOLOGICAL RENEWAL

How can downtown retailers compete with the shining new stores in suburban centers? The problem grows more acute with the recent rise of "superregional centers"—with such assets as large numbers of major stores, lavish decor, and climate-controlled environment. Most discussions of downtown revival center around new shopping malls, parking space, and improved transit. Most appeals to attract downtown shoppers have been commercial. All this misses the true problem of downtown. It's emotional. Our studies, based on hundreds of interviews, indicate such psychological factors as these:

1. The typical city lacks a strong, distinctive image. It's easy to "fall in love" with Paris, Rome, or San Francisco, but the drab sameness of many American cities precludes a strong emotional attachment. Yet most people have a strong desire and need for a downtown area with which they can identify.

2. Many citizens are ashamed of their downtown areas. They'd like to identify with a city that's distinctive, modern, and alert—an innovator in architecture, entertainment, and commerce. Instead, they feel that the real downtown makes the city appear hicklike, decrepit, and old.

3. Commercial appeals—"bargains galore"—are the wrong approach. Instead of bribing the shopper, downtown should woo, with love, and promote a feeling of "belonging" and being wanted.

4. People still associate downtown with business and government—stiffness and restraint, as opposed to fun, newness, and excitement.

Thus psychological renewal—the development of unique city "personalities"—should be the major aim of downtown efforts. Creating uniqueness may be a painstaking and difficult job. The answer can be found only by talking to people and doing a special study to determine the city's differences and individuality. It might be the development of a special city "style"—India, for example, has a red city, Jodphur, where most of the buildings have a reddish tint. It might be the rediscovery of city history—landmarks and typical architectural styles. It might be the development of "interesting" neighborhoods, such as New Orleans' French Quarter or Chicago's Old Town. Some American cities might be able to create an "old" and a "new" town, as many European cities have. The old section, specially set aside to keep or revive its charm and intimacy, represents a psychological retreat—not a museum, but an area for discovery and adventure. With such civic image building as the basis, cities could carry out such further efforts at psychological rejuvenation as these:

1. Create a feeling of participation and civic pride. Not only the leading businessmen of the downtown area should be responsible for reviving downtown; as many segments as possible should be involved. Efforts in this direction might include a contest for shoppers to suggest new ideas for better shopping facilities, invitations to women's-group leaders to talk to business leaders, films and lectures to encourage downtown salespeople to be friendlier and more courteous, and giving small retailers (shoe stores, stationery stores, etc.) their "day" with special promotions.

2. Don't make downtown a "foreign" territory. People complain that they don't feel at home downtown; there's little done to make the citizen feel welcome. Purely commercial appeals only make people feel "exploited." Bargain lures only further cheapen the image of the downtown area. A city can play host, not only to out-of-town visitors, but to its own people as well. Special days to welcome women and children and open houses and special courses at banks and libraries are possibilities. Downtown promotion should emphasize more than shopping: cultural events, interesting areas, and historical landmarks, for example, to make suburbanites feel less like strangers.

3. Eliminate the "Play at home, work here" image that too many modern cities seem to have. We need playgrounds for adults as well as children. Urban planners should look at recreational needs in a more systematic way. Why not have special areas for hi-fi enthusiasts, art collectors, etc.; special teen-age areas; or even a "children's city"?

4. Create cultural attractions. We can learn from the examples of Rome and other European cities, where the center of town is often used for fiestas and for all kinds of pageantry. Little of this is done in the United States. Special downtown "holidays" can contribute to the feeling of a throbbing, dramatically alive "urban heart."

5. Promote the idea of newness and change. Often downtown retailers defeat their own purpose by demonstrating a lack of faith in the area. Their downtown units grow shabby, while what's best and newest is re-

served for suburban branches. Downtown should set the pace—whether in fashion, music, radical building methods, or entertainment.

6. Think of a new name for the area; perhaps the very word "downtown" is outmoded—and sounds too difficult, old-fashioned, and businesslike. A new name—more suggestive of fun and variety and richer in imagery—may be needed.

COMMUNICATION IN THE "BIG" SOCIETY

City governments are increasingly recognizing a problem in addition to the heavy burdens of the tangible affairs of the metropolis: keeping the lines of communication open with their citizens. The individual's feeling of "Who cares about me?" and "Whom can I talk to?" obviously intensifies as cities grow larger and as their problems—and the bureaucracies designed to cope with them—grow more complex. Recently, a larger share of our motivational studies and recommendations has been devoted to creating new relationships between city governments and departments and the citizens around them.

The city of Vienna, for example, is now instituting a program to convince citizens that they aren't merely part of a neglected mass. The following are among the measures we recommended:

1. A series of open houses given in public buildings to allow people to meet members of the city council.

2. A children's program. Children can now ride along on nonhazardous trips on city fire engines.

3. A living symbol. Vienna's "Rathaus," or city hall, had a rusting symbol on its roof—a knight in armor—which we recommended be taken down. A real "Rathaus" man now walks through the neighborhoods of the city, ready to answer individuals' questions and hear their complaints.

4. Open phone lines. City officials are now all reachable by phone. If people aren't happy with a particular department, they can now talk back.

Companies, too, are beginning to face the need to build new kinds of relationships with their employees. Companies are growing bigger, and at the same time the employee's need for individual expression and his dissatisfaction with being bossed, with routine, and with insignificant job categories are increasing. Too many corporate communication programs designed to build "morale" have provided only one-way communication, allowing the employee no channel to speak up. For one company, for example, we suggested a new kind of "Muzak": allowing employees to take turns as disc jockey and provide entertainment interludes kidding the bosses. While morale has been considered a strictly personnel department concern, it becomes increasingly a marketing problem as well. Service companies, for example, know that their ability to compete depends on how well motivated their employees are to satisfy the consumer. This is just as crucial as bright advertising and up-to-date equipment.

THE FOURTH DIMENSION IN ENVIRONMENTAL PLANNING—SPATIAL TYPOLOGY

Individual psychological factors may be more important than physical or environmental ones. There may be space-oriented people, as opposed to intimate types. Some people may want or need to be more isolated and have more space around them; some people may want to be close to others. These are new factors that can be taken into consideration in new types of planning. People move to a country area with lots of acreage because they cannot afford space in the urban area, and they accept the necessity of traveling to their jobs. Some people think of their homes only in terms of shelter and protection and are less interested in the outside appearance or the location; they are inner-directed. Others consider their homes to be a status symbol, an investment to be lived in conspicuously; they are outer-directed. This knowledge can be utilized in planning. There might be different areas for inner- and outer-directed people.

We should recognize the importance of friends and family. Some people retain close contact with friends and family even when they have moved more than 20 miles away from them. Others are motivated by the availability of friends in their neighborhood.

Mobility is another factor. Some people never move. Others move at the slightest provocation. It would be important to know what factors help or hinder this mobility. The "triggerability" of people represents important factors in modern environmental planning.

Shopping centers of the future may have to use psychological orientation as much as functional practicality. Some people may desire adventure and discovery shopping. Some people see themselves as inhabitants of a country or a wider area; others, of only a small neighborhood. Just as there are nationalists and internationalists, there are those—depending on personality or other factors such as intellectual horizons—who see themselves as belonging to a limited area and those who think of themselves as citizens of the whole world. There are also "permanent" as opposed to "temporary" inhabitants. Some people, even after having lived in an area more than ten or fifteen years, still consider themselves only transients and foreigners. Others feel at home right away.

These are some new concepts which can and have been utilized in research to help develop a modern approach to the consideration of the fourth dimension in environmental and urban planning.

23

Helping People Decide

THE "UNDECIDED" VOTER—OR PEOPLE ARE NOT NEUTRAL

What the political polls that make newspaper headlines *don't* reveal may be the decisive factor in a presidential election. The polls count voters who've already made up their minds. However, the major challenge—as in brand competition—is winning the undecided. The Institute recently conducted an in-depth study of this group, as compared with decided voters. The findings shed light not only on problems of presidential elections but also on many problems of product marketing.

Undecided doesn't mean "neutral" Far from it. Preference studies usually lump the "don't knows" together. In actuality, people in the undecided group represent a broad spectrum of leanings ranging from very vacillating attitudes to those of people who've already practically come to a decision. Marketers can find some important truths about the undecided group, such as those discussed below.

What's bothering the undecided voter? To probe these feelings, a survey avoiding direct questions about preference was developed. The answers revealed significant findings about both candidates' images and the voters' psychological topography. Such questions as the following were included:

If you had to compare each candidate to an animal, which would you choose?

What kind of music best represents how you feel about each candidate: fox-trot, soul, rock 'n' roll, march, rhythm and blues, etc.?

Which candidate would our enemies like to see elected?

Which figure (jagged line, rectangle, spiral, scrawl) best represents your feelings about each candidate?

The questions also probed reactions to simulated newspaper headlines such as—"Defeat in Vietnam," "A Fourth Party," "New Riots," and "Peace and Prosperity." Some questions were included to indicate voter feelings about candidates (the one about comparing the candidate to an animal, for example), while others were intended to offer explanations for these feelings—allowing interpretation of the major psychological trends among the undecided.

Decision preventers Our study revealed that overall, the undecided group tends to be more quizzical and somewhat better educated than the decided group. Basically, the undecided voters do not yet feel "understood" by any of the candidates. Analysis of reactions showed three basic psychological segments in this group:

1. *The Visceral, or "Stomach," Thinker.* This type shows a classic response to frustration in aggressive physical action. He's characterized by a belief in quick solutions to international and social problems. He prefers a President who is an authoritarian figure. "Striking out" is his solution to elimination of problems, and he's a believer in the use of force. He's more likely to make descriptions of candidates which are stereotyped, simple, and emotional: "dirty rat," "wishy-washy." In 1968, this group trended in preference to George Wallace, Ronald Reagan, and, to a lesser extent, Richard Nixon.

2. *The Wishful Thinker.* This segment also longs for a "real leader" as President and wants problems taken care of for him in a decisive manner. In contrast to the visceral type, however, the wishful thinker's response to frustration is less striking out than regressing and partially rejecting reality. There are strong similarities to the confusion and dreaminess of adolescence. His verbal descriptions of candidates are more urbane and intellectualized than the visceral type's—but also simplified. While partly aware of the complexity of social and world problems, he retreats from these. He tends to have a more negative total outlook than voters in other groups and to believe that problems can be dealt with quickly if action is taken. He desires a more intellectual, masterly father figure as political leader. Such voters tended to lean toward McCarthy and slightly toward Rockefeller, for example.

3. *The Wholistic, or Realistic, Thinker.* This thinker's indecisiveness is probably influenced by his awareness of the complexity of issues, to which easy answers and "fatherly" candidates do not appear to be solutions. His descriptions of candidates exhibit less stereotypes and more balance and contrast: "a demagogue but sincere," "a cautious liberal." This group views the President's role as more like that of an orchestra conductor—a coordinating leader—than like that of a club-carrying martial figure or a superbrain. His views on issues fall into less rigid patterns. In 1968, this group tended to be most strongly attracted to Humphrey.

Politics' communications gap   Attitudes of undecided voters also reveal a communications problem for any candidate. Many of these (partially contradictory) feelings of the modern citizen also reveal important areas of which company-to-people communicators should also be aware:

1. Strong feelings of being left out and misunderstood—"No one cares about my problems." The communicator must become almost a therapist to help the individual understand himself and his world. This sense of alienation and resentment pervades a broad range of opinions—from those of "demonstrators" and their sympathizers to those of conservatives who see themselves as hard workers who don't get the attention they deserve because they are pushed aside by noisy lawbreakers.

2. Specific issues are not major criteria in choosing among candidates. By the time candidates begin making speeches, ideas have become too blurred for differentiation. Personality factors—symbolic and real—appear uppermost in voters' minds. To a lesser extent, experience is influential.

3. Skepticism and a resignation to the "realities" of politics. Vague and large promises probably won't sway the uncommitted.

In summary, the political findings tell us much about the approach to use when selling undecided consumers. It may be a mistake to direct messages of reassurance to customers who are already sold. It is the undecided —the unsold—customer who is the obvious and best prospect. Find out more about him—his attitudes, his preferences, his unvoiced choices. Shape the advertising to nudge his already trending favor toward your product or service.

24

Changing Habits

HOW TO CHANGE THE HABIT OF SMOKING

It is not taste alone that makes a person a habitual smoker. We have found that smoking is just as much a psychological pleasure as a physiological satisfaction. Here is a list of the motivations that need to be understood before effective communications can be developed:

1. Smoking is fun.
2. Smoking is a self-reward.
3. Smoking gives oral pleasure and sensual gratification.
4. Smoking is a modern hourglass that measures time.
5. Smoking is a substitute activity and counteracts impatience by making time pass faster.
6. Smoking can help make friends by breaking down social barriers. It can also be a sexual contact point between people.
7. Smoking, by making breath visible, satisfies the desire to create things (smoke rings, etc.).
8. Smoking satisfies the fascination with fire, which is itself a symbol of life.

9. Smoking provides a focal point for concentration when attention is important.

10. Smoking provides relaxation. It offers a rhythmic excuse for lingering.

11. Smoking is dramatized breathing, which relieves depression because it eliminates the shallow breathing which occurs when people are upset or depressed; it restores the normal rate of breathing.

12. Regularity of breathing, induced by smoking, helps to overcome the heavy respiration which is characteristic of anger.

13. Smokers identify with their own brand of tobacco.

14. Most smokers reject other brands of tobacco at first because it takes them awhile to get accustomed to another brand.

15. A full pack of cigarettes, a box of cigars, or a pouch of pipe tobacco signifies abundance.

In summary, smoking is now. It helps people to cope with life here and now. It offers gratification now. It is an existentialist expression of the pleasure principle—and, like all existentialists, smokers are prepared to die (now, if necessary) as a result of accepting the pleasures that life has to offer.

Once you grasp the basic principles of effective communication—and arrive at an understanding of the motivations that account for smoking—there is still the question, "What is to be done?" Because each smoker is different and each communicator is different, we cannot set down any rules that will be effective at all times and under all circumstances.

Here are ten practical suggestions for more effective communications and nonverbal devices which may help people cut down on smoking:

1. Accentuate the positive by pointing out that even the so-called smoker spends most of his time not smoking. Suggest that the smoker prolong these periods of nonsmoking. For example, if they usually last fifteen minutes, they might be extended to half an hour. The amount of time spent smoking could be reduced by 50 percent almost immediately.

2. Suggest that smokers merely stop buying cigarettes—and get smokes by "borrowing" from others instead. The embarrassment involved in begging cigarettes from others will minimize the "bumming" that goes on. The lack of instant availability will also reduce the amount of smoking.

3. Tell adults who are trying to cut down on smoking how ordinary people like themselves have faced the same problem and have succeeded. In addition, to make an even greater impression, try to collect testimonials from well-known people (TV or screen personalities, sports figures, people in the news) which describe in detail how they cut down on smoking.

4. One of the questions that smokers frequently ask themselves is,

"What will happen to me if I stop smoking?" This question should be anticipated—and answered in advance. The simplest answer (as well as the most convincing) is "Nothing." This simple device may communicate essential information, and it may counteract false popular stereotypes about withdrawal problems, too.

5. Artificially inflate the cost of smoking. (Market studies indicate that the amount of smoking decreased in Great Britain after the cost of tobacco was increased.) Suggest that the smoker obtain a "piggy bank"—perhaps in the shape of a heart—and contribute to the American Heart Association an amount of money equal to that spent for smokes. The association might even provide such banks to doctors for distribution to their patients.

6. Have sales campaign—like the one in which the girl scouts sell cookies—to provide American households with an artificially sweetened no-calorie candy that can be used as a substitute for smoking. This product might even be packaged in a very masculine fashion—which is unusual in the candy industry—and be promoted as a more modern kind of gratification. It might even be given a name such as Oral, and it might carry an endorsement by the American Heart Association. Valentine's Day might be the day set aside for sales—with the communications emphasis placed on gifts from women to men.

7. Recognize that communications should be tailored to the desires and beliefs of the smoker. For example:

  a. When communicating with teen-age boys, you might suggest that a real man does not smoke cigarettes anymore because that is too feminine nowadays. Perhaps a real man smokes a cigar or a pipe: suggest a pipe if the boy is interested in a profession or other intellectual occupation; otherwise, a cigar.

  b. In communicating with teen-age girls, you might suggest that boys really don't like kissing girls who smoke because the taste of tobacco is not really feminine. It might even be suggested that experienced women are careful about smoking—and do it only when they are not apt to be kissed.

  c. In communicating with adult males, you might suggest that cigarette smoking is now juvenile—an activity practiced mainly by teen-agers. Pipes and cigars can be suggested as more grown-up alternatives.

  d. In communicating with adult females, you might suggest that cigarette smoking is now associated with aggressive, competitive, almost masculine women and that real women don't smoke because it is not feminine.

8. Many communications made in regard to smoking and health are disregarded simply because they are stale. To gain acceptance for your communication, you must smash barriers by means of dramatic new ap-

proaches that have shock value, memorability, a fresh viewpoint, and a very modern flavor. Many communications from middle-class "do-good" organizations have become dated; people are tired—even bored—with their repetition of the same old messages. A new communications approach is needed, accompanied by other "why not?" devices that have flair, style, and imagination—even a degree of fun or sinfulness that will appeal to the modern, up-to-date person.

POSTPONEMENT—THE INTERNATIONAL DISEASE

"Yes, very interesting, I'll do something about it soon." This reaction may concern taking flying lessons, buying a new suit or a new pair of shoes, learning a new language, cutting down on smoking, cleaning up one's desk, or almost anything in our active life that needs to be taken care of. Some people are endowed by nature with immunity against the postponement bacillus. As was pointed out in the first part of this book, changing human nature is a big order, but it can be done. The purpose of this book is to break the process into tiny little morsels. Maybe we should create, as the Latin language so skillfully permits, a diminutive term: "changettes."

1. Start Five Things at the Same Time

Our puritanical heart is horrified at this thought. We have been told for centuries that once you start something, you are supposed to finish it. Modern psychology, however, shows that this never was true and certainly is not true now. We are much better off working at something as long as it interests us, if we have a choice, and then dropping it and switching to something else, then to something else, and then to something else again—and then eventually coming back to our first task. We are ready to admit that interest and involvement are the necessary ingredients of work motivation. Completing five started tasks is a lot easier than filling a vacuum. By the same token, parents have found it helpful to supply children who are going off to camp with writing paper on which the first line is filled in, reading "Dear Parents, I am fine." This leads to more letter writing than just giving the child blank sheets of paper.

2. Mental Rehearsal

As I pointed out in the first part of the book, going through the paces of a new experience brings it closer to you, helps you lose some of your fear, and makes it almost appear as if you had already started the new adventure.

3. Break the Big Task into "Taskettes"

If a Ph.D. candidate saw piled in front of him all the books he had to read in order to get his degree, he would be quickly discouraged and probably never achieve his goal. If he looks at one task at a time, however, he can get enough courage to feel that he can digest the little "taskette." In an experiment with agricultural workers, one group thinned out a row of beets which was interspaced with little red flags, and the other worked on a row without any visible interruption. There was considerably increased work efficiency among the group that could break the row of beets into smaller segments. If we had the courage, it would be a good idea to tear a book apart and concentrate on only one chapter at a time. We would buy a second one (which would please the publisher) to put in our library. Advertisers or sales executives often make the bite too big for their customers, thus discouraging them altogether. To sell life insurance more effectively, for example, first lure your prospect into having the medical examination, then into filling out various blanks, and finally into signing the insurance papers.

4. Retroactive Conversion

In the first part of this book, I mentioned that an effective technique is to use testimonials of people who have successfully overcome their difficulties and achieved their goals. If you want somebody to travel to Greece, don't spend so much time portraying the beauties of Greece, but instead concentrate on people who also hesitated but who now regret that they did. Billy Graham uses this technique very successfully. Political campaigns often make the error of inviting people to change their party affiliations, which is almost as difficult as changing religions. It would be so much better to invite them first to at least listen to some of the opposing arguments without having to commit themselves in any way. Showing people as witnesses who have gradually made this change represents another example of this retroactive conversion.

HOW TO GIVE THE DIETER A BETTER SHAKE

Most diet-food manufacturers don't understand the true motivations of the weight watcher. Most diet products now in existence are far from the ideal of what the consumer wants. A growing segment of the public is aware of the need for weight control, and many products in this field can rightfully be considered "growth" ones. But the problems of broadening the market and encouraging more than sporadic usage remain. Marketers have so far overlooked powerful appeals in promoting their products.

Health, for example, isn't a powerful motivation for dieting. Vanity is far more influential, as is a desire for youthfulness. The *biggest mistake* made in most diet-food advertising, however, is pitying the dieter. The typical ad assumes that dieting will be an ordeal and places too much emphasis on results—not on the process of dieting itself. Actually, dieting is "fun"—if of a slightly weird variety. This fun involves:

1. Sexual and erotic pleasure—self-flagellation.

2. Body awareness. Being starved is to many people almost as enjoyable as proof of their willpower as overeating and satiety.

3. A feeling of power and self-discovery, as the weight watcher learns what he or she can "take." There's also a sense of wonder as the pounds "melt away" and a "new" person seems to emerge.

4. The challenge of the fight for food. Today we are surrounded by easy, ready-to-eat foods. Dieting brings back the illusion of hardship, of pioneering, and of life among "real" things. The individual with a growling stomach can feel a sort of kinship with the hunter of old in search of meat.

5. Overcoming insecurity feelings that lead to overeating. The diet-food advertiser can offer therapy to the consumer by substituting the idea of fat, static security with that of agile mobility.

What's wrong with diet products? Typically, they try to imitate a conventional food. For example, advertisers claim that diet liquids taste like milk shakes. But they are really dull and uninteresting. The person who must watch his weight is someone who likes food—too much so, perhaps. Why, then, should he or she be satisfied with a pallid imitation?

The ideal diet food should offer a totally new experience in eating. It should offer adventure and new discovery in form, tactile interest, and flavor. The Swiss, for example, have developed types of dried beef and dry milk-alcohol combinations that appear to have no counterpart among natural foods. Diet-food packaging should also promote the idea of pleasure and adventure. Too much of it suggests medicine and is drab and middle-aged in image. Products for this market should also not be too "convenient." To reinforce the idea of something real being involved, some ritual of preparation should be necessary. Today's low-calorie foods also lack virility in their image. The dieter wants not rabbit food, but tiger food.

THE CRAZY, MIXED-UP WORLD OF THE OVERWEIGHT

To "calorie-conscious" persons, the world in which they live frequently seems like a very alien place—one certainly not made for them, but designed primarily for a race of slim, trim, active people whose bodies rarely get in their way. This is because the slender figure is the accepted standard of beauty to Americans, a concept aided and abetted by fashion designers;

stage, screen, and television; popular magazines; and the medical profession. Everywhere the overweight person turns, he is met by frustrations.
The abundance of food and delicacies is not for him, clothing doesn't
fit him properly, theater seats are tight and uncomfortable, participation
in sports is a chore, beds sag, chairs become loose and wobbly, girdles
squeeze, and sexual attractiveness fades.

In an effort to fit himself into his environment more comfortably, the
overweight person makes dieting a daily preoccupation. Here, more
problems arise. Efforts toward self-enhancement, social acceptability, and
better health are thwarted by psychological conflicts arising from the
withdrawal of food.

Our findings disclose that there are three types of dieters: those who
diet for medically compelling reasons, whose reactions tend to be less
negative and extreme than those of other types of dieters; those whose
dieting is self-imposed but who are not compulsive eaters; and those who
are restrictive dieters—guilt-ridden and anxious—for whom dieting is
cruel, tyrannical, and torturous.

Any attempt to sell a dietary preparation to "overeaters" must take into
consideration certain psychodynamic factors. Removal of food increases
feelings of anxiety and frequently creates feelings of depression. Consequently, it is important that efforts be made to change the negative
setting in which dieting is perceived and experienced. The self-discipline,
deprivation, and deliberate avoidance of certain cherished foods are at
variance with the growing present-day concepts of greater leisure, self-
indulgence, and the pursuit of pleasure. Dieting, however, is seen in a
role that is out of balance with these concepts. Advertising that translates
dieting into terms of modernity, pleasure, ease, and convenience is the
kind that is needed.

25

Creativity and Innovation

HOW "UPSIDE-DOWN THINKING" FREQUENTLY PUTS THINGS RIGHT SIDE UP

In analyzing selling problems, it is unfortunate that we are all too likely to start out by fighting new ideas with negative arguments. It is suggested that the same imagination used to prove that something can *not* be done be used in what I call "upside-down thinking."

For example, why shouldn't women sell automobiles? From a psychological point of view, a car is as much a female as a male symbol. The modern driver not only wants a car he can drive fast but also wants to feel "at home" in it; in a sense his car *is* "home" to him. That's why a married car buyer, whether he admits to it or not, usually likes to have his wife's opinion before making up his mind. This is because he knows deep down that his wife is inclined to think more rationally than he does and would therefore keep him from making a foolish choice.

In selling automobiles, a woman would play a similar role. Instead of being a kind of "seductress" as many might think, she actually would be a "wife and home economist" substitute. This would engender greater faith in a given make of car and make the car buyer easier to influence and sell. True, a woman might not understand all the complicated mechanics of a car. However, neither does the average male car buyer. Furthermore, it is such factors as the color of the car inside and out and its elegance, styling, and appointments—in other words, its fashion aspects —that really influence his purchase. And in this area a woman salesperson is far more likely to qualify as an expert, just as a salesman in a hardware store, who has a workshop at home and builds furniture for a hobby could be more helpful and persuasive when serving customers with the same interests. Similarly, in a clothing store a stout salesman could establish friendly relations more easily with corpulent customers.

In a study for a furniture company we found that it was advisable for the salesman to sit down with prospective buyers—more often than not young couples—in a simulated living room and, in a way, to play a "visiting game" there. This enabled the customers to "make friends" with the furniture and to get a taste of a more permanent association with it.

Carpet dealers in Morocco long ago discovered that is is more profitable first to serve customers peppermint tea, and thereby establish a feeling of sociability, than to immediately start talking about the merits of their products.

Our experience reveals that there are few sales situations which would not profit from a new, even if revolutionary, sales approach. The primary requirement is a loosening up of our more rigid, fixated attitudes toward the problem. *And what better way to do this than through the employment of upside-down thinking, in which the problem is deliberately viewed from an angle exactly opposite to the one customarily used.*

HELP YOURSELF, CAVEMAN

Does a man in a cafeteria line snapping up salad and pie think of himself as a hunter? This may seem far-fetched. But one of the basic appeals of self-service and quick-food restaurants is rebelling against what Freud calls the "discomfort of culture." Neither convenience nor speed is the most important factor. It's the *fun* of revolting against everyday eating— a Carnaby Street of the stomach. We are entering the area of hedonism in food, and the appeals of self-service should be understood by anyone involved in advertising and merchandising food products. More can be done to exploit the basic pleasures of helping oneself.

The primitive dinner   The leaping flames, the sizzle, and the aroma of meat cooking before your eyes in a fast-food restaurant create an excitement beyond that of the tray delivered in a formal eating place. They appeal to the desire to enjoy the primitive, relaxed eating ways of the caveman. (Mother may feel that "gracious living" is threatened, but still she condones it—just as she does when her husband barbecues dinner in the backyard.)

The informality, clatter, and odors of the fast-food and buffet-style restaurants gratify a deep human need for freedom and activity. For many Americans, formality seems to interfere with eating enjoyment. In the lively fast-food place, he can "feel himself." The appeal of informality might be extended to restaurants where the customer is encouraged to abandon knives and forks and eat with his fingers. Informality is related also to the attractive democracy of this type of restaurant. There are no bars as far as income, race, or nationality is concerned; one is apt to see "all types."

Gastronomic gadgetry   The customer is often confronted with machinery—vending machines, Automat boxes, beverage dispensers, rotisseries, infra-red broilers, etc. In some cases, the customer can operate the machinery himself. Not only is this fun, but it also appeals to the desire to control one's environment. And it satisfies a need in regard to modern technology—reassuring the diner that advances are not confined to outer space, but also consider the inner man and his everyday pleasure. However, the completely automatic restaurant, without some visible, personal touch, would not appeal to most people.

Participation   The man carrying his own tray is in control of his fate. The passive role—being waited upon—is alien to most Americans. The person who is dependent at home on his wife is likely to want to express his independence when dining out by waiting on himself. There's even the pleasant, sneaking feeling in the cafeteria line, while helping oneself and getting food immediately, that one doesn't have to pay—immediately, anyway. Self-service could also be carried into new areas: ladle your own soup from a big tureen, mix your own salad, or slice the meat for your own sandwich from an array of hanging sausages.

New experience   The self-service and fast-food restaurants offer the possibility of fulfilling a strong desire—that for discovering new kinds of food and enjoying eating in surroundings that aren't like home, e.g., eating standing up or in the car. Why not have places where one eats on the floor, while lying down, or while revolving on a merry-go-round?

The horn of plenty   In the fast-food restaurant, one is surrounded by a vast array of visible, touchable, smellable food—we're usually deprived of this in a conventional restaurant. There's a deep reassurance (like that which a full refrigerator provides) about being surrounded by food far in excess of what one can eat. That's why an empty vending machine or Automat box is so apt to be resented.

26

Combating Fear

WHO'S AFRAID OF THE BIG BAD COMPUTER?

Lots of people are afraid—as a result of misinformation and unrealistic thinking—of what computers *can* do, *are* doing, and *may* do. A psychological examination of the subject among the personnel of large companies using or planning to use computers revealed a number of significant factors that contribute to the confusion. Delaying tactics, negativism, and uncertainty were much in evidence, even though it was generally acknowledged that electronic data processing is becoming more and more of a necessity if a business is to keep abreast of the demands that technological change and competition are forcing upon it.

Price, for example, emerged as a convenient scapegoat for indecision, being frequently used by an individual as an excuse for not recommending a system that would replace something he had initiated and installed and with which he identified very closely.

The "glorified misery of choice" often arose—a so-called logical reason for hesitation in making a definite commitment. Determining which brand to install places decision-making individuals in the position of having to choose from among reputable, top-ranking companies whose products are known to be trustworthy and reliable.

"Buck-passing" rationalization, such as the claim that more careful investigation was needed or that preliminary preparations were inadequate, and the "let's wait for something better" syndrome, figured prominently in management's thinking about the matter.

Analysis of our research revealed the necessity for providing executives with the kind of reassurance and information that will support more positive thinking. Computer manufacturers seem to need a greater recognition of the prospect's own sense of importance; they need to show more interest in the peculiar nature of a prospect's problems and to provide more factual material regarding computers that have been used successfully in analogous situations and similar industries.

The weakest of the various sources of information and reassurances is advertising. Our findings indicate that there is a typical chain of decision making and that the men who make the decision—the office manager, the systems and procedures man, the controller, the tab supervisor, etc.—do not evince any strong reactions to advertising. A deeper understanding of the fears, anxieties, and apprehensions of this audience would enable advertisers to reach them more effectively "where they live."

27

Managing Others

NEW WAYS TO HEIGHTEN MANAGEMENT SKILLS

How can executives learn to be better managers? Management grows more complex every day and involves more information handling, bigger risk taking in new and unfamiliar product areas, heavier demands on available time, and a need for more effective communications, not only to customers, but also to levels above and below within the corporation. However, most training methods haven't kept pace with the needs of modern executives. Typically "canned" approaches, they attempt to fit the dynamic individual into present rules for performance. Moreover, most management training is hardly as sophisticated as the executives it attempts to teach, and thus it can't reach the prime management problems: improving decision making, creativity, and communications.

New System for Motivated Learning

For these reasons, we developed entirely new methods to help executives and salesmen improve their performance levels. This new system will not attempt to cram individuals into prescribed patterns, but rather to use their own traits in more creative, productive ways. The course will employ the latest motivational and management research, as well as such advanced technology as a videotape camera, multimedia projection, and new methods such as a three-dimensional Rorschach. It will include such new management theories as business decentralization into small entrepreneurial units, judging ability by the "band-of-potentialities" method, eliminating hierarchy, and speculative management. The course will concentrate on such vital areas as the following:

1. *Self-knowledge.* Initial sessions will encourage the individual to make a fresh recognition—and will occasionally startle him into doing so —of his own abilities and weaknesses: how they are changing and how they influence his mobility within the firm and his relationship with peers.

2. *Information Handling and Control of the Environment.* Every modern executive must grapple with masses of computer-generated and other information, and at the same time he must sharpen his perception —of his markets and of his own business associates. The Institute's course will suggest solutions to such problems as how to approach and "personally" research business areas that are totally unfamiliar, how to sharpen observation of changes in the world, and new methods of storing and retrieving data. The present filing system is a static one. What we want to teach is a more dynamic and immediately usable form of information handling. Information should be not only readily accessible but also helpful in generating and defending unusual approaches.

3. *Personal Organization.* The higher an executive moves in an organization, the less time he has, it seems, to think. Telephone calls, meetings, business travel, and ceremonial functions all are time-consuming. New techniques are needed to help the executive determine priorities, classify information in functional rather than superficial ways, and bring order into his increasing workload.

4. *Dynamic Technical Communication.* Modern executives are still communicating with their peer groups, superiors, subordinates, and outside business associates in outmoded ways. Do letters still have to be in letter form? Is it possible to streamline internal communications—to develop new electronic devices that will allow for less tie-up of valuable executive time and create a feeling of participation? Sessions will also delve into how to generate a flow of ideas from "below" in the organization.

5. *Interpersonal Relations.* Many executives and salesmen can gain by developing a more sensitive awareness in interpersonal relations. Too many of us are passive rather than active listeners, can be tricked by superficial signals into making rash judgments, and don't utilize all our senses in observing people and things. Interpersonal relations can also be

improved if the individual is confident, is not trying to "play a role," and comes across as a real person—problems for which the Institute has developed the new techniques of the "psychological mirror." Sessions will also include improving persuasive powers through "typology" of dialogue partners and gaining insights into one's own behavior during periods of psychological stress in order to cope without losing control.

6. *More Creative Thinking.* The modern executive has to make decisions, think problems through, and understand more and more complex issues. But intelligent decisions are frequently blocked by such factors as "misreading" other individuals' explanations and rationalizations, generalizing and label sticking as a result of a lack of proper information (or, frequently, a failure to ask insightful questions), trapping ourselves between two alternatives, and prejudice. Also, it is becoming increasingly important for modern executives to develop new ideas, which they often feel inhibited about doing because of fear of change, rules of what can and can't be done, and concern about personal censorship. A new methodology to free the individual in decision making and generating new ideas has been developed by the Institute.

Too much of a valuable executive's life is controlled by convention—the way his desk is organized, the manner in which his memos are written and distributed, supposed requirements for "selling" distributors and consumers, the products and outlets appropriate for his firm, the meetings he must attend, and the way his secretary keeps his files. Moreover, executives frequently don't have the time or skills to absorb enough fast enough—from their daily papers to their superior's speech and expressions. New strategies are needed in dealing with both people and facts.

28

Changing Beliefs

THE PSYCHOLOGY OF PRICING

You are about to launch a new product or service. How much should you charge for it? Assuming that manufacturing economics have enabled you to offer it at an especially low price, is it wise to put it on the market for as little as possible? Or, on the other hand, if, because of inflation and increased labor and production costs, you find that price increases are necessary, how high should you go? And, what is even more important, how should the price be explained to the buying public?

We have found, in working with consumer groups over the years, that the actual price usually plays a much less important role than the psychological aspects of pricing. Many years ago, a survey was conducted in Belgium by the then Finance Minister in which, on the basis of a number of actual test cases, the *psychological* role of pricing was made dramatically clear. An item that normally sold for 29 cents was advertised boldly: "*One* for 21 cents—two for 45 cents!" The experiment showed that most people took advantage of the "two for 45 cents" offer because the manner in which it was publicized made it look like a bargain.

Our studies show that there are three major elements of pricing which the seller needs to consider:

1. *Psychological Pricing.* When a leather substitute was being launched not too long ago, it was decided to charge more for shoes made of this new material than for comparable shoes made of leather. This made it appear to be a far superior product, in the eyes of the buyer, and not just a synthetic substitute. We have found that when an item is priced somewhat higher than might normally be expected, it is assumed that the higher price means higher quality and that the product is therefore more desirable.

2. *Cultural Reasons Affecting Pricing.* Very few men ever buy two or three suits at the same time. There are, of course, many reasons for this, among them the high price of quality clothing. However, more often than not we have found in our studies that there is a cultural reason for the consumer's reaction to the price of a product. When family incomes were considerably lower than they are today, the purchase of a man's suit took a sizable "bite" out of the budget, and to buy *two* at the same time was unthinkable. Today, even though the ratio between income and the cost of clothing has changed considerably, this psychological feeling still persists, and the purchase of more than one suit at a time is rarely considered, even though the buyer might very well be able to afford it.

3. *Interpretation of Price Changes.* We have also found that even more important than the price itself is how a price change is explained to the public. In a study for a tractor company we suggested that a higher-priced tractor be introduced by comparing its price with that of a *worker*, rather than with that of *other tractors.* Since farm workers are scarce and costly, the price of the tractor, when compared with the yearly wages of a good helper, seemed quite reasonable. Breaking down a price into cost per unit is another approach which usually works very well; for example, "You get forty cups out of every pound of Brand X Coffee. Yet even at this higher price, each cup costs you only one-quarter cent more—certainly little enough to pay for its superior flavor and satisfaction."

Playback from our psychological analysis of motivational behavior reveals very clearly that both price increases and price reductions are more acceptable when justification for the action is explained to consumers. Yet, as every marketing executive knows, it is not enough for a particular factor affecting the product to be true—it must also seem true. Nowhere is this principle more applicable than in the handling of price differentials.

MONEY IN A GOLDEN AGE

The role of discretionary spending in the affluent society is often discussed. Overlooked is the fact that affluence also creates discretionary saving. Insurance, savings funds, the stock market, and mutual funds all have tougher competition today because the consumer has more freedom of choice about his savings dollars—and new attitudes about money.

Decline of "morality"   A large American company recently asked us to discover why its younger employees started to withdraw money from their pension funds after a few years to speculate on the stock market. Fund regulations stipulated either complete maintenance or withdrawal, and many members were being lost. Our recommendation was to allow partial speculative membership. This was based on our findings that many people, especially young people, are no longer interested in old-fashioned, puritanical savings.

Our studies further indicate that affluence also eliminates the vital motivation of worry about the future. Perhaps one reason for today's "generation gap" is the fact that young people feel the future is assured —"The government or someone will take care of me." Therefore, they feel free to indulge in the luxury of present revolt. Even older people feel frustrated at the realization that they need have little anxiety about the future, and they continue the habits of accumulation—and worry. Governments today—seldom consistent "savers"—also upset traditional thinking about money.

Hazards of safety   "Safety" of investments is becoming a less believable, less desirable claim. In an inflation-oriented, unpredictable world, there's a growing realization that no form of savings or investment is 100 percent safe. Insurance companies have already felt the pressure of desire for "growth" rather than stability. All this means that financial institutions today must tune communications to new attitudes:

1. *Moral Reasons for Saving Won't Get You Far.*   "You really should save" takes all the fun out of it. Savings should be promoted for fun and adventure aspects. Among the ideas we've suggested are "crazy-money" accounts and catalogues showing the increasingly exciting merchandise that can be obtained by maintaining one's account for longer periods. Savings should perhaps be related also to newer goals of inner satisfaction and growth—leading to a period of greater inner freedom. Savings institutions should perhaps themselves be freed to offer combined speculative and sober types of accounts combining adventure with stability.

2. *Individuality.*   Many financial firms have little distinctiveness in the consumer's mind. All savings banks tend to offer the same services and to blur together, for example. One solution might be more segmented approaches. Savings banks might concentrate on definite sectors of the market—career girls, industrial workers, etc. Perhaps savings programs could be individually geared to differing personality types and goals. Brokerage firm prospects could probably use some psychoanalysis to aid them in figuring out their real investment objectives.

3. *Fear of the Intangible.* Even educated people still feel subconsciously that cold cash is "safer" than such abstract forms of money as stock, carloads of wheat, etc. Related is the fear of loss of control. Here, educational efforts would help. Many ad and editorial campaigns now aim to educate, but mostly they fling facts at the consumer that are unrelated to the individual problems and motivations for investing. What good does it do a small investor to know what a floor trader is, for example? More should be done also to relate the significance of government and big-business moves to the individual's money. Lack of control may also be a problem as the "cashless" society draws nearer; prepayment of bills may be convenient, but many people won't want the bank messing around with their hard-earned dough.

4. *New Service Concepts.* Banks have played the "friendly" theme almost to the point of unbelievability. It may be that friendliness is actually a less desirable image than that of the worldly but approachable financial expert. Many types of financial institutions talk about becoming broad "family financial centers" and advisers—but few have delivered. Young people especially need advice in financial and investment programming—special "under-thirty" departments might be one idea. Financial services might also bring firms closer to their communities—opening facilities for meetings, holding investment classes, and even sponsoring concerts. Baby-sitting service while Mother's in the vaults might be offered.

THE NEW PSYCHOLOGY OF DRESS—AND UNDRESS

Today fashion plays a crucial role in the marketing of products from lipstick to tires and radios. But this can be a dangerous game. It's not merely a matter of the rapidity of change of styles and fads themselves. Marketers must understand the deeper changes taking place in the psychological meanings and benefits of fashion. Moreover, apparel marketers themselves must be aware of significant new opportunities to enhance the excitement of their products and communications.

Visual rivalry   Smart, up-to-the minute dress means that one is with it—one is "in the race." Wearing yesterday's style is almost like being left behind in school, like not participating. Fashion should make increasing use of the appeal of staying "competitive" by being modern and up to date.

Your own thing   In many recent studies we discovered that today, young people especially no longer dress for proper role playing—they don't wear "banker's gray" or "Madison Avenue sincere." They want their apparel to be the outward, visual expression of their individuality. The old adage about how "clothes make the man" has been superseded. Clothing manufacturers and stores could gain by stressing the fact that their products are specifically designed to bring out the consumer's individuality. Psychological "typologizing" might help gear styles to various personality types.

Projected creativity   Most people have a deep wish to express their creativity—but lack artistic talent. Selection of clothing and other products, however, represents an easy form of projected creativity. Marketers might emphasize the "bravery" it takes to own certain models. Moreover, fashion involving participation—completion through individualistic activity—will play a growing role in the future.

Self-discovery   The purchaser of a new blouse rushes to the mirror. The reason is deeper than to see "how it looks." It's to discover what transformation, what new aspect of personality, is revealed. Buying new clothes has an element of "intoxication" about it.

New youth   Each new fashion is an antidote against age and decline. We strip off the old and feel renewed—at least on the outside. Fashion is one of the oldest fountains of youth.

The new "outer limits"   Many of our studies show acceptance of new technology and methods that don't even exist yet—new kinds of closures, materials with chips of metal woven into the fabric, plastic combinations, and molded apparel, for example.

"Instant" dress   Greater convenience—clothing that is easy to put on and take off—is a major desire, according to our studies. We have already seen such developments as dresses with built-in bras and slacks with built-in girdles. Why not have thermostatically controlled fabrics that adapt themselves to temperature changes or more convenient fasteners than buttons or hooks and eyes?

"Lover" styles   Americans today are part of a titillation culture. We no longer need to hunt for food, eat merely to stay alive, or dress simply to stay warm. More and more products we use are ticklers and titillators, elements of self-stimulation. Clothing that appeals by means of its "inner feel" may well be on the way, for example, dresses with caressing linings —or ones that tickle—or pocket linings that provide a tactile adventure.

Outdated fashion language   Typical fashion language—words such as "chic" and "smart"—has by now lost its "excitability" and no longer commands attention or interest. A new, fresher kind of communication is needed. For example, instead of presenting a dress as "washable," labels might declare, "Yes, you may—I'm washable." Part of such new fashion language should involve a greater use of imagery to move beyond the purely verbal. One dramatic way of evoking the softness of a fabric, for example, might be to illustrate a dress laid out on a rock.

HOW TO MOTIVATE REPLACEMENT PURCHASING

In many areas in the United States and in some European countries, the problem of market saturation has become a rather serious one. The woods are no longer filled with families who do not yet own a refrigerator, a television set, and countless other big-ticket items. Modern merchandising and marketing methods have enabled us to track these families down and nail their purchase orders to the barn door! So, *how* do you get a housewife with a rheumatic refrigerator to decide that it's time for a replacement? The answer, so far, has been through the development of new models and new improvements in products—or obsolescence. However, because this is no longer enough, here are some psychological techniques which we have found to be effective:

1. *Replace "Squirrel" Psychology with Renewal Philosophy.* Probably one of the major differences between consumer psychology in Europe and that in America is that the European, because of background, training, and experience, likes to hold onto things as long as possible. Americans, on the other hand, prefer to discard many things after a few years of ownership. This is due partly to high servicing costs, which cause a family to get rid of many items once they begin to need frequent repairs or do not function efficiently any longer. Since restoring an item to its original state of operation often costs almost as much as buying a new one, most families prefer to replace a product with a more up-to-date one. Economists seem to agree that this throw-away philosophy is largely responsible for our rapidly developing economy.

Europeans still need to change their attitude in this respect, and we find that to a limited extent they are doing so. We have learned that by openly discussing the advantages of this throw-away philosophy—and by analyzing the deeper reasons for it—a change of attitude can often be brought about. What is involved, of course, is a basic feeling of insecurity which many Europeans still have—the fear of being deprived, of starving, of someday being reduced to the bare necessities of life. Having lived through two ravaging world wars, they have trouble shaking off a subconscious fear that they may again be put into a similar kind of situation. There is a definite feeling of guilt associated with throwing things away; it is almost comparable to the reluctance most civilized people have about stepping on an old piece of bread lying in the road.

What we have therefore tried to do regarding the advertising of some of our European clients is to suggest the pleasures of throwing things away. This is an almost antimaterialistic kind of attitude. Furthermore, it tends to free the mind of the nagging feeling that perhaps it would be better to get rid of obsolete, outmoded possessions and not continue living in fear of what might happen.

2. *Help Others in a More Practical Way.* It used to be customary to give used clothing to less fortunate relatives or to donate it to a charitable institution. This is one way of relieving guilt feelings and obtaining justification for the purchase of new products. However, this form of absolution is becoming more and more difficult. Despite economic problems, it is quite likely that these relatives are now more able to buy the clothing they need. So we have emphasized that throwing out old things and buying new ones helps to keep the economy going, reduces unemployment, and is a much more efficient way of living.

3. *Create a Specific Life Cycle.* We have found that in some cases, products are not thrown away and replaced by new ones because many people simply do not know how long one is supposed to keep a still-functioning appliance or car. Through the creation of a definite life cycle for various types of products, this uncertainty can be eliminated, and a more rapid replacement cycle can be established. By pointing out that most people find it economically unwise to keep a new car longer than three years at the most and that it is much more satisfactory to buy a new refrigerator every five or six years, replacement can be accelerated.

4. *Suggest Multiple Ownership.* A further device which works very well is to point up the advantages of owning more than one refrigerator, more than one vacuum cleaner, more than one car, additional television sets, and even two *homes*—one of which should be a *vacation* home. Despite the obvious logic of multiple ownership, many of our studies show that countless men don't even have enough shoes or enough suits to meet their everyday needs!

Extending this idea, book publishers might very well suggest the purchase of two books of the same title—one to be torn apart and only several chapters taken along on a trip and the other one for the library shelf at home. And, incredible as it may seem, buying a tube of toothpaste for *each* member of the family is another possibility which has not been properly exploited.

Product replacement should not be left to just technological and aesthetic obsolescence. A clearer understanding of the deep-rooted psychological reasons for deferment of purchasing needs to be obtained in order to motivate more frequent buying. Only by understanding these hidden reasons more thoroughly is increased product penetration of saturated markets possible.

CHILDHOOD MEMORIES CAN MAKE OR BREAK ADULT ATTITUDES

Many of our studies show that far too little consideration is given to the fact that many of the buying attitudes we have today were created ten, twenty, thirty, or more years ago—during childhood! We have therefore found that an analysis of the conditions affecting behavioral development during childhood frequently leads to a clearer understanding of why adults act the way they do in the marketplace.

In various studies of dentifrices we found that there are at least three major types of toothpaste users and that their buying habits are derived from childhood training. The first of these we call the *antiauthoritarian* type. This individual was forced, by his mother usually, to pay very strict attention to his teeth. He submitted to this maternal coercion only superficially, however, and now revolts against the necessity of brushing his teeth. The toothpaste he seeks is one that will help him get the job done as easily and quickly as possible, and he is not too worried about cavities.

A second type, the tooth hypochondriac, represents another reaction pattern to childhood coercion. Rather than fight back, this person not only submitted to the pressure, but went Mother one better by becoming even more concerned with his teeth than she intended him to be. This is a typical pattern of neurosis. Very often it is combined with physiological aspects of tooth problems, wherein it is difficult to determine which came first—the cavities and then the concern or the concern and then the cavities. This person is very likely to reach for semimedicated dentifrices. We were able to demonstrate in many of our studies that these customers represent the typical buyers of toothpaste containing ammonia, fluoride, or chlorophyll and of similar types of dental products.

The third type is the social conformist. He, as our studies showed, was trained by his parents in a more permissive fashion. He was told that brushing one's teeth is like getting washed up and is part of the normal, not too serious aspects of civilization. There is therefore no need for this individual to fight back later in life. He tends to take a rather nonchalant attitude toward brushing his teeth and will buy a toothpaste which will assure social acceptance but which doesn't make any particular promise to control cavities.

Bread is another product which has a strong childhood tie. In a study for Arnold Bakers we were able to demonstrate that even though many people today do not remember from personal experience the *aroma* of homemade bread, nevertheless the bread eaten in one's childhood holds very cherished memories. Evoking it again in advertising proved to give very good results.

Our tests also revealed that Ovaltine is another product most people recall, often with negative feelings because of having been forced in childhood to drink it against their will. They did not dislike the taste, but they remember the coercion. We recommended that special advertising emphasis be put on its satisfying, delightful, and beneficial qualities. Results? Good!

Even in car buying we found that the experience of the very first car a person owned as an adolescent can act as a very powerful motivation. When we suggested that Plymouth use a drawing of an old jalopy with the headline, "Do you remember when? . . ." we had a most effective ad.

On the basis of our findings, we feel that it is most important not to overlook childhood experiences when talking to grown-ups. Freud was right—our personalities are formed much earlier than we think, and the effects of our early experiences stay with us literally to the end of our days. And they don't weaken. If anything, they become even stronger as we grow older.

29

Promoting Mobility

HOW TO PERSUADE MORE PEOPLE TO TRAVEL

The travel business has been one of the "booms" of the past decade. Increasingly larger numbers of airline passengers to Europe and the Far East are reported yearly. But there is actually a far greater potential for the travel business than has yet been tapped by its promoters. For instance, a third of the people who can afford to never take vacations away from home. A large number of so-called vacations are highly conformist: a jaunt to the same old lake or a relative's house in another city year after year. At least 60 percent of the population has never been on an airplane. The majority of the public has never stayed in a hotel or motel overnight.

How to jolt the consumer out of his inertia? Travel promoters—agents, airlines, government tourist bureaus, etc.—must recognize the true motivations surrounding travel—or nontravel. Simply presenting the facts, however alluring, may not in any sense move the customer. Deeper and possibly unexpected emotional responses may be involved. For example, an initial market study to determine why more Europeans weren't visiting the United States disclosed that Europeans considered this country too expensive. Our deeper probing, however, revealed that this was merely rationalization. Europeans were actually afraid of facing what they thought would be their own future—a more urbanized, depersonalized industrial world.

Stay versus go   The question of travel is related to a basic ambivalence within the human personality—a conflict between the security of routine and the desire for adventure. On the one hand, we like to know exactly what to expect each day, and we resent incursions on our routine. On the other hand, we also become bored if things repeat themselves in the same pattern each day, and we secretly hope for change. Thus, although the physical dangers of travel have generally been eliminated, it still involves psychological dangers—an uprooting of firm ideas and prejudices and a shaking up of orderly routine. Yet traveling to a place with too many of the "comforts of home" isn't very interesting. Americans do not consider Canada an important goal for travel because it is not too different from the United States.

The explorer within us   One of a traveler's most disappointing experiences is to have to tell friends that a place was too much like another one he's visited. Similarly, travel advertising can err by showing pictures of "anyplace" situations—the beach that could be in Miami, Israel, or Rapallo. The promise of uniqueness—offering the traveler the chance for discovery—has strong appeal. In describing his special discovery, the traveler proves to himself that he is indeed a unique individual. We all want to go places where "no one else" has been (certainly not all those "tourists")—or at least become part of an elite that can exchange confidences about secret places.

The new self   Any form of travel results, psychologically, in revealing new insights, in making the individual see himself in a different light. One is surprised to discover another side of himself that he never suspected existed. The travel marketer should therefore promise the fulfillment of such wishes. Too much travel advertising concentrates on historical sites, food, and other outward appeals of travel. The real, more hidden motivation is this discovery of the unknown (and possibly freer) self.

A "philosophical" exchange may be another appeal of travel. Recently in the United States we have been undergoing a period of questioning of our goal- and achievement-oriented culture. The traveler, in a way, is secretly hoping that the strange and different country may represent the answers to his questioning and clarify his own ideas. He is curious to discover how other countries—perhaps those oriented more toward contemplation and enjoyment of life—can "manage."

Misunderstanding often adds to the traveler's feeling of being an outsider. Perhaps he may feel that he is being scrutinized in an unfriendly fashion. In our surveys, we find that the traveler prefers an airline, a hotel, or a country that makes him feel liked and accepted. Recently, France has developed a negative image in this respect—giving tourists the feeling of being unwanted, overcharged, or even cheated. Often such difficulties can be prevented by explaining host-country customs to visitors.

Sell the "hangover" The best part of the trip may come after it's over —when sore feet, rain, and other inconveniences are forgotten and the traveler can think back on his experiences. The true value of a trip should be measured not in just days spent or miles traveled but in the aftereffects. An exciting two weeks may have more meaning and value than years of repetitious, ordinary living. The travel promoter should dramatize this "surplus" value of a good trip.

TUNE IN TO THE PSYCHE OF THE JET-AGE TRAVELER

As Americans grow more mobile—a trend the jumbo jets will accentuate —hotels, motels, and other travel-service businesses would do well to make a fresh appraisal of their customers and their methods of operation. Two things seem necessary: (1) Hotels should change their image from that of large, anonymous places, almost indistiguishable from city to city and often with intimidating personnel, to that of individualized ones, just as manufacturers today have to give products unique personalities, and (2) hotels should become more people-oriented and understand the true motivations of their guests.

When he comes to a hotel, the individual, is not the same person he is at home. He has been uprooted in a psychological sense; he desires the security which may be engendered by liberal doses of pampering, which he would never require in his own house; and he regresses to a more infantile level. He may be content with one towel at home; his dream in a hotel is to be supplied with many. In the same way, the person who is neat and orderly at home may become negligent and sloppy in a hotel, dropping ashes on the carpet, scattering his clothes, etc. To be truly satisfied, the traveler needs more than cleanliness and attractive surroundings. The following are several ways in which hotels might individualize and humanize themselves in the traveler's mind, catering to his psychological as well as physical needs:

1. *"Instant Welcome."* Creating the sense of individualized concern for the traveler might begin at the registration desk. The clerk might ask whether the person needs extra blankets, chairs, etc. The guest might be asked to fill out a form indicating the kind of room he'd like—with or without a view, near the swimming pool, etc.

Once in his room, the traveler typically feels unfamiliar and disoriented, and he has to discover how things "work" by trial and error. To take possession, so to speak, he turns knobs, opens and shuts doors and windows, inspects the bathroom, etc. Welcome here might be a room "orientation guide"—telling the guest how to use the air conditioner, where to look for the laundry bag, and how to order food or extra pillows—perhaps with an invitation to relax and unpack instead of "living out of a suitcase" and to make himself feel at home. Hotels should also be more conscious of the many details which may spoil the traveler's opinion of an otherwise plush, modern operation. Such things as locks that don't work easily and maids who constantly appear at the door annoy the guest out of all proportion.

2. *On the Town.* Many hotel rooms provide information about restaurants, theaters, and sightseeing in the city, but such guides are seldom organized in a convenient way. Answers to questions such as what places are open late at night for food or entertainment, how one gets there, and what hours the principal stores in town are open might be answered in a specially prepared booklet. The traveler of today is also more sophisticated than his counterpart in the past. He wants to see more than the "typically tourist" museums and monuments. The hotel might also provide up-to-date information on city politics, the newest urban renewal projects, new businesses in the area, interesting neighborhoods, and other things that would give the traveler a deeper "feel" of the city.

3. *Check-out Convenience.* Frequently the traveler must check out of his room several hours before he's leaving town, particularly if he's on a business trip. It might be feasible for hotels to fill this hospitality gap with special rooms where luggage might be stored and the traveler could relax after vacating his room.

4. *Raiding the Icebox.* Although the traveler wants to feel pampered, he sometimes doesn't like to be waited on continuously. Some hotels are beginning to furnish in-room refrigerators and vending machines for drinks, coffee, and snacks for the traveler who'd like "a little something" but doesn't want to bother with room service.

5. *Sociability.* Single travelers and even couples often would like to sit down to chat casually with other people. Why couldn't hotels emulate cruise ships, providing a "hospitality hour" during which people might, if they wished, get acquainted?

6. *Better than Home.* The hotel guest wants more than the "comforts of home"—he's seeking luxury and adventure. Sauna baths, swimming pools, breakfast in bed, and even such little touches as providing bath oil to encourage the kind of lazing one never has time for at home all contribute to the sense of adventure. The strictly "commercial" hotel will

increasingly lose out to the one that fulfills the traveler's desire for super-comfort.

TRAVEL MARKETING: NEW "DESTINATIONS" NEEDED

Outmoded vacation concepts are still being promoted by airlines, resort developers, hotels, and tour operators. Vacations have always been considered a "rest"; this idea stems from the days when most people engaged in hard physical labor in their daily lives. Today we are increasingly a society of white-collar workers, office thinkers, and—even in the factory—supervisors of automated equipment. New vacation concepts must be developed to meet entirely different physical and psychological needs.

"Psychological" vacations are what's really needed—mind expansion, rather than lying on beaches. The ideal vacation today should allow the individual to live differently from the way he does in his everyday life—to escape his habits and find his true or undiscovered self. There is also the "runaway" aspect: The vacation should be psychotherapy to help the person cope with the modern world. Such "trip" concepts could be developed as:

1. *The "Opposite" Vacation.* Many men have a sense of artificiality and role playing in office jobs. The most refreshing vacation for them might be one that is physically oriented—on a farm or a fishing boat. The dress, food, and activities would all be radical departures.

2. *"Learning" Vacations.* Such holidays would offer the benefit of self-achievement. Special tours could combine leisure time in interesting places with education in hobbies—painting, flower growing, languages, sports (most ski and golf tours are aimed at people who are already experts—not those who'd like to learn), or even pressing wine in bare feet as a participatory means of learning a new culture.

3. *Personalized Tours.* Why not have a computer system which would match an individual's psychological requirements, life-style, and budget with the ideal vacation environment? Or the more daring vacationer might be sent on a trip "into the blue"—with no idea where his plane or cruise ship is taking him until he arrives. Planned lack of plan in itself would appeal to some segments of the travel market.

4. *"Experience" Resorts.* More novelty and a sense of enjoying a new kind of life even without being far from home might be offered by resorts. The resort might be a place to fulfill dreams—to live like an admiral or a Gypsy, for example. More personal involvement could be achieved by "renting" guests their own garden plots to till during their stay, or tropical resorts could let guests pick their own oranges for juice. Resorts

could also create more of a sense of awareness with unconventionally shaped beds and other furnishings. The new "floatels," which let vacationers choose whether to go off on their own in houseboats or be part of a resort community, offer interesting psychological directions.

MOVING TRAVEL RETAILERS INTO THE JET AGE

As more and more of the general public has the money and leisure time to spend on vacation travel, the travel agency business should logically be the one to benefit. The travel agency is the convenient place, for inexperienced pleasure seekers particularly, to seek advice and help with plans. But travel agencies are missing many opportunities to live up to their potential. What could be improved?

1. *Closed-door Policy.*   Some agencies are so anxious to avoid casual "shoppers" that their offices appear too forbidding. The atmosphere and organization give the impression that if you're not ready to sign on the dotted line, forget it. Agencies should look friendlier—they should suggest, "C'mon in and browse."

2. *"Sampling" Is Needed.*   The agency office should suggest some of the new experience of travel in other lands and other sections of the United States. Unfortunately, many are merely cluttered and drab. Foreign music, art, fashion, and even snacks might help.

3. *Money Confusion.*   Airlines spend a lot to tell consumers that travel agencies don't charge for their services—but the idea still hasn't come across to many people. Agencies themselves should make it clear that services are paid for largely by commissions.

4. *Promote, Promote.*   A vast range of promotional techniques are available to encourage the idea that the agency is a comfortable, easy place to shop for travel ideas. A "destination of the month"—with appropriate displays of posters and informative material from airlines and hotels—could create atmosphere and provide a continuing source of interest and suggestions to potential travelers. Fashion shows, open houses to meet a visiting celebrity, and more intriguing mail-order ads—for example, "C'mon down" cards that are mailed from the Bahamas—are other possibilities.

5. *Build an Image with a Specialty.*   Most agencies now look quite a bit alike and appear to offer similar ranges of services. Agencies could create more distinctiveness for themselves by specializing, in addition to their normal activities, in youth travel, honeymoons, ski trips around the world, ultraluxurious tours, or a particular part of the world, for example.

6. *Helping Consumers Plan.*   Many people hardly know when to start planning vacation trips. Agency advertising and signs should help—by

suggesting winter ideas in summer, and vice versa. Often by the time people get around to deciding where to go, it's too late to make reservations.

7. *Create Local Travel "Clubs."*   This could both draw customers in and establish the agency as an important travel idea center. For example, the agency could offer travel savings plans, similar to banks' Christmas clubs; perhaps the coupon book could include a puzzle showing a beach scene that becomes totally visible when the proper amount has been saved.

8. *Travel Marketers Could Do a Better Job.*   Most travel marketers send travel agents so much promotional material that their basements are stacked high with brochures. More consideration might be given to promotion aimed at bringing customers to agents. Itinerant musical shows, foreign-food demonstrations, and "orientation seminars" for families ready to travel are possibilities.

WHY PEOPLE MOVE (MIGRATION MOTIVATIONS)

When asked directly, people say they move because of lack of work in an area or for economic reasons of various types. We used a motivational depth approach, letting people talk at great length in nondirective interviews. We found a number of much more vital reasons for migrating than the financial ones alone.

Even money has a deeper meaning, however. A laborer who moved from Coruthersville, Missouri to Chicago told us:

> You mean what I want most? I want a decent living. I want a decent job. That means a job that will pay me enough to take care of my family. I'd be well pleased with a good job. Then I could manage to get the rest of the things I want, the things we really need—like my own place to live in and clothes. And I know one thing—I would send my wife to a good doctor or hospital. She's been kinda sickly and I wasn't able to send her to one down home.

Making a living is not measurable in dollars alone. Human dignity is involved. The surroundings where I made my home up to now are my enemies. By changing my surroundings, I increase my chances of success.

Various cities seemed to offer different attractions as goals for migration.

In spite of the above, the respondents by no means showed that they viewed city life through rose-colored glasses. They were very well aware that city life holds its own unique hazards, especially for blacks. Nevertheless, the hostile environment of the cities, with their slums, crime, poverty, and so on, appeared to most of our respondents to be composed more of material obstacles than psychological burdens. In contrast, the respondents seem to feel that both psychological and material burdens were involved in remaining in a small Southern town. In spite of its problems, the city is apparently seen as an environment which offers the individual some chance to manipulate his destiny and improve his own chances in life.

Recent history has done more to dull the attraction of the cities than bad housing or poverty ever could. One of the city's main attractions—relative freedom from restraint—has been undermined by the growing feeling that the city is a place of rioting and looting. Detroit, in particular, seemed to be strongly associated with extreme violence by all our respondents.

In their replies to a very general question about what other people might say if they decided to move, the respondents tended to be very defensive. Some apparently interpreted it as a question of who had the right to tell them what to do. This interpretation is, of course, a unique function of the Southern environment. One of the ways to assert one's independence from the old ways is to show that one can leave.

However, a series of deeper psychological factors are more important than the obvious but nevertheless significant motivations of migrating for reasons of survival. By understanding these motivations, which became clear as we analyzed our depth interviews, we were able to arrive at additional avenues for influencing migration in a positive way. These possible solutions are, of course, steps to be taken in addition to the many approaches of an economic nature, such as providing more opportunities for employment.

1. "I Am Dreaming a Dream"

We asked our respondents to describe to us what they considered the good life to be. Most of the time the dreams were modest enough. Moving seemed a way to get closer to these dreams.

A housewife from Elm City, North Carolina, described her dreams in the following way:

> You mean the good life, like the way I'd make a living and everything like that? Let me think about that a minute. One of my boys ought to answer that. They are always dreaming up things.
>
> Well, I would like to have a job being a seamstress making $125 a week, eight hours a day, five days a week, and go to church every Sunday and prayer meeting on Tuesday. I'd like to have a nice brick home of my own —oh, I'd love that [*throws back head and laughs delightedly*]. I'd love six rooms and a bath and a half. That's my dream. I'd need two baths, wouldn't I, with all my children? I wouldn't want expensive furniture, just nice, and I'd want a good job to meet all the payments on it. I would like a den and big kitchen all made together and a big room for my boys with single beds

so they wouldn't be kicking one another in their sleep. Oh, I could talk all the time about that house I want. Most of all, I want my house in the country—still stay in the country. I would like an electric stove and cabinets all around the kitchen. I would want all my boys and girls to get a college education, those that are left at home—well, Von and Linda, too; it's not too late for them—at a good college, not just any college, but the best. I could make out with the car I got and the TV we got. I don't want to be rich. I just want a good living. Everybody started saying 'Color TV! Color TV.' But I'm satisfied with my TV. I want to work for my living, but I want a good living.

This is the way the wife of a tenant farmer described her day:

I get up about 5:30 A.M. if I don't oversleep. The first thing I do is wash my face and hands. Then I fix our breakfast and dinner both, and while everybody else is eating, I eat too. Lots of times I don't sit down to eat breakfast because I'm busy cooking and waiting on the children. I eat fast at breakfast. Other times, too, I reckon.

After breakfast I drive to town or close-by farms to pick up hands who will help us that day. I take the boys [*her sons*] to the field or the barn if they're working far away from the house and it's on my way.

As soon as I get back with the helpers, we start to work at the barn or in the field, wherever the work has to be done that day. Around ten or eleven o'clock they send me to the store to get refreshments—Nabs and Pepsis, whatever they call for. I go to the house at 12:30 and warm up dinner. We start eating about 1:30 and about quarter to two I go and get the hands to start back to work. [*James, her husband, has taken them to their houses or to the store, or wherever they eat their dinner.*] I figure I have about fifteen minutes to eat and rest at dinnertime. I leave the dishes and cleaning up till suppertime.

After I pick up the hands, we go back to work at the barn or in the field and work till six, sometimes seven o'clock. I take the hands back to town or wherever they live, and then I come back home.

Everybody has a job to do at the house then. My job is to cook supper. The girls and me clean up the kitchen after we eat. At night I shuck corn or shell beans, things like that, so I won't take long to fix dinner the next morning.

I get a good bath and watch TV till after eleven-o'clock news. Then I go to bed and get up the next morning and start all over again.

2. Freedom from Control of Small-town Restrictions

Our respondents indicated that one of the things they resented most was a lack of freedom within the small-town atmosphere. Everybody watches what they do. What they are dreaming about is to have complete individual freedom. The big city in the North seems to hold this promise:

It's bigger. You can get lost. I mean Chicago is big, and Caruthersville is just a small town. You don't see no farms around here. I don't know.

3. Being Reborn

The region where one is born is like a mother. In order to migrate, you have to tear yourself loose. Mother had to be denied. You are choosing a new relationship, a new origin. There is a considerable amount of guilt involved, almost as if one had betrayed one's own mother. The unsuccessful migrant feels that he is being punished for having abandoned his origin and legitimate "motherland." If he successfully overcomes this separation, it is symbolically a form of rebirth for him.

A laborer in a bicycle factory who moved from Arkansas to Chicago commented:

> Well, we weren't doing too well where I was, but finally when I first thought about moving, my cousin was visiting his mother from Chicago, and he was talking about how well he was doing. I really wasn't thinking about moving right then, but I started thinking about what I was doing there. Well, I was working in a factory there on and off, mostly off. I wasn't doing no good where I was, and he told me how good he was doing, so then the last time I got laid off, I just thought about moving to see if I could do better.
>
> When I moved, I wasn't doing nothing, and after I thought about what my cousin told me, I thought maybe I could do better if I moved here. I thought about it, but I knew if I stayed down there I couldn't do no better. They won't let us—I mean the folks that has the jobs and the factories and things like that. I also thought about my kids coming up, and I want them to have more schooling than I got. Yep, that's the main things I thought about.

4. Playing God (Antifatalism)

"I am stronger than fate; I can tear myself loose from what destiny had in store for me." This feeling is frequently expressed. Moving is a form of antifatalism: "I am defying my natural destiny." The migrant has to be an activist because his natural tendency would be to stick to the accustomed little things of everyday life.

There is a mixture of exhilaration and fear at the same time. A maid from Virginia described her first experiences this way:

> I was scared and excited at the same time. Wondered if I would get off at the right time and scared to go out on the street and catch a cab and afraid of what the cab driver might do and where he might take me. I wondered if the people thought I was a little country girl or not. The city was fantastic to me.

Migrants are optimists   There is a tendency to look down upon migrants as shiftless people without roots. In reality, people who have the courage to start anew are like the original immigrants to the United

States. You have to have a considerable degree of stamina and self-confidence and an optimistic belief in the future to go through the traumatic experience of changing your life completely. What the migrants complain about is that they are treated as if the opposite were true.

5. Destroying the Past

One of the respondents told us quite dramatically that before leaving, he destroyed all his minor possessions. He did not want to be reminded of the past: "We took only the clothes on our backs along. We left everything." The way it is explained is that it is almost a ritual bath, a sort of cleansing. The past is dirty and slowed you down. Unlike a child who may take a doll or a little possession along on a trip to provide security and the comfort of things known and familiar, the migrant wants to break all ties. True, he drifts in the new surroundings toward peer groups. He is interested in meeting people who come from the same background or the same kind of neighborhood. At first, however, everything that reminds him of his "prison" is rejected.

6. Fresh Start

When the migrant arrives in his new surroundings, the very first contacts he makes are extremely important. One of our respondents stated: "I got the wrong address from a man I asked. He was not even a white man. But after that everything went smoothly."

The newcomer judges people as to whether or not they welcome him and are ready to give him a chance. He is nervous and partially hostile. If he becomes disappointed, he is likely to turn against people in authority, whom he blames for his frustration. He expects to be loved and welcomed. Since this is often not the case, this disappointed love turns easily into aggression and physical violence.

A physical education instructor from Augusta, Georgia, said this:

> One of the things I have always wanted is to be free to think and decide to do just those things I would care to do and would enjoy. I have always wanted this freedom to go places without restriction. I have needed to do certain things no matter what anyone thought about it. I think that I would like very much to remain single for awhile. I tried to be married, but there were too many restrictions, and I feel that I don't wish to have these restrictions in marriage or in no aspect of my life. So the best kind of life would be one where I could be free to move about anywhere without being discriminated against or without having to have a thought about whether I really will be accepted by everyone. In my hometown there are so many ways the black man is told that he is not on the same par with the whites. It's hard to take. I wouldn't want to continue my life in the South. This is the kind of life I wouldn't want.

7. Moving Up

The migrant we interviewed usually belonged to an underprivileged group. The new "country" he moved to was supposed to lift him up to a new social class. He felt that if he stayed where he was, it would be very difficult to become socially mobile. The chains of the accustomed group would hold him back. Moving to Chicago, Detroit, or any other Northern city meant at the same time reaching a higher social level.

A student from North Carolina dreamed about moving to Washington, D.C.:

> One of the things I always wanted in life was to have a car of my own. Finally my brother helped my sister build a better house for us. I always thought something might happen to me before I grew up. I thought I might have an accident or something like that. I never really looked forward to a good life. I guess I didn't know what to look for. As for being worse, I don't think that things could be much worse for my family in any way. My mother has always had to work, and my father has always had to work in the tobacco warehouse as a truck driver and sometimes as a helper. My mother would work as a cleaning woman in a doctor's office. She still works there now. My father isn't working because he's sick.

8. Personal Growth

Cutting the ties with "Mother," with friends, and with familiar sights can and often does involve a feeling of having become independent and having matured. Migration is not only a discovery of a new world but also a discovery of a new aspect of one's personality. Recognition, which came automatically from one's friends, has to be rearned with the new group. Values which seemed to be accepted before suddenly do not operate any longer:

> Before I came to the city, I lived with my grandparents, who are getting up in age. I enjoyed living with them, except they were very superstitious and believed in so many things I don't believe in. If your nose itches someone is coming, or you will get a letter; a black cat crosses your path, and it's bad luck; break a mirror, and it's seven years of trouble; don't sweep after dark; the corns on your toes hurt, and it's a sign of rain. They were very strict with me, which I didn't mind too much because there wasn't any place to go outside of church. Of course I knew this was for my own good. It was very dull and lonesome living in a small town like Mullins with old people who don't think as I do. They were unable to give me as much spending money as I wanted. Of course, my parents sent me money from Chicago and came to see us each summer. We had a phone, and they would call us every weekend and would write often.

9. Social Growth

"I met many new people, people I would never have associated with in my old bailiwick," said one migrant. Making new friends from the same social stratum is a new experience, but even more important is the fact that the migrant often has the chance to make new acquaintances who are on a different social level. Naturally it can also happen that the new social group is below the level the "mover" was accustomed to.

People often see cities and famous people on TV. Their curiosity has been aroused through the mass media. They want to see for themselves now.

A typist from South Carolina said:

> In Chicago, you can get good jobs. I have met some friendly people here, there are many places to go for amusement, and there are good school systems and some very nice churches. I saw some nuns for the first time since I've been in Chicago. Chicago has many ways of transportation. I believe New York is somewhat like Chicago, only I don't believe it offers as many opportunities as Chicago does. These are popular, important cities, and people are always going to them for vacations. Lots of rich people go to New York to get the latest styles in fashion and to see the Empire State Building.

PRACTICAL APPLICATIONS

Obviously, financial opportunities should be increased so that it would be unnecessary for people to move. But the purpose of our study was to uncover other, deeper reasons for moving and to see how they can be utilized.

1. Understanding Motivations for Moving

I have listed various psychological factors that are influential in making people migrate. Anyone concerned with practical measures to help migrants should develop a deeper understanding of such motivations as guilt feelings, aggression, and hostility resulting from becoming uprooted.

2. Moving by Staying Where You Are

If the desire to break away from familiar surroundings influences people to migrate, it might be helpful to let them taste a new environment by establishing, for example, Northern fairs in the South.

A "Chicago is coming to you" exhibit might give many people firsthand contact with a new "home." Some may be stimulated to move; others, particularly if all the negative factors of the new surroundings are also shown, may be influenced to stay where they are. If only a change of environment is needed, it might be possible experimentally to have people move into different neighborhoods.

3. Training Course for Potential Migrants

Before people move, they could take a course which would prepare them for the new possibilities, professionally and psychologically. Many could be screened and persuaded to stay home and use their newly learned skills right in their own neighborhood. In such a course attempts could also be made to rid people of many old attitudes and prejudices—to get them to really start fresh.

Some potential migrants want to move, but don't really have enough courage to move completely, to change their personalities also. Such a course would help them to develop a "fresh-start" attitude. It could also serve as a training ground for people who could help the migrant either before he makes the decision or after his arrival.

Booklets or TV programs should be developed for the purpose of discussing some of the less obvious reasons for migrating as outlined here. The result could be a change in attitudes on the part of the migrants as well as in the new community when they arrive.

A systematic attempt could be made to duplicate many of the psychological goals of migration in the present neighborhood. Various experimental social innovations could be tried. Giving people a feeling of a fresh start, for example, could be achieved by setting up special classes for groups of people who are ready to move and to discuss with them how they can approach their lives right now with the purpose of achieving a feeling of a fresh start.

30

Creating Involvement

DEVELOPING A NEW SELF-CONCEPT

Even though those magnificent men and their "thinking machines" (computers) have now made possible automatic ordering and inventory control—and have thereby appreciably reduced the need for certain types of selling employees—the great task of pushing products along the distribution pipelines of America is still going to have to be done through nose-to-nose confrontation by flesh-and-blood salesmen.

While a mechanical device can be galvanized into immediate action through an electronic impulse, salesmen can no longer be made to increase their productivity by grabber-smasher pep talks or periodic absorption of product information churned out by the marketing department. Even the lure of a bigger commission, a fat bonus, or incentives such as color TV sets or two weeks on the Riviera don't, in my estimation, really go to the heart of the problem.

The objective, I feel, should be to help the salesman develop a fresh and more richly rewarding self-concept. And what is this self-concept? It is not, strangely enough, what the salesman is, but *what he thinks he is!*

It is an organized conception of the self based on such things as past experiences, present status, ideals, and, most important of all, the salesman's own estimate of his relationship with others.

Because of a pronounced psychodynamic drive toward ego fulfillment, salesmen are most productive when they are convinced they are doing something worthwhile for the customer, and thus directly or indirectly for the world. At the risk of sounding somewhat impractical, I have become convinced that one of the oldest and, at the same time, most modern ways to motivate salesmen effectively is to appeal to their *idealism*.

In a study for a leading shoe company we found, for example, that it was desirable to make it clear to the shoe salesman that he should become something of an expert on the human foot. This feeling of expertise enabled him to overcome some of the negative feelings he might have about stooping down and handling customers' feet. We suggested that in fitting shoes he should make every effort, through the careful, almost caressing way in which he handled the foot, to demonstrate that he was extremely interested in the customer's well-being. Through such considerate action he was, in effect, saying to the customer, "I fully appreciate just how concerned you are with your feet and your foot problems, and I want to do my best to see that the shoes I sell you give you the utmost in comfort and satisfaction." His self-concept should be one of service through superior skill and knowledge.

For a furniture company, we pointed out that salesmen should be helped to understand that buying furniture is very often one of the first joint acts of a young couple and that in a sense it is almost as though the salesman is a psychotherapist or marriage counselor. When salesmen adopted this attitude, the job took on much greater significance and interest. This was sound motivation because the salesman was no longer just selling furniture, but had developed a new self-concept which made the job one of real importance.

To increase sales of women's gloves, we recommended that instruction in the psychology of gloves be given to saleswomen, along with information about the significance gloves have for various people, the history and origin of gloves, the role they played in battle in the middle ages, etc. Again, this made the salesperson feel as though she was an authority regarding the product and caused her to alter her self-concept. Ego enhancement was the motivation here.

In a study for a cosmetics manufacturer, we were asked to determine how girls acting as demonstrators of the company's products felt about their jobs. We found that while the commissions they were earning were of course important, what really gave them the greatest sense of satisfaction was the realization that through their efforts they were helping other women to look more beautiful and attractive—which, in turn, had a most salutary effect upon their marriage, relationships with friends, and sense of well-being.

Regardless of the field in which a salesman operates, his role might very well be compared with that of the old-time evangelist, who sought by exhortation, explanation, and solicitude to convince others of the lasting benefits of his proposal. His self-concept was that of being an appointed representative of the Almighty, and his greatest satisfactions grew out of a feeling of the importance of his mission in life. So whenever salesmen hit the glory trail to convert prospects into purchasers, their productivity can be greatly increased if care is taken to see that their inner needs—for status, for recognition, for respect—are met.

31

Controlling Emotions

CHANGING ONE'S MOOD

Many mistakes in important foreign policy decisions have been made because one of the parties involved was in a bad mood. In management, controlling one's mood is probably more important than many elaborate techniques that can be put on complicated charts. Yet the technique for controlling mood is frequently neglected, and moods themselves are difficult to determine and to define. One of the most nefarious aspects of this nebulous phenomenon is that it can be blamed easily on outward circumstances—having gotten out of bed on the wrong foot, having missed a train, having a torn collar button, or finding out that your suit is stained. The truth of the matter is something completely different. Very often being in a bad mood is a form of weapon. I feel I have been neglected, taken for granted, and not paid attention to; I conjure up a bad mood, and voilà—I am noticed again.

In advertising and selling not enough attention is paid to you—the consumer. In a sales training course, the pupil is taught all kinds of subtleties of human relations, but seldom how to cope with the ill temper, the general grouchiness of the customer he is encountering. And yet probably more sales have been killed by this intangible form of sales resistance. What would the humor doctor recommend? In one of our looks into the future, we suggested that the home of the next few years include a "decompression chamber" into which the tired husband could withdraw, with or without alcohol, just to be left alone for awhile until he can face his family with their problems. Modern trains taking people to work or bringing them back from work might well think of such a possibility in the form of a special "decompression" car.

Of course, everybody has his own moods and ways of reacting. It might be a smart idea to develop for yourself a mood barometer and chart on it your high-pressure and low-pressure systems, just as the meteorologist does. You could then trace back to see when and under what circumstances your good or bad mood "tempests" occurred.

There are a number of remedies for a bad mood which seem to work:

1. The easiest one is to let your ill humor run its course, but limit it to a definite period of time—one or two hours.

2. Acknowledge to yourself and to others that you are in a bad mood. This in itself has a therapeutic effect. It shows the silliness of permitting such a fragile and undefinable phenomenon to control your actions.

3. Think of something very pleasant that has happened to you. Remind yourself how temporary a bad mood usually is. Remember that it will pass and that in a few hours you will feel quite different. We also derive a certain pleasure from feeling hurt and hurting ourselves and others with a bad mood. Recognizing this may in itself contribute to a partial cure.

4. Manager, factory supervisors, teachers, salesmen, and people in the field of communications in general should have a series of emergency steps prepared to use when they are in a bad mood, just as a pilot knows in advance what to do in case of bad weather. This could include a reminder not to make any decisions, not to start an important discussion, not to judge somebody else's work, and not to start a sales discussion while in this mood.

5. Many accidents occur because people are in a bad mood. Safety organizations might be well-advised to teach people not to drive when they are upset and to spend ten minutes cooling off. The same thing applies to operating dangerous or delicate machinery. Many times instructions are torn up in anger because one mistake is piled on top of another one or tools are broken. The right thing to do in such a situation is to stop and take a ten- or fifteen-minute breather until one has calmed down.

CHANGING FATALISM INTO PLANFUL, SCIENTIFIC PROCEDURE

Suppose you want to sell a farmer on the idea of applying herbicides in a systematic fashion. He, however, feels (with some justification) that the success or failure of his crop depends on so many different factors, such as weather, rainfall, the spacing of rain and sun, and, to a very large extent, luck. Therefore, it appears to him that applying herbicides is costly and unnecessary. Farming is basically gambling. People in many other occupations have a similar attitude. People in their private lives very often are guided by fatalistic attitudes. The Muslim religion, for example, is based on Kismet, the will of Allah. When decision making becomes too complicated, we may leave it up to superstition, an influence beyond our own individual lives. We surrender our human prerogative of independence. Changing this attitude will depend on understanding what is behind fatalism.

To a large extent fatalism is a form of escapism. It relieves the individual from a feeling of responsibility. If things go wrong, he can state that there was nothing he could have done about it anyway. Fatalism is basically perilous. Accepting the responsibility is strenuous, unpleasant, and dangerous. The only way we can succeed in changing such an attitude is to illustrate to ourselves that acceptance of responsibility is sweeter, more agreeable, more rewarding, and more apt to lead to success than fatalistic behavior. A diary in which debriefing is being done (as after a trip by the astronauts), a sort of tracing back of events in the person's life, can be one healthy procedure for avoiding fatalism. It demonstrates that we can influence many of our everyday occurrences with more careful long-range planning. People often get lost when they plan to visit friends for the first time, and so they continue home. If they simply looked at a map of the neighborhood and decided on the best and shortest way of getting to the correct address, they might save hours of lost time and avoid a lot of aggravation and embarrassment.

By taking more time and accumulating additional facts, you can often make a decisive and conscious decision rather than a haphazard and fatalistic one. The Apollo astronauts had to trust somewhat to luck, but they kept this attitude to a minimum and made sure that all eventualities had been taken into consideration beforehand. It could be that many fatalists who love to satisfy the gambling instinct would lose all interest in their actions if the outcome could be influenced in a much more definite fashion. This can be remedied by adopting the gambler's language when you are trying to teach him how to reduce the odds. Even with careful planning for the use of an herbicide, for example, you still leave enough uncertainties to satisfy a subconscious pleasure in gambling. Even the scientific farmer has to gamble to a considerable extent with weather and other uncontrollable factors.

MOOD AND MASS COMMUNICATION

At great cost, exhaustive media studies are conducted to establish beyond the shadow of a doubt that one publication or one network is more influential than another. Legions of weighty statistics are unloosed to prove that readers' or viewers' incomes are at an all-time high and that because of this, their buying resistance is obviously at an all-time low. Or an imposing array of figures is thrown into the fray to show that because of superior education, readers or listeners have a sharp eye for quality and an equally keen ear for value! Stacks of such studies have accumulated on the desks of space and time buyers all over the world, and our studies indicate that they are of somewhat limited value in determining just how productive a given medium may be.

The reason for this, in my estimation, is that in putting together these audience profiles, one very important element is omitted—the *mood* the reader or listener brings to the medium. In a study for CARF, the Canadian Advertising Research Foundation, our evaluation of the four in-home media—TV, radio, magazines, and newspapers—indicated that to a very considerable extent, the effectiveness of the different media depends upon how skillfully the mood of the advertising message is integrated with the fluctuating feelings of the audience.

We found that the morning period, from the time of awakening until work began, was almost completely monopolized by radio. Here, the dominant interest was in getting a fast, factual wrap-up of *news*. During the working day (except for housewives and students) the newspaper was a prime factor. Here, the interest in news broadened considerably to include comment and editorializing. For housewives, the role of radio subtly changed from a dominant one in the morning to that of a background companion throughout the day. Here, commercials needed to practically "jump out" of the loudspeaker in order to snap listeners out of their more indifferent attitude. In the afternoon, magazines moved into the picture prominently, as a short breath-catching "break" in the daily schedule or as a source of cooking, decorating, or self-improvement information.

Evenings, of course, were given over to more leisurely newspaper reading and to television. Evening television means *entertainment* to most people—the mood is reposeful. As a result, there is a strong disinclination to think very hard about *anything* at this time! Before retiring, many again turned to magazines or radio for a kind of quiescent "nightcap." Altogether, our studies revealed that each medium occupied a very special place in the routine of the home and that the overall effect was more complementary than competitive. However, there was considerable evidence that media effectiveness varies with the level of education. The higher the education, the greater the reliance on print media.

In a recent study in England, we were concerned with the creation of a special publication for a very carefully selected and circumscribed audience—the intelligent English woman. Our analysis showed that she is interested in realism and that her psychological, economic, and sociological milieu forces her to look upon life in a much less romantic fashion than her sisters of a previous generation. We found her to be more forthright, perceptive, and given to planning her life with care and understanding. She no longer desires or feels she could afford to play the role of a pampered, lovable doll. All these things dictated a completely different kind of content, one wherein the editorial *mood* would correspond as closely as possible to the woman reading the magazine. When launched, this publication, called *Nova,* met with immediate success because it was specifically designed to meet the needs and reflect the feelings of the audience for which it was being published.

Media research of the future will need to pay more attention to the dominant attitudes of people as they mentally plug into the power lines of mass communication. It's not only where people live, how much education they have, and what the family income is that influences response —it's also how well the medium succeeds in capitalizing upon the mindset or mood of the audience at the moment of contact!

32

Overcoming
Psychological Barriers

OVERCOMING THE "PSYCHOLOGICAL" BARRIER
TO UNITED STATES GOODS IN OVERSEAS
MARKETS

American exports strive to be competitive in price, quality, and performance—but what about psychological competition? Often overlooked, psychological competition has become an increasingly important factor in export marketing.

The psychological barrier confronts United States exports in a variety of ways. Take food as an example of how it operates. In virtually every European capital it's easy to find Japanese, Italian, French, and German restaurants. But rarely do people see a truly American restaurant. Although they are well acquainted with a variety of foreign food styles, persons living abroad are not always familiar with American-style food, and this lack of awareness of a good product creates a barrier to American food exports. With aggressive promotion, however, it's possible to offset this psychological hurdle—not only in food but in fashions and other types of products as well.

It is important to remember that the United States, in addition to having developed a superior technical "know-how," has also become a cultural leader—in modern art, architecture, and many other areas. Jean-Jacques Servan-Schreiber makes this point clear in *The American Challenge*. It's a vital selling point, and to compete psychologically, the United States should put more "oomph" in its sales effort by putting greater stress on its style and uniqueness in many fields.

In furniture, for example, American designs are practical, lightweight, and psychologically mobile. Young people everywhere appreciate these qualities. The American manufacturer nevertheless often feels inclined to use the word "continental" to praise his American designs—despite the recent popularity of Early American styles in continental Europe.

We encounter psychological competition head-on in the field of fashion. The label "Made in U.S.A." is really far superior to "Made in Britain." The cut of slacks and pants made in England does not compare with the superb fit of American garments. The lightweight materials used in men's clothing produced in this country are also appreciated abroad. To my knowledge, however, no American manufacturer has yet dared to advertise that these are typically American virtues. Shoes are another example. American shoes do a marvelous job of combining comfort and practicality with outstanding style and appearance.

Compared with the typical European, the average American is an individualist. Yet for decades Americans have been accused of being "conformists." And despite his individualism, the American has often failed to speak out in his own behalf and has permitted prejudices against his so-called conformity to exist.

As another facet of psychological competition, we should debunk other false stereotypes about the United States. For example, we should attack the misguided notion that the United States is just a materialistic society. The exact opposite happens to be true. Compared with people in other countries, the average American is much less attached to material possessions. He lives in a throw-away civilization. Unfortunately, the term "throw-away" still carries a negative connotation; however, retention of useless and outdated products is clearly detrimental, and the American talent for discarding such products is worthy of appropriate publicity.

Not enough has been done to dispel the misconception that all American cities are identical ("carbon copies") and dull. Tremendous changes are taking place everywhere in the United States—often giving each city more individuality—but people abroad remain largely ignorant of what has been happening. They don't know that imaginative projects like New

York's Lincoln Center have many advantages over their counterparts abroad.

It has been recommended that the American exporter try to adapt himself to foreign markets. But it is equally important to realize that the foreigner does appreciate American uniqueness. Too often foreigners have complained about a lack of uniqueness in American styles, criticizing us for being too eager to please and for "playing the chameleon."

If American exports are to find even more acceptance abroad, the United States exporter will need to radiate more self-assurance—but without arrogance or boastfulness. First, however, he will have to convince himself that he really has something to offer beyond competitive prices and quality. Only then will there be a major step forward toward even greater confidence in America's export wares. The ultimate result should be greater acceptance of United States products by customers abroad.

In today's world many products are becoming more and more international. True internationality, however, does not require anonymity. Volkswagen is an international product, and yet everybody knows that it is made in Germany.

American products can and should contribute more to the variety and beauty of modern life. It is important to provide buyers of American exports with the opportunity to feel that they are enjoying the wide choice of products and services offered by "one world." Instead of feeling overwhelmed by economic "Yankee imperialism," customers and prospects abroad will be flattered by the attention you pay to them.

HANDMADE VERSUS MACHINE-MADE

In the United States more and more products are being accepted that have been manufactured on a mass basis. In other countries there is still resistance. Building costs are extremely high—unnecessarily high—in many European countries because windows, doors, and many other building materials are still made by hand. Twenty to thirty thousand carpenters are busy nailing, planing, and carving windows and doors by hand. The commercials show a salesman demonstrating fifty or sixty models made by the factory, and then to top it all he walks through several of the glassless, empty window and door frames during the demonstration. In doing so he nurtured one of the major fears—the fear of lack of human concern. Our recommendation on the new commercials was to show a carpenter who has just finished a window and is giving it its last touch, thus conveying to the viewer that even in a window factory, where windows are made by machines, they also benefit from human concern and have a soul.

The field of synthetics lacks, to a very large extent, folklore. No princess is clad in nylon. Nylon or orlon products have no soul. Wool, linen, cotton, and many of the so-called natural products, although they are machine-made too, are much closer to real, natural handmade things. Our modern industrialization requires changing human attitudes in such a way that we can begin to accept the fact that machine-made products are not necessarily inferior to those made by hand. Without such a change in attitude many modern developments in the direction of progress are impossible. When American factory-made ice cream was introduced to the city of Vienna by the Sealtest Company, a cry of indignation arose at first, until the people tasted the product and had to admit that it was by far superior to what they had been used to eating. In blindfold tests, which we conducted ourselves, people were asked to compare so-called Grandma's homemade ice cream with machine-made ice cream; again and again, they preferred the factory-made product; they found the real homemade ice cream to be full of chunks, somewhat salty tasting, and lacking the rich quality of the machine-made product.

How does one convince Frenchmen to accept conveniently packaged cheeses with the same enthusiasm they had for the confusing variety of unwrapped cheeses displayed at the markets until now? How does one go about persuading people, without forcing them, to change their point of view and to accept the fact that they are living in the twentieth century? Create the assurance of creativity. Despite or because of the machine, there is room for creative contribution.

"MAN-MADE" MATERIALS VERSUS THE "DREAM OF NATURALNESS"

Our world is growing more and more filled with synthetic fabrics, plastics, and substitute products of various types. Many of these are superior to the natural ones: detergents, Corfam, Formica, and Dacron, for example, offer advantages over their natural counterparts—soaps, leather, wood, and cotton.

Yet consumers keep going back to nature as the ideal. We speak about "genuine leather," "real wood," and "real soap." In many of our studies we find again and again that when people are questioned about their favorite products, the natural ones come first to mind. Even our choice of words is significant. We distinguish between the "real thing" and the "man-made," "synthetic," or "substitute" material. This is illogical: Plastic derived from lactic acids and milk is as real as wood, and detergents derived from chemical elements are as real as soap, which is derived from other chemical elements.

Why do we have this feeling about "real" products, as opposed to man-made ones? There is no doubt that this "dream of naturalness" exists and represents a powerful advertising appeal. It probably comes from deep down, from the "animal within us." Psychologists speak of "alienation" as one of the diseases of the modern world. Getting back to the real things, the things we knew about in our animal past, gives us a feeling of security and is a cure for this alienation.

On another level, it is almost as if we still don't quite believe in the achievements of modern technology: "It's too good to be true" and "One of these days we are going to discover that we're right back where we started, in the days of the caveman." Going back voluntarily, by using natural products, is a way of telling ourselves that in case of emergency, we can survive with the simple things.

Our analysis shows that there are a number of deep appeals in the "real" things. To most people, they have depth; they live; they are imperfect; they change; they have warmth. They also have history, folklore, and many personal associations and experiences attached to them. If we are ever to gain acceptance for the so-called ersatz products, we shall have to surround them in advertising with the same aura that natural things have. They have to acquire depth, aliveness, changeability, and imperfection. We are somehow afraid of the glossiness, smoothness, and machine-made characteristics of Formica when compared with the knots, unevenness, and warmth of wood.

Another area which will require study concerns fairy tales and legends in which the hero surrounds himself not with leather, wood, and steel but with modern materials. Maybe someday the seven-league boots will have to be made of Corfam, and Siegfried's sword of Duraluminum.

HOW TO SELL "SINFUL" PRODUCTS SUCCESSFULLY

One of the most persistent trends emerging from our recent studies is the drift toward a more hedonistic society. We see it in attitudes, actions, and purchasing habits—especially in the buying of "sinful" products. Which ones are they? They are the products that come in conflict with puritanical morals. Liquor, candy, cigarettes, fattening foods, cola drinks, coffee, and the "a-go-go" women's clothes and cosmetics. Obviously, these aren't really "bad"; they are simply symbols of pleasure-seeking, live-for-today life.

Here are five recommendations for selling "sinful" products:

1. *The Perfectly Good Excuse.* Provide rationalization—build up a reason for using the product that sounds good. For example, people drink to get drunk or at least to "feel good." No one admits this, of course. Thus the astute marketer will see that his brand of liquor is associated with

acceptable motives like "cocktail hour U.S.A.," festive occasions, and socializing.

2. *"I Deserve This."* Justification is another way of cloaking a "sinful" product in acceptable dress. Make the user believe he has a right to enjoy, that he deserves to pamper himself at times: "My life is tense," "I need a pick-me-up," "Candy gives me energy," etc. Many products that suggest indulgence and luxury can thus become "needs." They help people *cope* with modern society.

3. *Doesn't Everybody Do It?* Many an alleged "sinful" product receives a resounding stamp of approval simply because using it becomes the thing to do—or because it can't be wrong if everyone uses it. Sinning in groups is less sinful. Drinking alone is abhorred, but in company it's perfectly all right. Eating candy from a box by yourself is wrong, but pass it around, and everything's fine.

4. *Surround It with "Poetic Sizzle."* An obscene novel can be presented as an "artistic achievement" if it's properly promoted. A strong after-dinner coffee becomes a "unique taste experience." A martini made with expensive English gin is sophisticated. A bawdy play becomes a "sociological experiment in theatre."

5. *Sin in Style.* It is currently fashionable to emphasize one's individuality. This makes it easy to enhance a "sinful" product with an aura of creative distinctiveness. A drink made with a "double twist of lemon" is no longer a "slug of whiskey"—it's a creative cocktail. A call girl who picks her patrons carefully is less immoral than one who isn't so choosy. A person who enjoys rich, fattening foods gets away with it if he eats with the gusto of a gourmet.

In short, sell "sinful" products with a psychological sizzle. Give people an excuse for enjoying them.

33

Political Attitudes

FOR POLITICIANS: IT'S THE "AGE OF TRUTH"

Politicians, perhaps even more than marketing men, are apt to look to the records of the recent past for clues as to what makes the "sale." Presidential and other candidates must realize, however, that much has happened to public attitudes and motivations in past years. Techniques which have succeeded in the past won't work anymore. The candidate who isn't alert to current public feelings or who uses outmoded campaign methods won't get far. Here are some bipartisan suggestions for anyone running for office:

1. Don't be a radio hero—on TV. Politicians are not using the modern communication potentialities of television. The candidate gets up and talks, and he thinks that's enough to persuade people or change their thinking. The "stand-up" candidate might just as well be on the radio. Many devices are open to the candidate on TV; for example, he can use models (showing what an ideal school or classroom would look like) or the "documentary" (showing the candidate in the slum or cornfield listening to the slum dweller or farmer explain his problems in his own words).

Symbolic techniques might be used to explain dry or difficult points—how the budget would be allocated, the "domino" theory, etc.

2. "Orating" is outmoded and even dangerous for the candidate. Our studies show that people are more suspicious than ever of generalizations, flag-waving phrases, and purple prose. Young people are especially put off by such language. Today's successful politician must avoid puffery and use ordinary, current language.

3. The "ideal" candidate is out. No one expects a candidate to be a perfect human being, with answers to everything, these days. No one will believe in a candidate who never has made an error and never will. Self-mockery and admitting past mistakes are more believable, more in tune with what people want today.

4. People are searching for real insight into the candidate's thinking. The moment that gets the most attention is when the speech is over and the candidate thinks, for a split second, that he's "off camera." Creating an atmosphere of honesty—of a look at a real person—is necessary. Speeches should be as "ad lib" and unprepared-sounding as possible. Showing the candidate at home—when his wife asks, "What are you *really* going to do about that problem, Honey?"—is another possibility. With the complexities of today's problems, such breaks from the pat routine of speeches might make it easier for candidates to convince the public of the lack of quick, easy solutions and present realistic assessment of problems.

5. People would still like to be inspired, but they are warier than in the past of "promises." The successful candidate should get down to the nitty-gritty—he should be specific and level with his audience.

6. Candidates should make a greater effort to talk to and understand the unconvinced. For instance, many people might switch parties when they vote if they could somehow justify this to their friends. The candidate should show that he understands this hangup. People in general today are seeking, more than ever, the "real person" as their leader. They'd like to understand the candidate's true motivations.

MOTIVATING VOTING BEHAVIOR

We are still suffering from the illusion that most voting is done on a purely intellectual basis. Here are a number of pragmatic approaches, which don't require interfering with a political platform, that we have utilized and developed in local and national elections.

We recommended the following concrete steps to local politicians:

1. Stress the importance of local elections—the fact that in the final analysis local elections concern you much more than national elections because they touch your pocketbook, your profession, and your future.

2. The modern voter is frustrated. Politicians have made too many promises that have not been kept. Distribute a calendar in which you underscore specific promises—what you intend to do three months after election or six months after election. Attack the frustration directly: "Why should you believe me? Don't believe me. Ask me for proof of what I really intend to do."

3. Particularly in rich counties use biting sarcasm: "We are so rich that we have a man on our payroll who does nothing. We just pay him because it looks good."

4. Too many people use their votes just to get rid of their frustrations. A mayor, a local candidate, and also a national candidate can point out that this is infantile behavior. Exploding, wanting to solve everything in one stroke, is just another form of escape.

5. Stress the fact that you are a problem solver—that you do not know all the answers but that you know how to get at the problem.

6. Influence the actual voting decision in a conditioned-reflex form. On posters or in ads show a red or blue ribbon attached to the lever with the candidate's name on it. At the moment of decision, the moment of truth, when the voter is about to pull the lever, he will be reminded of the ribbon and of the candidate's name, which he has continuously associated with it.

34

Down the Psychological Walls between People

Many radio programs and books are devoted to daily gymnastics for the purpose of conditioning the body. I suggest that in order to bring about a change of attitude such as better understanding between people, similar mental exercises might be desirable. We cannot expect the unification of Europe or the world to be carried through by state organizations, politicians, or special civic groups. In the final analysis, each of us will have to make his contribution by bringing about, through systematic training, a change in his own views and patterns of thinking.

When I was in Japan some time ago, I went to a variety show. There was standing room only. I suddenly noticed that everybody was looking at me, and with a never-before-experienced shock, I discovered that I was at least a head taller than all the people around me. I am not a particularly tall individual, but suddenly I realized what being taller than the others means. I felt isolated, and I literally attempted to draw my head down between my shoulders so as not to be so painfully conspicuous.

In order to change one's attitude, two preliminary steps are necessary. First, one has to be aware of his own peculiarities and those of other people; second, one has to understand their origin, the reason for their existence. Then and only then can a proper therapy, cure, or technique for changing such attitudes be brought about. I do not advocate that all people should behave alike or use their hands the same way or have the same facial expressions and the same mannerisms. This would indeed create a boring uniformity. But what is necessary is that we stop evaluating—usually in a negative way—other people's slightly different behavior. When a German observes Frenchmen or Italians, he is struck by the fact that their gestures are more or less livelier than his own and that they underscore their speech with decisive hand and arm movements. On the other hand, Latins are inclined to look upon the Scandinavians, English, and Germans as rather stiff because they do not use the secondary three-dimensional drama of gestures. One useful exercise might be to have a Frenchman try for an hour or two to use the more restrictive and restrained hand movements of a German and to try to speak one hour every day in this fashion. Similarly, a German might want to practice the livelier gestures his Latin fellow Europeans are accustomed to. In this possibly primitive fashion, a first attempt could be made to develop an awareness of differences and to experience "below the navel," as it were, and not just intellectually, how even such a slight thing as hand gestures may influence one's outlook on life.

For a European coffee company we introduced the idea of suggesting that people in different countries serve an Italian breakfast, a French breakfast, or a German or Dutch one. This may be another interesting and rewarding exercise. If possible, subscribe to a number of European magazines or a newspaper which covers European news. Another good idea might be for national newspapers themselves to introduce one or two pages of news that concerns problems of development of European unification. If it is true that Germans in general are well organized, it might be interesting to practice a similar orderly classification of one's daily tasks or to arrange one's desk in a rather symmetrical and what in a prejudicial fashion might be called Prussian manner and to find out how this affects one's work and one's outlook. The effect of many such exercises might be similar to that of the exercise recommended to the young Peace Corps volunteers to help them become accustomed to Arab ways, as discussed earlier in the book.

Religious cleavages are extremely important ones. Many people have never witnessed a Catholic religious service because they themselves are not Catholics. The same thing is true as far as members of other religious groups are concerned. Participating in such ceremonies, particularly when this is done without any preconceived notions or prejudices, can often lead to a much greater appreciation of an otherwise foreign and therefore threatening phenomenon. It would be very desirable to have such a loosening up of cultural and religious frameworks take place from childhood. This would not lead, in my opinion, to a lack of security or a dangerous weakening of one's ties with the group he is born into. On the contrary, an honest comparative appraisal of the values your own group represents and the values of the differing groups would take place. In most circumstances, a strengthening of belief and loyalty would stem from it.

The mother trying to train her family to think and feel European could quite easily introduce a German meal or have a German day when mostly German food would be served. On other days, foods of other countries could be introduced. Much of the work that we have been doing for commercial companies is already pointing in this direction. We have tried to introduce Germans to French cheese. Similarly, French companies have been very much interested in replacing wine with milk as a preferred beverage for children.

The success of a number of these ideas, of course, would depend on the readiness of the average individual and family to accept the goal that bringing up one's children as good Europeans is at least as desirable as bringing them up as good Christians or with the proper moral and ethical standards. Too much in our daily education, unfortunately, is still directed toward making good Frenchmen, Swedes, Germans, or Englishmen out of children rather than stressing the fact that while such national differences are amusing, interesting, and have historical justification, they are only minor differences. If a mother is really interested in working for peace, the best way she can get started is to eliminate from her daily conversation as many references as possible to what a good German or a good Spaniard is supposed to do.

What we are really talking about is the necessity for changing our daily environment and as many of the inferences that surround us as we can. Walking down the street in Zurich, for example, one is struck by the number of signs that stress Swiss banks, Swiss fashion, Swiss art, and Swiss this or that and the lack of references to the European aspect. The same thing is true, of course, in any European country. How can Europeans be encouraged to get accustomed to the idea that Switzerland—or France or Italy—is only a part of Europe and not an independent unit on its own? A relatively simple device is to add the designation *Europe* to addresses on mail being sent to Italy, France, Switzerland, or any other European country.

At one point, although this may be an even wilder dream, the "one Europe" idea might be replaced by the concept of a globe that has no boundaries. The process of unification has to take into consideration the total environment in which we live. Every company, for instance, that subscribes to the idea of one world should study what it can do to imbue its employees, from the moment they arrive at work until they leave to go home again, with the thought of the entire globe as a new object of patriotism.

Too many schoolbooks still extol the powers of national heroes. The average Frenchman still admires Napoleon without really being told that he should be looked upon as a clever man who tried to unify Europe but who tried to do it by force, similar to the way Hitler did, although in a less cruel and barbaric fashion. A commission might be profitably set up which would study European schoolbooks from the viewpoint of whether or not they perpetuate, according to my belief and the theme of this book, the dangerous disease of nationalism. To continue with a chauvinistic teaching of history is a little bit like inoculating people against a disease and at the same time contaminating them with the very bacillus that the vaccine is supposed to fight.

We'll need heroes. What have we done to portray the international man, the globetrotter, the person who can adjust himself to different cultures and who feels at home in many different countries, the really modern political James Bond? Instead we are using such terms as "stateless" and the "man without a country"—almost making it a moral offense not to believe in a fatherland. Our parks and museums are full of statues of people who in one way or another tried to prove the superiority of one country over the other and supposedly fought victorious battles; instead, they should feature statues of those who tried to unify Europe and the world.

In school, French children should be asked to draw pictures of Germans, for example, and describe them. It would be the teacher's duty to point out fallacies, to combat prejudices with facts, and to prove that not all Germans are punctual, that German railroads are often as late as French or Italian ones, and that the world's largest hydroelectric dam can be found not in Germany or Sweden but in France. In other words, one of the major jobs (starting within each individual family and then continuing automatically throughout the school years) would be to destroy our silly notions of permanent national characteristics. There is no school subject that couldn't stand such revision. Certainly our history lessons and our geography lessons would benefit by having European concepts introduced into them. Children should learn to draw the borders of Europe in addition to those of their own country. I realize that European geography is taught up to a point, but usually much more attention is paid to the detailed information about one's own country.

Even such terms as *l'èstero* in Italian leave a feeling of strangeness and danger connected with a foreign country. We often have unconscious prejudices against people in other cultures, and these people are very observant and sensitive on this point. In Morocco my wife and I met a local carpenter who had done some work for our son, who was then with the Peace Corps. We shook hands with him, talked for awhile, and walked off. When we met him again he told us that he preferred us to the parents of another Peace Corps volunteer. He was convinced, he said, that they looked down on him and that we did not. These parents had been very nice and could not be directly accused of any prejudices. Yet in further discussions a fascinating detail came to light. This rather primitive, uneducated carpenter had observed that the other parents, particularly the mother, had wiped their hands after having shaken his. We had not done so. To him this was subtle proof, more powerful than any kind of verbal protestation, that they had a deep-seated feeling of contempt mixed with fear. How often do we do similar things as far as people of other nationalities are concerned?

Several years ago I observed a group of Germans taking a night tour of Paris. While they were obviously enjoying the sights of Paris at night, they discussed with one another the degeneration of the French and complained continuously of the lack of organization of the sightseeing tour. Had they been asked in a direct interview whether they were prejudiced toward Frenchmen, they would definitely have denied it.

A good exercise would be to make a soul-searching attempt to find out how we really feel about people of other nationalities. If an Italian or a Spaniard is late for an appointment and we happen to be from a more northern part of Europe, do we attribute this to his nationality, or do we blame the particular individual? It could be part of our daily mental gym exercises to stop ourselves every time we are tempted to make a prejudiced observation.

While each individual and each family can contribute enormously to such a reorientation, much of the job could be done by large organizations. I mentioned before the possibility of each office doing its share to fertilize the ground for the development of world consciousness. Newspapers could have sections stressing all those new items which indicate a continuing development in the integration of Europe. Airlines and railroads, which people use to cross national boundaries, could provide booklets that sell the idea of Europeanism. These might be little brochures reminding people to check themselves as to whether or not they are carrying psychological contraband into the foreign country in the form of prejudices, negative attitudes, and an unwillingness to really adapt themselves to the different customs.

Very important in this respect is the fact that nationals understand their real psychological characteristics. Extreme chauvinism often has its origin in a real feeling of inferiority. There are a number of European countries that suffer from such symptoms. They belong, in a sense, among the underdeveloped countries, if underdevelopment does not refer simply to economic factors. We found in many studies that Spaniards, for instance, often have—and often in an unwarranted fashion—a feeling of inadequacy as far as their products are concerned. The Greeks, the Turks, and even the Italians and Portuguese show similar symptoms. There is a mysterious invisible dividing line between north and south. The victims of discrimination in the southern part of Europe have begun to accept some of the prejudices against them. It is almost like the situation that Arthur Miller describes in his play *Incident in Vichy*—the Jews have been accused for so many hundreds of years of being greedy, aggressive, and money-minded that they have begun to believe it themselves.

It is this feeling of not being free or accepted that results in attempts to balance a negative exaggeration with a positive one. Schools, newspapers, transportation companies, and all leaders in public life can help combat this wrong form of nationalism by first building up the feeling of equality. Only when the inhabitants of all the countries of Europe begin to feel that they are equal partners and that no one is superior or inferior to anyone else can we hope to achieve a true psychological community of Europeans. Just as in Adlerian individual psychology the patient is first made really aware of his inferiority feelings in order to make it unnecessary for him to overcompensate these feelings, some sort of therapeutic courses might have to be set up starting in school for those members of the European community whom we can suspect of having such secret fears.

Tests could easily be worked out that would bring these doubts out into the open. For example, readiness to accept criticism of one's own country might be considered such a psychological measure. We can ask for a Spaniard's reaction, for example, to being told that Spain is the most backward country in Europe. How would he defend himself? He would have one of two possible responses, both of them equally neurotic and proof of insecurity—accepting the accusation, or overcompensating with a feeling of nationalism. In school discussions or even in newspapers and magazines an analysis could be conducted as to what the right kind of attitude ought to be in connection with such inferiority feelings.

Another major new medium of mass communication is, of course, the film. All over the world attempts should be made during movie performances, which are attended by millions of people, to propogate the idea of the unification of Europe. Some of the quizzes and tests which we have recommended could be adapted for use in shorts and newsreels. One possibility might be to show ten individuals, each of whom is of a different nationality. The movie public would be asked to guess which one is an Italian, a Frenchman, a German, etc. Since my thesis is that it is very difficult, if not impossible, to determine specifically to what group a person belongs, the point could be made in subsequent solutions to the quiz that we are guided by prejudices. Another quiz could consist of asking people to identify persons of different nationalities on the basis of their actions. We might show a very loud group of people and ask moviegoers to guess their nationality.

We tried such a test on a limited basis and found, for instance, that in France, the loudmouthed people were thought to be Germans; in Germany, they were thought to be Frenchmen. Another test in newsreel form might show people with various mannerisms—neat, organized, systematized, erratic, volatile, cold, and restrained, for example. Then the audience would be asked to identify their nationalities. The therapeutic effect would consist in the recognition that many such prejudices are completely erroneous and not based on fact at all.

The unification of Europe will not take place by itself. It has to be engineered. I have tried in this chapter to show what each individual and each family can do on a day-to-day basis and how their efforts can be aided by small and large organizations. Needed in all these attempts is an understanding of the motivations, resistances, and fears behind all our professed beliefs. It is only if we control these unconscious motivations that we can achieve a successful unification of Europe.

35

How to Produce
Unification of the World
and Peace

We live at a mental distance from ourselves and one another. It is a challenge, therefore, to shorten this distance. If we become more successful in recognizing the motives common to all Europeans, we shall be more inclined to act in the same direction. Cooperation depends on *mutual* understanding and respect. If someone does not understand what motivates *you,* he is more likely to be intolerant of you and your goals.

Understanding of one's own motivations and those of others leads to a balanced personality—one which is flexible and cooperative. In the past, lack of insight has contributed to our failure to achieve democratic cooperation and unification. Our goal of maturity can be achieved only if each individual has learned to *trust* his judgment and intelligence—and that of others, too. Suspicious people are immature, unhappy, neurotic, and insecure. Our democratic procedures are inefficient without insight and maturity.

Is there a danger, however, that we shall become stereotyped? Not at all. A study conducted at the Brussels World's Fair, where we asked people of various nations to describe and evaluate one another, showed that people judge nations not so much by their *superiority* in one field or another as by their *uniqueness*. Real understanding will result in a strengthening of differences, rather than in a reinforcement of similarity.

Removing mental blocks   Even as social scientists, businessmen, or political leaders it is difficult to free ourselves from preconceived ideas, superstitions, and fears. How much more difficult must it be for the average person? Mental blocks cause much of our resistance to new concepts. For example, tests have shown that we often fail to solve a *simple* problem if we have been led to expect a complicated solution. Most of all, we suffer from *illusions* of rationality. To deal with these illusions and blocks, a *new perspective* is often successful in "turning the tables." By standing on our heads, we frequently discover new concepts, previously blocked. Similarly, getting others to "stand on their heads" will enable them to overcome mental blocks. For example, role playing can be useful. If the French consent to play the role of the Germans for awhile, some of the common concepts begin to "make sense" to both.

Setting goals "step by step"   Putting *distant* ideals and goals in front of people is not enough. It is also important that the long-range goals of democratic unification be translated into immediate objectives so that these goals become less elusive than they seemed at first.

A series of step-by-step goals may be achieved where a single "long-range" goal fails to be reached—because we take human nature into consideration when we set goals step by step. It does not help, for instance, to stress the ultimate desirability of balanced diets if this is not accompanied by short-range goals, which also motivate people to overcome their desire for an unbalanced diet.

Independence has to be similarly broken down into daily activities resulting in the acceptance of responsibility. With each such small experience of independence we come closer to the real, more permanent behavior of independence and personal freedom.

Creating a bandwagon effect   Persuasion can also be facilitated through testimonials and reference to a growing movement. For instance, the Peace Corps program was generally well received in all parts of the world. People responded to these *individual efforts* because they respected the movement behind this program—the fact that thousands of others had joined.

The authority of the mass media of communication creates a feeling of a mass movement. Television, radio, and magazines afford the opportunity to reach millions of people for educational purposes and to give them the feeling that they are not alone in their efforts. People change more easily if social pressure is exerted. They must feel that others are in the same boat and that they act and decide similarly.

Retroactive conversion   A very effective method of persuasion is to present a communication from a "satisfied customer"—a testimonial from someone who has learned the lesson. Most of us appreciate assurance *in advance* that something is really worthwhile if the person who has tried it (before we do) is a credible source of assurance. The witness who gives "testimony" is an important cog not only in our legal system but also in our everyday lives. The witness may be just an ordinary person, but he has experienced something which we can only wonder about. The raw recruit is anxious to listen to the old veteran! The soldier on his way to Vietnam is interested in combat films, for example.

Unification represents a major change in one's way of life. People who have made this change, like the Swiss or other European executives who have to sell or operate in many different countries, are important witnesses. We can emulate them and be inspired by them.

Defining the structure   Ideas are abstractions, but they may still have "structure." In promoting growth, for example, it helps to know that growth is not akin to a straight line, but may be thought of as a rising spiral or a series of rises and plateaus, much like a spiral staircase. When structures are used, concepts—whether old or new—are much more easily assimilated.

In a study for *Time* magazine, we found that concepts presented as structures were easily perceived by the reader. For instance, a pendulum can be used in describing the *historical development* of labor-management relations. At first, the pendulum swings from extreme to extreme—from aggressive management to aggressive union. Over the years, the arc of the pendulum decreases, as compromise takes place. Thus, industries with a *long* history of labor-management relations are usually more "stable" than industries in which unions or guilds are battling for a foothold. The structure is helpful in bringing about understanding of a variety of situations by means of a single, underlying concept.

What is the structure of unification? It is akin to a dynamic line; it is related to real life. Life is changing. Only swimming along with the torrent of daily events provides real security, dynamic security. Seeking protection and barricading oneself must lead to maladjustment. The society which permits people to live their lives fully and to realize the utmost potential of their personalities is definitely better than the one which protects people and makes them dependent, as does the narrow, nationalistic one.

Many methods can be employed to show people the road to greater political independence and unification, without defeating the ultimate aim of greater personal maturity. These methods must pass two tests:

1. They must be based on sound scientific knowledge of human beings, the learning process, and motivation.

2. They must be compatible with the ultimate aims of greater personal maturity.

In other words, both the *means* and the *ends* must be democratic as well as effective. The possibility of finding the right solution hinges on our willingness to heed the ancient admonition: "Know thyself."

Unification depends on greater communication. Each group that becomes a member of the final, unified, larger group must be able to respond to that group. Unification is a gradual learning process, which would have to take place even if a United States of the world could be created by edict. This psychological integration might as well take place before as after the fact of unification.

I have tried to group practical recommendations in several major areas:

1. What you can do tomorrow alone?
2. What you and your friends can do?
3. What commercial and civic organizations can do?
4. What national governments can do?

1. What You Can Do Yourself Tomorrow

How do you think of yourself? As a Frenchman, a German, or a European, or as a world citizen?

  a. Train yourself to think more frequently as a European rather than a German, a Frenchman, or an Italian.

  b. Check your manner of speaking and your general outlook in regard to the philosophy of a unified Europe.

  c. Try to train yourself to use the word "European" whenever you can, rather than "German," "French," or "Italian."

  d. Try to really understand the psychology and the national characteristics of other individuals. Do you really know how a Frenchman lives? How an Italian lives? What motivates him? What interests him?

  e. How often have you invited foreigners into your family circle?

  f. Learn European languages.

  g. Spend time in another European country, but don't stay in an international hotel. Make it your business to really "live" differently.

  h. The next time you are about to generalize in a positive or negative sense about "all Germans," stop yourself. Are you justified in making these statements, or are your simply upset by the behavior of one German?

2. What You and Your Friends Can Do

People often make the mistake of stressing the *content* of an idea without being concerned about the other person's motivation. Consequently, a lot of lessons are never learned because the motivation is weak—and nobody does anything about it. The next time the unification of Europe or the world is being discussed, don't laugh at it; *give encouragement.*

I have become interested in programmed instruction because it provides a unique opportunity to address the problem of student motivation. We devised a sort of "preamble" to various instructional courses in which we increase the motivation to learn at the very beginning of the course, and also at the start of each new lesson, by showing how the student would benefit from the lessons to be learned. With this encouragement, the student is more receptive to new ideas. Without encouragement, he may not learn at all.

To state the desirability of unification is not enough. The citizen has to be encouraged. He has to be told that European unification is not too difficult to achieve. He has to have the rewards of this personal freedom described to him as a powerful incentive and motivation:

a. Admit in discussions that most stereotypes are wrong—even those which sound right and good from your own viewpoint. If you are a German, for instance, admit that it is not true that all Germans are efficient or well-organized.

b. Use your influence in schools and in your teaching techniques at home to show children that Europe and one world is a living truth. Use similar approaches in talking with your friends or your children about unification of Europe.

c. Whenever possible, send your children, for at least some time during vacations or the school year, into a foreign country.

d. Organize people-to-people programs where German families invite French families or schoolchildren, establish correspondence, etc.

e. Create small "international" cocktail parties to permit people to understand one another better, despite their ethnic differences.

3. What Organizations Can Do

a. Gasoline companies could start printing European or other maps on which national borders are sketched in a less forbidding and more temporary fashion. These maps should leave out frontiers of European countries. Teach people to think in terms of the total concept of Europe. It would even be possible to introduce a European road comparable to the Pan American Highway.

b. Many European and international establishments are directly involved in the Common Market. They could be approached to help in promoting through their advertising the idea of a unified Europe.

c. Banks could create a world gold piece. They could propagate the concept of a general European and world currency.

d. A world capital should be created.

e. A world museum for the *achievements*—not only the wars of the world—could be emphasized.

f. Textbooks should be rewritten so that much greater emphasis is put on the joint growth and development of the world, rather than on wars.

g. The various historical attempts to unify Europe and the world should be portrayed as correct in concept but incorrect in terms of the techniques used, inasmuch as they employed military means.

h. Increased ease of travel should be sought. Customs officials should be continuously influenced to make the crossing of borders within Europe even easier.

i. A world passport could be created that would be shown simultaneously with the national passport. Publicity could be created around the idea, and Europeans could become accustomed to the idea of carrying one inter-European passport with them.

j. Travel exhibits where people could find out about each other should be organized.

k. World societies should be created for specific professional groups; all physicians, all lawyers, or all architects, for example, could be asked to unite.

Bibliography

Almond, Gabriel A.: *The Appeals of Communism,* Princeton University Press, Princeton, N.J., 1954.

Baker, Stephen: *Visual Persuasion: The Effect of Pictures on the Subconscious,* McGraw-Hill Book Company, New York, 1961.

Bauer, R. A.: *The New Man in Soviet Psychology,* Harvard University Press, Cambridge, Mass., 1952.

Barnouw, Erik: *Mass Communication,* Clarke, Irwin & Company, Ltd., Toronto, 1956.

Bertalanffy, Ludwig von: *General System Theory,* George Braziller, Inc., New York, 1968.

Blake, Robert R., and Jane S. Mouton: *Corporate Excellence through Grid Organization Development,* Gulf Publishing Company, Houston, 1968.

Brinton, Crane: *Anatomy of Revolution,* Random House, Inc., New York, 1957.

Brown, J. A. C.: *Techniques of Persuasion,* Penguin Books, Inc., Baltimore, 1963.

Brown, Roger: *Social Psychology,* The Free Press, New York, 1965.

Bursk, Edward C.: *How to Increase Executive Effectiveness,* Oxford University Press, London, 1953.

Carnegie, Dorothy: *Don't Grow Old Grow Up!* E. P. Dutton & Co., Inc., New York, 1956.

Cetron, Marvin J.: *Technological Forecasting: A Practical Approach,* Gordon and Breach, Science Publishers, Inc., New York, 1969.

Charlesworth, James C.: *Mathematics and the Social Sciences,* The American Academy of Political and Social Science, Philadelphia, 1963.

Cofer, Charles N., and Mortimer H. Appley: *Motivations: Theory and Research,* John Wiley & Sons, Inc., New York, 1964.

de Ropp, Robert S.: *The Master Game,* Delta Publishing Co., New York, 1968.

Dichter, Ernest: *The Strategy of Desire,* Doubleday & Company, Inc., Garden City, N.Y., 1960.

———: "Seven Tenets of Creative Research," *Journal of Marketing,* vol. 25, no. 4, April, 1961.

———: "The World Customer," *Harvard Business Review,* vol. 40, no. 4, pp. 113–122, July–August, 1962.

———: *Handbook of Consumer Motivations,* McGraw-Hill Book Company, New York, 1964.

———: "Discovering the 'Inner Jones,'" *Harvard Business Review,* vol. 43, no. 3, pp. 6–10, p. 157, May–June, 1965.

———: "How Word-of-mouth Advertising Works," *Harvard Business Review,* vol. 44, no. 6, pp. 147–166, November-December, 1966.

———: *Nationalism Is a Disease,* Edizioni Ferro, Milan, 1967.

———: *Warum Eigentlich Nicht* (Why Not Management Principles), Lorch Verlag GmbH, Frankfurt am Main, Germany, 1971.

———: *Creativity for Managers,* Cassette Course, National Extension Services, Newport Beach, Calif., 1971.

Fisher, Roger: *International Conflict for Beginners,* Harper & Row Publishers, Incorporated, New York, 1969.

Flesch, Rudolf: *The Art of Clear Thinking,* The Macmillan Company, New York, 1951.

Gagne, Robert M.: *Psychological Principles in System Development,* Holt, Rinehart and Winston, Inc., New York, 1962.

———: *Management by Motivation,* American Management Association, New York, 1968.

Gellerman, Saul W.: *Motivation and Productivity,* American Management Association, New York, 1963.

Glasser, William: *Reality Therapy: A New Approach to Psychiatry,* Harper & Row, Publishers, Incorporated, New York, 1965.

Graham, Robert G., and Clifford F. Gray: *Business Games Handbook,* American Management Association, New York, 1969.

Haefele, John W.: *Creativity and Innovation,* Reinhold Publishing Corporation, New York, 1962.

Huizinga, Johan: *Homo Ludens,* Beacon Press, Boston, 1950.

Hunter, Edward: *Brain-washing in Red China,* Vanguard Press, Inc., New York, 1951, 1953.

Jay, Antony: *Management and Machiavelli,* Holt, Rinehart and Winston, Inc., New York, 1967.

Kepes, Gyorgy: *Education of Vision,* George Braziller, Inc., New York, 1965.

Korzybski, Alfred: *Science and Sanity,* Science Press Printing Co., Lancaster, Pa., 1941.

Levi-Strauss, Claude: *The Savage Mind,* The University of Chicago Press, Chicago, 1966.

Lockley, L. C.: *The Use of Motivational Research in Marketing,* National Industrial Conference Board, Inc., Department of Studies and Business Policy, Booklet 97, New York, 1960.

Lucas, Darrell B., and Steuart Henderson Britt: *Advertising Psychology and Research: An Introductory Book,* McGraw-Hill Book Company, New York, 1950.

Maltz, Maxwell: *Psycho-cybernetics,* Prentice-Hall, Inc., Englewood Cliffs, N.J., 1960.

Mann, John: *Changing Human Behavior,* Charles Scribner's Sons, New York, 1965.

Marrow, Alfred J., David G. Bowers, and Stanley E. Seashore: *Management by Participation,* Harper & Row, Publishers, Incorporated, New York, 1967.

————: *Motivation in Advertising: Motives That Make People Buy,* McGraw-Hill Book Company, New York, 1957.

Martineau, Pierre: "It's Time to Research the Consumer," *Harvard Business Review,* vol. 33, no. 4, pp. 45–54, July–August, 1955.

Mason, Joseph G.: *How to Be a More Creative Executive,* McGraw-Hill Book Company, New York, 1960.

Meerloo, Joost: *The Rape of the Mind,* The Universal Library, Grosset & Dunlap, Inc., New York, 1956.

Merton, Robert K.: *Mass Persuasion: The Social Psychology of a War Bond Drive,* Harper & Brothers, New York, 1946.

Meyerhoff, Arthur E.: *The Strategy of Persuasion,* Berkley Publishing Corporation, New York, 1965.

Middleman, Ruth R.: *The Non-verbal Method in Working with Groups,* Association Press, New York, 1968.

Moroni, Rolf: *Kybernetische Automation Morgen,* J. P. Bachem Verlag GmbH, Koln, Germany, 1969.

Newman, Joseph W.: "Put Research into Marketing Decisions," *Harvard Business Review,* vol. 40, no. 2, p. 105, March–April, 1962.

Nicolaides, Kimon: *The Natural Way to Draw,* Houghton Mifflin Company, Boston, 1941.

Olds, James: *The Growth and Structure of Motives,* The Free Press, New York, 1956.

Osborn, Alex: *Your Creative Power,* Charles Scribner's Sons, New York, 1948.

Pawlikowski-Cholewa, Harald von: *Marcel Marceau,* Overseas Publishers, Vaduz, Liechtenstein, 1963.

Peter, Lawrence J., and Raymond Hull: *The Peter Principle,* William Morrow & Company, Inc., New York, 1969.

Ruesch, Jurgen, and Gregory Batison: *Communication, 1951,* The Vail-Ballou Press, New York, 1951.

Sanford, Nevitt: *Self and Society,* Atherton Press, Inc., New York, 1966.

Sargeant, William: *Battle for the Wind,* Doubleday & Company, Inc., Garden City, N.Y., 1957.

Schon, Donald A.: *Displacement of Concepts,* Tavistock Publications Ltd., London, 1963.

Schutz, William C.: *Joy: Expanding Human Awareness,* Grove Press, Inc., New York, 1967.

Servan-Schreiber, Jean-Jacques, *The American Challenge,* Atheneum Publishers, New York, 1968.

Siegfried, André: *Nations Have Souls,* G. P. Putnam's Sons, New York, 1952.

Simon, Herbert A.: *The New Science of Management Decision,* Harper & Row, Publishers, Incorporated, New York, 1960.

Skinner, B. F.: *Science and Human Behavior,* The Macmillan Company, New York, 1953.

Smith, George Horsley: *Motivational Research in Advertising and Marketing,* McGraw-Hill Book Company, New York, 1954.

Smith, Gudmund J. W., and Andrews Lund: *Women Workers in Industry,* SNS, Stockholm, 1954.

Smith, Henry Clay: *Sensitivity to People,* McGraw-Hill Book Company, New York, 1966.

Taft, Jessie: *Dynamics of Therapy in a Controlled Relationship,* 1962.

Uris, Auren: *Mastery of Management,* Dow Jones–Irwin, Inc., Homewood, Ill., 1968.

Watson, James D.: *The Double Helix,* Atheneum Publishers, New York, 1969.

Weitz, Henry: *Behavior Change through Guidance,* John Wiley & Sons, Inc., New York, 1964.

Westfall, Ralph: "The Use of Structured Techniques in Motivation Research," *Journal of Marketing,* vol. XXII, no. 2, p. 125, October, 1957.

White, E. B.: *A Subtreasury of American Humor,* G. P. Putnam's Sons, New York, 1962.

Wolstrup, Preben: *Die Strategie der Propaganda,* Transtropa Press, Copenhagen, 1962.

Young, J. P.: *Practical Techniques of Executive Development and Advancement,* Halstead Press, Sydney, 1965.

Index